the TRUMAN YEARS

The Reconstruction of Postwar America

J. Joseph Huthmacher
Richards Professor of American History
University of Delaware

The Dryden Press Inc.
901 North Elm Street
Hinsdale, Illinois 60521

Contents

Introduction

Harry S. Truman, whose tenure as president spanned the post-World War II years 1945-1953, was born in Lamar, Missouri, on November 8, 1884. Raised on his grandfather's farm, and living later in the town of Independence until his father's livestock dealership floundered at the turn of the century, Truman was a shy youth whose frail physique and bookish habits set him apart from his peers. Perhaps seeking compensation, Truman wished to go to West Point after graduating from high school, but his poor eyesight disqualified him. Instead, after five years of pursuing various odd jobs in Kansas City, Truman went back to his grandfather's relatively prosperous farm, and there he lived and worked for nearly a decade. During these years Truman matured markedly, developing self-assurance and easy-going friendliness. He joined the Masons and became a worker in the local Democratic party organization. He also soldiered in the National Guard, and when World War I came served competently as a captain of artillery, apparently well-liked by the men he commanded. By age thirty-four, when the war ended, Truman's personality and manner had taken on the jaunty, outgoing characteristics that were to flavor his future career.

For a while after returning from the war Truman operated a men's clothing store in Kansas City—a venture that proved more socially and politically than financially rewarding. By now politics had become Truman's chief avocation—perhaps as much for the comradeship it provided as for the status and power. In 1922 he ran for and won his first political office—a seat on the county court—as the candidate of the notorious Pendergast machine, whose support Truman accepted pragmatically. "You can't get anywhere in politics around Kansas City unless you work with the machine," he once remarked to a friend. Truman worked with the machine until the imprisonment of its leader brought about its demise in 1940. Yet during the 1920s and early 1930s, as Truman rose to be the presiding judge of Jackson County (the chief administrative officer in charge of public works, roads, welfare agencies, and the like), he won a reputation for honesty and efficiency as well as for party regularity. His increasing percentage of the vote in successive elections indicated that he was learning to satisfy and reconcile the demands of the various components of his heterogeneous constituency—inhabitants of Kansas City as well as the farmers and townspeople among whom he had grown up, the Irish Catholics and other minority groups of the metropolis, Masons and Baptists like himself, and the various economic interest groups.

Truman's loyalty and service to the Pendergast machine were rewarded with nomination to the United States Senate in 1934, a banner year for Democrats across the country. During his first term in Washington he operated on the fringes of power, as a freshman congressman traditionally should. But he rendered reliable support to President Franklin D. Roosevelt's New Deal program and, perhaps because of the growing influence of blacks in St. Louis, he even voted for pioneering civil rights measures being pushed—without presidential blessing—by the most advanced New Deal reformers.

The senator from Missouri also lent firm support to the administration's foreign policies, and as war clouds gathered overseas in the late 1930s the former captain of artillery became an ardent proponent of military preparedness against the "small and vociferous pacifist group" that sought to frustrate the president's defense program. "The better we are armed, the less chance we have of getting mixed up in this [war]," Truman maintained in 1940. "We are facing a bunch of thugs, and the only theory a thug understands is a gun and bayonet."

The disaster at Pearl Harbor seemed to confirm Truman's stance on behalf of preparedness. Thereafter he continued to emphasize the need for a strongly armed America whose strength in arms would likely persist in the postwar power vacuum, although he now supplemented that reliance with indorsement of an international organization which, having an international police force at its command, would be capable of helping to restrain threats to the world's peace. That Truman already harbored fears regarding one possible source of such threats seems certain: in 1941, after Hitler invaded Russia and while the proposal to extend American Lend-Lease aid to the Soviet Union was pending, it's said that Truman once suggested, with an uncharacteristic degree of humor, that the United States should help the totalitarian belligerent that gained the upper hand in the contest, "and that way let them kill as many as possible." "Neither of them think anything of their pledged word," Truman added at this early date. Nonetheless, after the United States and Russia joined forces in the fight against Hitler, Truman refused to speculate publicly over such "secondary" issues as the future of American-Russian relations. Instead, he referred to the Communist power as "that brave ally."

By 1940 Senator Truman, adeptly practicing the arts of the politician-broker, had widened his power base in Missouri sufficiently to win re-election despite the breakup of the Pendergast machine. Fortune smiled on his political destiny once again when, in 1941, Truman was appointed to head the Senate's Defense Investigating Committee, which was charged with ferreting out waste and favoritism in the awarding of war production contracts. During the next three years the Truman Committee won a reputation for fearlessness and constructive action, while its chairman earned national reputation and added political stature. The stage had been set for Truman's elevation to the executive branch of government.

By 1944 Vice-President Henry A. Wallace had fallen into disfavor not only with the southern wing of the Democratic party (because of his views on race issues), but also with some of the party's most important big-city bosses (because of his alleged radicalism). Although Wallace remained the favorite of the party's more advanced liberals and the CIO leadership, advisers convinced President Roosevelt that Wallace's renomination could only damage the party's ticket. Casting about for a substitute, Roosevelt, with the prompting of Democratic National Chairman Robert E. Hannegan of St. Louis, became increasingly impressed with the credentials of the senator from Missouri: his newly-won prestige as chairman of the Defense Investigating Committee, his support of "sane" New Deal liberalism, his border-state background, and his ultimate acceptability to all of the party's warring factions (grudging as it might be in some cases), which was taken to be a reflection of his political shrewdness. And so as convention time neared Roosevelt let it be known that he would be "very glad" to run with Harry S. Truman (or with Supreme Court Justice William O. Douglas).

On the first vote in the vice-presidential balloting Truman's main support came from big-city bosses close to Hannegan; on the second roll call many Southern delegates climbed aboard his bandwagon, and Truman won the nomination. After the fact liberal and labor spokesmen delivered their endorsements. Wallace himself pronounced the winner a reliable progressive, and Sidney Hillman of the CIO declared that "if we hadn't been for [Wallace], we would have been for Truman." The *New York Times* characterized the nominee as "a realist sympathetic to the problems of various groups rather than . . . the doctrinnaire or the zealot." The terms were as yet unfamiliar in 1944, but a present-day editorialist might have described the situation by observing that in choosing their second-place candidate the Democrats had sidetracked a potential "polarizer" of the electorate in favor of a "consensus" politician of the pluralist school. In any event, the event was big with meaning for the future of American society.

Truman was allowed to suffer—or enjoy—the traditional obscurity of the vice-presidency for a scant three months after inauguration day in January 1945. During that time he received little schooling that might prepare him for the contingency that gave his office its chief importance; the press of events as the war in Europe rushed toward its end left Roosevelt little time to groom a successor even if the president had chosen to operate that way—and, characteristically, he had not. Then, on April 12, the worn-out chief executive expired at Warm Springs, Georgia. Summoned to the White House and informed of the news, a suddenly humbled Harry Truman took the presidential oath. At that moment, Truman later observed, "the moon, the stars, and all the planets fell on me."

Regardless of the talents, experience, and personality traits he brought to the job, the president who presided over the postwar reconstruction of America—and of the world—was bound to achieve an important, if controversial, place in history. The readjustment of American society from a wartime to a peacetime basis would inevitably and immediately pose hard policy alternatives, and memories of post-World War I reminded Americans of the crucial importance of the choices made. Moreover, while many people envisioned simply a return to the conditions of the 1930s once the war ended, prescient ones were uneasily aware that the war had set in motion portentous influences that would challenge old assumptions and usher in a new phase of American development—in terms of the economy's amazing productivity, in demographic patterns, in ethnic and racial relations, in political alignments, and in the realm of spiritual, social, and cultural values. Looming ahead, too, were the vast problems of international politics opened up by the disruption of the prewar balance of power, the disintegration of prewar empires, the introduction of nuclear weapons, and by American commitments to a "large policy" in the world arena and to the establishment of a system of collective security based on the United Nations. These latter commitments already enjoyed bipartisan acceptance— Franklin Roosevelt succeeded where Woodrow Wilson had failed—and thus it was assured that World War II would effectively end *American* history as something distinct from *world* history. It was to these vast transformations that Harry S. Truman—the product of a Missouri farm, the Pendergast machine, the border state region, of pluralistic New Deal welfare statism, and with an ingrained distrust of totalitarian systems—applied his political experience and personal talents between 1945 and 1953.

Almost inevitably, foreign affairs confronted Truman with the most pressing problems he faced upon assuming office. Perhaps not so inevitably, they continued to dominate his administration throughout its duration, owing to the degeneration of Russian-American wartime collaboration into a situation of distrust, competition, and Cold War. Within a few months of April 1945, both Germany and Japan had surrendered. But in the meantime Russian behavior, particularly in those East European countries the Red Army occupied, re-kindled the new president's old suspicions regarding the reliability of totalitarian collaborators. Within a short time he had adopted a "get tough" policy toward Russia, aimed at "liberating" East Europe from the Communist presence. But Truman's tough exhortations and pronouncements failed to dislodge the Russians and, facing up to the limits circumstances placed on the exercise of American power, Truman by 1947 had settled for a policy of "containing" Russian and Communist influence to the limits it had theretofore attained. Containment pressures, it was hoped, would eventually compel the Communists to give up their expansionist ambitions and thus create a situation where "peaceful coexistence" would be possible.

In pursuit of containment Truman innovated policies ranging from the Marshall Plan of large-scale economic aid for Europe to a makeshift airlift to keep beleagured Berlin supplied; from America's first peacetime alliance (the North Atlantic Treaty Organization) to the Point IV program of technical assistance to emerging Third World countries. In 1950 containment also dictated that the United States engage in a "hot war" of outright armed conflict to curb alleged Communist aggression in Korea. Indeed, under Truman and his successors America's self-assumed containment responsibilities were expanded to virtually globe-girdling proportions.

The Cold War also produced important domestic repercussions, the most immediate being in the area of internal security. Obligated by his oath of office to safeguard the national security, and confronted by several undoubted cases of Soviet espionage, Truman inaugurated a loyalty program which, he affirmed, afforded due protection to the rights of individuals. Goaded by charges from the right that he was "soft on Communism," the president gradually tightened his security program. At the same time, as China "fell" to communism and as the Russians ended America's monopoly over atomic weapons, many Americans verged on hysteria in their determination to root out the domestic agents of the Communist "menace." Increasingly, public and private institutions, personalities, and programs came to be weighed in the scales of pro- and anti-communism, culminating in the wave of "McCarthyism" that swept the country between 1950 and 1954.

Thus, for more than a generation the Cold War and its repurcussions became a central influence, if not *the* central one, in the lives of Americans. It is not surprising, therefore, that interest in tracing the origins of that pervasive phenomenon runs high among the nation's historians and students. Nor is it surprising that, as in the case of most efforts to probe the causes of profound historical developments, explanations of the nature of the Cold War have become more subtle and complex, rather than simpler, with the passage of time, as the selections in the first section of this volume attest.

At the outset, during the Truman years and for some time thereafter, most Americans and most American historians accepted the "official" interpretation of the Cold War developed by the administration to explain and justify its policies. According to this version, America's wartime vision of a peaceful and progressive postwar world, built on the principles of collective security sanctioned by the United Nations and continuing Big Power collaboration, was shattered by the resurfacing of Russian ambitions to foment revolution and achieve conquest on behalf of communism's cause. The United States' political, economic, and military responses to this threat represented her assumption of leadership among the "peace-loving" peoples of the world in defense of self-determination and other "democratic" values. This is essentially the position that Arthur Schlesinger, Jr. continues to occupy in his article which is reprinted here, although his defense of American policy has been updated to take into account some of the criticisms that have been lodged against the "Liberal Establishment" position in more recent years.

In the 1950s, various forms of "revisionism" began to make headway among historians of the Cold War. A growing number of them adopted the view, suggested even earlier by Hans Morgenthau, Walter Lippmann, and some others, that postwar Moscow-directed challenges to American interests in Europe represented manifestations of specifically *Russian,* rather than *Communist,* ambitions. The Cold War had originated as a relatively narrowly limited affair, therefore, and America's early responses had been correct and successful ones. But the United States should not make the mistake of escalating the Cold War to global proportions, for America could not realistically undertake to play "policeman to the world."

Much more radically revisionist was the position that held the United States, rather than either Russia or communism, responsible for beginning the Cold War. Under the leadership of Professor William Appleman Williams, a leftist school of diplomatic historians portrayed American foreign policy as essentially a function of the nation's capitalist socioeconomic system. At least since the late nineteenth century, according to this interpretation, American foreign policy consistently aimed at creating an international polity that would be most conducive to American business expansion and commercial penetration. To those among the emerging "New Left" who pushed the Williams thesis to its most extreme implications, the Cold War thus represented only the latest and most ambitious outburst of American economic imperialism—an imperialism reinforced now with the power of nuclear energy.

During the 1960s the revisionists' arguments gained increasing acceptance, especially among the young, in an atmosphere made hospitable to skepticism by the "thawing" of American-Russian relations, growing American involvement in the Far East and other distant parts of the world, mounting pressures for social reform at home, and the emergence of the New Left as an articulate element in American society. Many of the revisionist and New Left motifs are sounded in the extract from the writings of Rexford G. Tugwell that is included in this volume. Tugwell's analysis, moreover, takes off from a particular touchstone—the alleged departure of

President Truman from the policies that a wise and competent Roosevelt had devised for the postwar world, a contention which is itself explored at the beginning of Schlesinger's article.

More recently, too, historians have begun to re-explore the relationship of the Truman administration to McCarthyism. And while earlier writers were inclined to portray the president as a staunch defender of civil liberties against the McCarthyite onslaught, investigators like Athan Theoharis, whose conclusions are reprinted here, have identified Truman's own anti-Communist stance—in his foreign policies, in his political strategies at home, and in his often flambuoyant rhetoric—as a precursor that prepared the way for McCarthy's free-swinging crusade. Perhaps one senses in such writings, particularly when they emanate from writers on the left, a judgment that Truman and the Democrats therefore deserved the calumnies and the political hurts that the Republican senator from Wisconsin visited upon them, as in the presidential campaign of 1952.

The Cold War and the exigencies of foreign policy considerations also played a large role in determining the fate of Truman's domestic legislative program, as both articles in the second part of this volume make clear. In view of his previous record, it seemed natural enough that Truman should advocate a resumption of New Deal reformism at the war's end, and in a September 1945 message to Congress the new president spelled out a legislative agenda that gave familiar substance to the skeletal "Economic Bill of Rights" that Roosevelt had promised earlier. Yet Truman obviously lacked FDR's charism when it came to such matters, and some of Roosevelt's ardent admirers doubted the sincerity of Truman's commitment to their cause. During his first two years in office he seemed to "go slow" on domestic reform proposals, even as he "got tough" with the Russians, and he seemed too much at home with conservative advisers like his Secretary of the Treasury, John W. Snyder, and his Secretary of Commerce, Charles Sawyer.

But if such were the case, the Republican victory in the mid-term congressional election of 1946 jolted Truman off dead-center. Thereafter he broadened the inherited New Deal program to include civil rights measures, federal aid to education, national compulsory health insurance, and a new agricultural program designed to give higher prices to farm producers, and lower prices to urban consumers, at one and the same time (the Brannan Plan). Now Truman gave himself over to the influence of the band of liberal advisers—Special Counsel Clark M. Clifford, Federal Security Administrator Oscar Ewing, Leon H. Keyserling of the Council of Economic Advisers, and others—who had previously been forced to contest with the Snyder group for the President's ear. During 1947 and 1948 he smote the Republican Eightieth Congress for its failure to enact his program, during the 1948 presidential campaign he "gave 'em hell" on its behalf, and in his 1949 inaugural address he formally conferred his own "Fair Deal" label on the updated agenda of reform he had adopted. Although the outbreak of the Korean War in mid-1950 forced the

President to soft-pedal his home-front crusade for progressivism, he nonetheless kept up rhetorical pressure for Democratic commitment to it until the end of his term in office.

In an article reprinted in this volume, Richard E. Neustadt thoroughly assesses Truman's record of victories and defeats in his campaign for domestic reform, pointing out in partial explanation of the president's failures that "there was no time . . . when Truman's Administration . . . could afford to trade a major objective in the foreign field for some advantage in the domestic. Consistently, it was, and had to be, the other way around." Nevertheless, Neustadt does credit Truman with success in keeping his party officially committed to the reform impulse, and in keeping the social problems against which his program was aimed prominently within the purview of the national conscience.

Barton J. Bernstein's views, as presented in the article that follows, offer a stark contrast to Neustadt's. Even had there never been a Korean War, and had Truman succeeded in winning adoption of the whole Fair Deal intact, he feels, the result would still have fallen far short of solving the real problems that beset American society. The liberal assumptions upon which Truman built his Fair Deal—and indeed, upon which the whole tradition of modern American reform has been based—provided only blinders, rather than broad vision. Obviously, Bernstein's frame of reference dates from a more recent perspective than the 1940s afforded, and his indictment of the Truman administration's shortcomings really adds up to an indictment of the American people and their history. Nevertheless, Bernstein does pose fundamental questions of the kind that are more frequently being asked of that history today.

Another reason for Truman's failure to win enactment of more of the Fair Deal program, in addition to the high priority given to foreign affairs, was the persisting strength of the conservative coalition that had come to dominate Congress during the twilight years of the New Deal. Composed of conservative Republicans and conservative southern Democrats, the coalition rode high after 1938 despite nominal Democratic control of Capitol Hill. In an effort to break the prevailing deadlock Truman adopted the "go-for-broke" tactics urged upon him by Clark Clifford's liberal strategy board in the 1948 campaign, treating the country to the free-wheeling whistle-stop campaign that is so colorfully described in this volume by journalist Cabell Phillips.

Yet, according to Samuel Lubell in the selection that follows the Cabell piece, Truman was supremely fitted by background, training, and experience to preside over just the very kind of stalemate that gripped the country in those years (and for years thereafter). He was the "typical" American politician insofar as a member of that breed is defined as one whose role it is "to raise all issues but to settle none." Truman's "upset" victory in 1948 thus comes to be understood not as a popular uprising in support of further Fair Deal innovation, but rather as a conservative

reaction on the part of those interest groups the New Deal and the Truman administration had succeeded in placating, groups that viewed the Republicans as a
"radical" rear-guard threat to the status quo. This might help to explain why,
despite his personal triumph at the polls, Truman's efforts to win enactment of the
Fair Deal proved little more successful after 1948 than before. And in thus describ-
ing Truman as "the man who bought time," Lubell too poses a profound question
when he asks, "In whose favor has time been working?"

Most authorities regard the beginning of the Korean War in June 1950 as the
event that dealt a death blow to President Truman's domestic Fair Deal program,
and that conflict undoubtedly dominated the president's and the public's attention
during the remainder of his term. Regarding the North Korean invasion of South
Korea as a Moscow-directed move that represented a peripheral challenge to
America's containment policy (an interpretation now subject to serious question),
Truman—with the United Nations' blessing—responded by dispatching General
Douglas MacArthur's armed forces to repel the invaders. After recovering ground
lost in the original setback, MacArthur's operations proceeded smoothly and by
October 1, 1950, the North Koreans had been pushed back across the 38th parallel
border. The Truman administration—again with the UN's backing—now decided to
bring about by arms the reunification of Korea, an objective that had hitherto
eluded political settlement. And so MacArthur's forces moved northward. But when
they approached within fifty miles of the Yalu River boundary between Korea and
China at the end of October, Communist Chinese battalions swarmed into battle
and nearly expelled the UN forces from Korea altogether.

At this juncture General MacArthur renewed his request that the administration
take a number of military steps—including a blockade of mainland China, the
bombing of enemy bases north of the Yalu, and employment of Chiang Kai-shek's
army—designed to apply pressure on the Communist Chinese. When MacArthur
continued to espouse his proposals publicly after the administration vetoed them,
Truman decided, in April 1951, to remove the general from his command on the
grounds of preserving civilian control over the military. MacArthur returned to the
United States amid tumultuous acclaim, while Truman's popularity sagged to a new
low.

A subsequent congressional hearing fully aired both sides of the Truman-
MacArthur controversy, as described in the selections reprinted in this volume.
John W. Spanier, endorsing Truman's insistence on *limited* warfare as a legitimate
weapon against peripheral Communist probings, presents the administration's case
in a favorable light. Alvin J. Cottrell and James E. Dougherty, on the other hand,
while withholding total endorsement of MacArthur's program, point up the manner
in which the Communists took advantage of the seeming indecision implicit in the
administration's "half measures" in order to prolong the war and employ psychological pressures designed to wear down the American people's will to persist in the

contest. In the long run the significance of the debate boiled down to the vital question: "In whose favor does time work, within the context of 'limited war'?" Certainly events that have ensued since the early 1950s, and particularly the United States' involvement in Vietnam, have produced further evidence on that subject.

Truman left office in 1953 under a cloud as dark as that which had attended Herbert Hoover's departure from the White House twenty years earlier. Communism, corruption, and Korea—troubles that Republican orators laid at the door of the Truman administration—together with the immense popularity of General Dwight D. Eisenhower, the Republican candidate for president, had combined in the 1952 election to bury Truman's would-be Democratic successor, Adlai E. Stevenson, under an avalanche of votes. Yet Truman's reputation staged a remarkably quick comeback, and in retirement at Independence, Missiouri, he soon came to be looked upon as a colorful, but respected, elder statesman. Once in office the Republicans, despite their campaign-inspired attacks on the Democrats' containment policy, continued to follow Truman's foreign policies in essential respects, and the Eisenhower administration finally concluded the Korean War in 1953 on truce terms similar to those Truman had hoped to attain. At home, meanwhile, Eisenhower proclaimed himself a "modern Republican," sang the praises of "moderate progressivism" (or "progressive moderation"), and acquiesced in most of the economic and social reforms that the New Deal and Fair Deal had placed on the statute books. Increasing signs of affluence muted partisan and interest-group strife, and convinced many Americans that the country's remaining social problems were well on the way to solution under the status quo. "Celebrationist" historians stressed the importance of "consensus" in America's past and de-emphasized the role of "conflict." Celebrationist publicists like Frederick Lewis Allen, from whose writings an excerpt is reprinted here, hailed the nation's blend of mixed enterprise as not only the key to understanding America's own "Big Change" for the better in the twentieth century, but also as a model other peoples of the world might imitate as an alternative to totalitarian patterns. To many Americans of the mid-1950s, then, the state of the American "system" seemed to be very good indeed.

In these happy circumstances Harry Truman was acclaimed, in the words of historian Eric Goldman, as the "leader of containment foreign and domestic." He had thwarted incipient isolationism so that Communist expansionism might be held in check, and he had thwarted conservatism so that the New Deal might be consolidated and carried forward. In brief, Truman had seen to it that post-World War II did not duplicate post-World War I. In recognition of that accomplishment, as late as 1962 the man from Independence was voted into ninth place in the "near great" category of America's presidents by a group of the nation's leading historians and social scientists who were polled by Arthur Schlesinger, Sr.

Pervasive as it was, however, the good feeling of Americans in the 1950s was not universal. Conservatives still awaited their chance to run a "real" Republican for president—one like Senator Barry Goldwater of Arizona, who upbraided Eisenhower's modern Republicanism as "a dime-store New Deal"—while writers like Russell Kirk described *The Conservative Mind* (Chicago, 1953) and formulated *A Program for Conservatives* (Chicago, 1954). At the opposite end of the spectrum, native Marxists further refined their doctrines so as to accommodate the latest turns in the seemingly unpredictable American experience (see Guide for Further Reading).

A particularly independent and stimulating dissent from the celebrationist consensus was entered by sociologist C. Wright Mills in his study, *The Power Elite* (New York, 1956), a selection from which is reprinted in this volume. During and since World War II, Mills maintained, an elite group composed of defense-oriented industrialists, the military, and submissive administrative politicians, spawned by the nation's persistent wartime and Cold War preoccupations, had assumed control over the vital decision-making processes of American society. By 1961 even the retiring President Dwight Eisenhower felt compelled to issue a warning of some sort against the waxing influence of the military-industrial complex. And during the turbulent decade that followed, a virtual flood of studies appeared for which Mills' work served as the departure point. The Pentagon-Wall Street-Washington-dominated America they depicted bore little resemblance to the democratic, equalitarian, pluralistic, affluent, and nearly-fulfilled system Frederick Lewis Allen and his many imitators had portrayed a short time earlier.

As time progressed many liberals themselves—dismayed perhaps by the all-too-obvious failure of the New Deal-Fair Deal of liberalism to solve the problems of modern industrial society—turned a more skeptical eye toward the precepts and practices of their tradition's own recent heroes. One such critic was political scientist Theodore Lowi, whose writings are sampled in this volume. Disillusioned with the pragmatism and opportunism that characterized the "broker state" under Roosevelt and Truman (and their successors), Lowi regarded the "interest group liberalism" they fostered as constituting not only a betrayal of the *public* interest but also as the progenitor of an administrative state, operating on the basis of fluctuating administrative law, alien to popular participation and control in government. Pluralistic welfare-statism might placate well-organized pressure groups and salve the politicians' consciences, Lowi seemed to contend, but it did not and could not accomplish the important things that needed doing.

Whatever verdict history may in the end pronounce on the state of the American system, it is clear that Harry S. Truman will not bear the sole responsibility for it. In all things having to do with his regime, he was an inheritor of immediately past policies, and limited also in his freedom of action by the cultural bounds established during three and a half centuries of American experience. He inherited both the postwar international power vacuum that accompanied the end of World War II, and the deep-seated American revulsion against communism that seemed to make a "hard line" against Russia imperative; both the deadlock that had stalemated American democracy since the late 1930s, and the long-held American definition of politics as "the art of the possible." He did not inaugurate the benign welfare state applauded by Frederick Lewis Allen, nor did he complete its construction. He did not originate the military-industrial complex or the system of interest group liberalism feared by C. Wright Mills and Theodore Lowi, nor did his administration mark the termination of their influence.

Yet it is clear that the problems of the postwar years, and the particular ways in which Truman met them, exerted a powerful effect on future American development—and on today's and tomorrow's world. He presided over the American government during much of what was, in Eric Goldman's words, a "crucial decade." In the realm of international affairs he was the foster father of the containment policy, and the guardian of the "limited war" tactic. At home he advanced an updated New Deal, while attempting to adapt it to a new economic base and to new social and ethnic demands. Yet in most cases Truman sought to temporize conflict, postpone confrontation, and trust to time as the great healer. Indeed, perhaps the most common theme uniting the various commentators represented in this volume is the question, "In whose favor has time been working" during the Truman years and under his successors? Implicit in some of their writings, at least, is the conclusion that leaders more willing to confront hard questions, rather than those seeking to sidestep them, might serve the nation better.

Today's students and voters will have to ponder that problem in determining what the character of American leadership shall be in the 1970s and during their own lifetimes. In doing so, they may find it fruitful to weigh the American experience during the postwar years and arrive at their own tentative conclusions concerning the value of Harry Truman's presidency. Only time can deliver the definitive verdict, of course. But as historians and citizens, we now have enough evidence and perspective on the Truman years to begin to analyze and judge.

The Clash of Contemporaries

"I believe that it must be the policy of the United States to support free peoples who are resisting attempted subjugation by armed minorities or by outside pressures."

President Harry S. Truman to Congress
March 12, 1947

"No nation, however strong, has the universal world power which reaches everywhere."

Walter Lippmann
"Today and Tomorrow," May 8, 1945

"We are reckoning with a force which cannot be handled successfully by a 'Get tough with Russia policy.'... The tougher we get, the tougher the Russians will get."

Henry A. Wallace
September 12, 1946

"Our present negative policies will never end the type of sustained offensive which Soviet Communism is mounting. . . .

John Foster Dulles
Life, May 19, 1952

"I have in my hand 57 cases of individuals who would appear to be either card carrying members or certainly loyal to the Communist Party, but who nevertheless are still helping to shape our foreign policy."

Senator Joseph R. McCarthy
February 20, 1950

". . .Under the guise of American ideals the old New Deal has been revived . . . The Federal Government comes forward again as Santa Claus himself, with a rich present for every special group in the United States. . . ."

Senator Robert A. Taft
January 8, 1948

". . . People are sick and tired of your empty pronouncements regarding civil rights. The nation has made itself ridiculous long enough by meddling in foreign countries while callously disregarding its manifest duty at home."

A citizen to President Truman
November 26, 1951

"No occupant of the White House since the nation was born has taken so frontal or constant a stand against racial discrimination as has Harry S. Truman."

Walter White
Executive Secretary, NAACP, 1952

"We know the kind of government we have now. It's tired. It's confused. It's coming apart at the seams . . . It cannot give this nation what it needs most—what is the real issue of this election—unity."

Governor Thomas E. Dewey
Campaign speech, 1948

Part One   THE COLD WAR: INTERNATIONAL AND DOMESTIC DIMENSIONS

Chapter 1 **NOTHING COULD SATISFY STALIN'S PARANOIA**

Pulitzer prize-winning historian who has written extensively on the age of Roosevelt, ARTHUR SCHLESINGER, JR. currently holds the Albert Schweitzer Chair in the Humanities at The City University of New York. In the essay that follows, Schlesinger surveys the events of the early Cold War period, and generally sustains the interpretation of those events as developed by the Truman administration. How does Schlesinger deal with the criticisms of the so-called "Liberal Establishment" interpretation that have multiplied in recent years? What factors does he emphasize in sustaining the position that "blame" for the Cold War still resides primarily in the Kremlin?

The Cold War in its original form was a presumably mortal antagonism, arising in the wake of the Second World War, between two rigidly hostile blocs, one led by the Soviet Union, the other by the United States. For nearly two somber and dangerous decades this antagonism dominated the fears of mankind; it may even, on occasion, have come close to blowing up the planet. In recent years, however, the once implacable struggle has lost its familiar clarity of outline. With the passing of old issues and the emergence of new conflicts and contestants, there is a natural tendency, especially on the part of the generation which grew up during the Cold War, to take a fresh look at the causes of the great contention between Russia and America.

From Arthur Schlesinger, Jr., "Origins of the Cold War," *Foreign Affairs*, XLVI (October 1967), pp. 22-52. Copyright 1967 by the Council on Foreign Relations, Inc., New York. Reprinted by permission of *Foreign Affairs*, October 1967. Footnotes omitted.

Some exercises in reappraisal have merely elaborated the orthodoxies promulgated in Washington or Moscow during the boom years of the Cold War. But others, especially in the United States (there are no signs, alas, of this in the Soviet Union), represent what American historians call "revisionism"—that is, a readiness to challenge official explanations. No one should be surprised by this phenomenon. Every war in American history has been followed in due course by skeptical reassessments of supposedly sacred assumptions. . . .

In the case of the Cold War, special factors reinforce the predictable historiographical rhythm. The outburst of polycentrism in the Communist empire has made people wonder whether communism was ever so monolithic as official theories of the Cold War supposed. A generation with no vivid memories of Stalinism may see the Russia of the forties in the image of the relatively mild, seedy, and irresolute Russia of the sixties. And for this same generation the American course of widening the war in Vietnam—which even nonrevisionists can easily regard as folly—has unquestionably stirred doubts about the wisdom of American foreign policy in the sixties which younger historians may have begun to read back into the forties.

It is useful to remember that, on the whole, past exercises in revisionism have failed to stick. Few historians today believe that the war hawks caused the War of 1812 or the slaveholders the Mexican War, or that the Civil War was needless, or that the House of Morgan brought America into the First World War or that Franklin Roosevelt schemed to produce the attack on Pearl Harbor. But this does not mean that one should depolore the rise of Cold War revisionism. For revisionism is an essential part of the process by which history, through the posing of new problems and the investigation of new possibilities, enlarges its perspectives and enriches its insights.

More than this, in the present context, revisionism expresses a deep, legitimate, and tragic apprehension. As the Cold War has begun to lose its purity of definition, as the moral absolutes of the fifties become the moralistic clichés of the sixties, some have begun to ask whether the appalling risks which humanity ran during the Cold War were, after all, necessary and inevitable, whether more restrained and rational policies might not have guided the energies of man from the perils of conflict into the potentialities of collaboration. The fact that such questions are in their nature unanswerable does not mean that it is not right and useful to raise them. Nor does it mean that our sons and daughters are not entitled to an accounting from the generation of Russians and Americans who produced the Cold War.

The orthodox American view, as originally set forth by the American government and as reaffirmed until recently by most American scholars, has been that the Cold War was the brave and essential response of free men to communist aggression. Some have gone back well before the Second World War to lay open the sources of Russian expansionism. Geopoliticians traced the Cold War to imperial Russian strategic ambitions which in the nineteenth century led to the Crimean War, to Russian penetration of the Balkans and the Middle East, and to Russian pressure on

Britain's "lifeline" to India. Ideologists traced it to the Communist Manifesto of 1848 ("the violent overthrow of the bourgeoisie lays the foundation for the sway of the proletariat"). Thoughtful observers (a phrase meant to exclude those who speak in Dullese about the unlimited evil of godless, atheistic, militant communism) concluded that classical Russian imperialism and Pan-Slavism, compounded after 1917 by Leninist messianism, confronted the West at the end of the Second World War with an inexorable drive for domination.

The revisionist thesis is very different. In its extreme form, it is that, after the death of Franklin Roosevelt and the end of the Second World War, the United States deliberately abandoned the wartime policy of collaboration and, exhilarated by the possession of the atomic bomb, undertook a course of aggression of its own designed to expel all Russian influence from Eastern Europe and to establish democratic-capitalist states on the very border of the Soviet Union. As the revisionists see it, this radically new American policy—or rather this resumption by Truman of the pre-Roosevelt policy of insensate anti-communism—left Moscow no alternative but to take measures in defense of its own borders. The result was the Cold War.

These two views, of course, could not be more starkly contrasting. It is therefore not unreasonable to look again at the half-dozen critical years between June 22, 1941, when Hitler attacked Russia, and July 2, 1947, when the Russians walked out of the Marshall Plan meeting in Paris. Several things should be borne in mind as this reexamination is made. For one thing, we have thought a great deal more in recent years, in part because of writers like Roberta Wohlstetter and T. C. Schelling, about the problems of communication in diplomacy—the signals which one nation, by word or by deed, gives, inadvertently or intentionally, to another. Any honest reappraisal of the origins of the Cold War requires the imaginative leap—which should in any case be as instinctive for the historian as it is prudent for the statesman—into the adversary's viewpoint. We must strive to see how, given Soviet perspectives, the Russians might conceivably have misread our signals, as we must reconsider how intelligently we read theirs.

For another, the historian must not overindulge the man of power in the illusion cherished by those in office that high position carries with it the easy ability to shape history. Violating the statesman's creed, Lincoln once blurted out the truth in his letter of 1864 to A. G. Hodges: "I claim not to have controlled events, but confess plainly that events have controlled me." He was not asserting Tolstoyan fatalism but rather suggesting how greatly events limit the capacity of the statesman to bend history to his will. The physical course of the Second World War—the military operations undertaken, the position of the respective armies at the war's end, the momentum generated by victory, and the vacuums created by defeat—all these determined the future as much as the character of individual leaders and the substance of national ideology and purpose.

Nor can the historian forget the conditions under which decisions are made, especially in a time like the Second World War. These were tired, overworked, aging men: in 1945, Churchill was 71 years old, Stalin had governed his country for 17 exacting years, Roosevelt his for 12 years nearly as exacting. During the war, moreover, the importunities of military operations had shoved postwar questions to the margins of their minds. All—even Stalin, behind his screen of ideology—had become addicts of improvisation, relying on authority and virtuosity to conceal the fact that they were constantly surprised by developments. Like Eliza, they leaped from one cake of ice to the next in the effort to reach the other side of the river. None showed great tactical consistency, or cared much about it; all employed a certain ambiguity to preserve their power to decide big issues; and it is hard to know how to interpret anything any one of them said on any specific occasion. This was partly because, like all princes, they designed their expressions to have particular effects on particular audiences; partly because the entirely genuine intellectual difficulty of the questions they faced made a degree of vacillation and mind-changing eminently reasonable. If historians cannot solve their problems in retrospect, who are they to blame Roosevelt, Stalin, and Churchill for not having solved them at the time?

Peacemaking after the Second World War was not so much a tapestry as it was a hopelessly raveled and knotted mess of yarn. Yet, for purposes of clarity, it is essential to follow certain threads. One theme indispensable to an understanding of the Cold War is the contrast between two clashing views of world order: the "universalist" view, by which all nations shared a common interest in all the affairs of the world, and the "sphere-of-influence" view, by which each great power would be assured by the other great powers of an acknowledged predominance in its own area of special interest. The universalist view assumed that national security would be guaranteed by an international organization. The sphere-of-interest view assumed that national security would be guaranteed by the balance of power. While in practice these views have by no means been incompatible (indeed, our shaky peace has been based on a combination of the two), in the abstract they involved sharp contradictions.

The tradition of American thought in these matters was universalist—that is, Wilsonian. Roosevelt had been a member of Wilson's subcabinet; in 1920, as candidate for Vice-President, he had campaigned for the League of Nations. It is true that, within Roosevelt's infinitely complex mind, Wilsonianism warred with the perception of vital strategic interests he had imbibed from Mahan. Moreover, his temperamental inclination to settle things with fellow princes around the conference table led him to regard the Big Three—or Four—as trustees for the rest of the world. On occasion, as this narrative will show, he was beguiled into flirtation with the sphere-of-influence heresy. But in principle he believed in joint action and remained a Wilsonian. His hope for Yalta, as he told the Congress on his return, was that it would "spell the end of the system of unilateral action, the exclusive alliances, the spheres of influence, the balances of power, and all the other expedients that have been tried for centuries—and have always failed."

Whenever Roosevelt backslid, he had at his side that Wilsonian fundamentalist, Secretary of State Cordell Hull, to recall him to the pure faith. After his visit to Moscow in 1943, Hull characteristically said that, with the Declaration of Four Nations on General Security (in which America, Russia, Britain, and China pledged "united action . . . for the organization and maintenance of peace and security"), "there will no longer be need for spheres of influence, for alliances, for balance of power, or any other of the special arrangements through which, in the unhappy past, the nations strove to safeguard their security or to promote their interests."

Remembering the corruption of the Wilsonian vision by the secret treaties of the First World War, Hull was determined to prevent any sphere-of-influence nonsense after the Second World War. He therefore fought all proposals to settle border questions while the war was still on and, excluded as he largely was from wartime diplomacy, poured his not inconsiderable moral energy and frustration into the promulgation of virtuous and spacious general principles.

In adopting the universalist view, Roosevelt and Hull were not indulging personal hobbies. Sumner Welles, Adolf Berle, Averell Harriman, Charles Bohlen—all, if with a variety of nuances, opposed the sphere-of-influence approach. And here the State Department was expressing what seems clearly to have been the predominant mood of the American people, so long mistrustful of European power politics. The Republicans shared the true faith. John Foster Dulles argued that the great threat to peace after the war would lie in the revival of sphere-of-influence thinking. The United States, he said, must not permit Britain and Russia to revert to these bad old ways; it must therefore insist on American participation in all policy decisions for all territories in the world. Dulles wrote pessimistically in January 1945, "The three great powers which at Moscow agreed upon the 'closest cooperation' about European questions have shifted to a practice of separate, regional responsibility."

It is true that critics, and even friends, of the United States sometimes noted a discrepancy between the American passion for universalism when it applied to territory far from American shores and the preeminence the United States accorded its own interests nearer home. Churchill, seeking Washington's blessing for a sphere-of-influence initiative in Eastern Europe, could not forbear reminding the Americans, "We follow the lead of the United States in South America;" nor did any universalist of record propose the abolition of the Monroe Doctrine. But a convenient myopia prevented such inconsistencies from qualifying the ardency of the universalist faith.

There seem only to have been three officials in the United States Government who dissented. One was the Secretary of War, Henry L. Stimson, a classical balance-of-power man, who in 1944 opposed the creation of a vacuum in Central Europe by the pastoralization of Germany and in 1945 urged "the settlement of all territorial acquisitions in the shape of defense posts which each of these four powers may deem to be necessary for their own safety" in advance of any effort to establish a peacetime United Nations. Stimson considered the claim of Russia to a preferred position in Eastern Europe as not unreasonable: as he told President Truman, he "thought the Russians perhaps were being more realistic than we were in regard to their own security." Such a position for Russia seemed to him comparable to the preferred American position in Latin America; he even spoke of "our respective orbits." Stimson was therefore skeptical of what he regarded as the prevailing tendency "to hang on to exaggerated views of the Monroe Doctrine and at the same time butt into every question that comes up in Central Europe." Acceptance of spheres of influence seemed to him the way to avoid "a head-on collision."

A second official opponent of universalism was George Kennan, an eloquent advocate from the American Embassy in Moscow of "a prompt and clear recognition of the division of Europe into spheres of influence and of a policy based on the fact of such division." Kennan argued that nothing we could do would possibly alter the course of events in Eastern Europe; that we were deceiving ourselves by supposing that these countries had any future but Russian domination; that we should therefore relinquish Eastern Europe to the Soviet Union and avoid anything which would make things easier for the Russians by giving them economic assistance or by sharing moral responsibility for their actions.

A third voice within the government against universalism was (at least after the war) Henry A. Wallace. As Secretary of Commerce, he stated the sphere-of-influence case with trenchancy in the famous Madison Square Garden speech of September 1946 which led to his dismissal by President Truman:

> On our part, we should recognize that we have no more business in the *political* affairs of Eastern Europe than Russia has in the *political* affairs of Latin America, Western Europe, and the United States. . . . Whether we like it or not, the Russians will try to socialize their sphere of influence just as we try to democratize our sphere of influence. . . . The Russians have no more business stirring up native Communists to political activity in Western Europe, Latin America, and the United States than we have in interfering with the politics of Eastern Europe and Russia.

Stimson, Kennan, and Wallace seem to have been alone in the government, however, in taking these views. They were very much minority voices. Meanwhile universalism, rooted in the American legal and moral tradition, overwhelmingly backed by contemporary opinion, received successive enshrinements in the Atlantic Charter of 1941, in the Declaration of the United Nations in 1942, and in the Moscow Declaration of 1943.

The Kremlin, on the other hand, thought *only* of spheres of interest; above all, the Russians were determined to protect their frontiers, and especially their border to the west, crossed so often and so bloodily in the dark course of their history. These western frontiers lacked natural means of defense—no great oceans, rugged mountains, steaming swamps, or impenetrable jungles. The history of Russia had been the history of invasion, the last of which was by now horribly killing up to twenty million of its people. The protocol of Russia therefore meant the enlargement of the area of Russian influence. Kennan himself wrote (in May 1944), "Behind Russia's stubborn expansion lies only the age-old sense of insecurity of a sedentary people reared on an exposed plain in the neighborhood of fierce nomadic peoples," and he called this "urge" a "permanent feature of Russian psychology."

In earlier times the "urge" had produced the tsarist search for buffer states and maritime outlets. In 1939 the Soviet-Nazi pact and its secret protocol had enabled Russia to begin to satisfy in the Baltic states, Karelian Finland and Poland, part of what it conceived as its security requirements in Eastern Europe. But the "urge" persisted, causing the friction between Russia and Germany in 1940 as each jostled for position in the area which separated them. Later it led to Molotov's new demands on Hitler in November 1940—a free hand in Finland, Soviet predominance in Rumania and Bulgaria, bases in the Dardanelles—the demands which convinced Hitler that he had no choice but to attack Russia. Now Stalin hoped to gain from the West what Hitler, a closer neighbor, had not dared yield him.

It is true that, so long as Russian survival appeared to require a second front to relieve the Nazi pressure, Moscow's demand for Eastern Europe was a little muffled. Thus the Soviet government adhered to the Atlantic Charter (though with a significant if obscure reservation about adapting its principles to "the circumstances, needs, and historic peculiarities of particular countries"). Thus it also adhered to the Moscow Declaration of 1943, and Molotov then, with his easy mendacity, even denied that Russia had any desire to divide Europe into spheres of influence. But this was guff, which the Russians were perfectly willing to ladle out if it would keep the Americans, and especially Secretary Hull (who made a strong personal impression at the Moscow conference) happy. "A declaration," as Stalin once observed to Eden, "I regard as algebra, but an agreement as practical arithmetic. I do not wish to decry algebra, but I prefer practical arithmetic."

The more consistent Russian purpose was revealed when Stalin offered the British a straight sphere-of-influence deal at the end of 1941. Britain, he suggested, should recognize the Russian absorption of the Baltic states, part of Finland, eastern Poland, and Bessarabia; in return, Russia would support any special British need for bases or security arrangements in Western Europe. There was nothing specifically Communist about these ambitions. If Stalin achieved them, he would be fulfilling an age-old dream of the tsars. The British reaction was mixed. "Soviet policy is amoral," as Anthony Eden noted at the time; "United States policy is exaggeratedly moral, at least where non-American interests are concerned." If Roosevelt was a universalist with occasional leanings toward spheres of influence and Stalin was a sphere-of-influence man with occasional gestures toward universalism, Churchill seemed evenly poised between the familiar realism of the balance of power, which he had so long recorded as an historian and manipulated as a statesman, and the hope that there must be some better way of doing things. His 1943 proposal of a world organization divided into regional councils represented an effort to blend universalist and sphere-of-interest conceptions. His initial rejection of Stalin's proposal in December 1941 as "directly contrary to the first, second, and third articles of the Atlantic Charter" thus did not spring entirely from a desire to propitiate the United States. On the other hand, he had himself already reinterpreted the Atlantic Charter as applying only to Europe (and thus not to the British Empire), and he was, above all, an empiricist who never believed in sacrificing reality on the altar of doctrine.

So in April 1942 he wrote Roosevelt that "the increasing gravity of the war" had led him to feel that the Charter "ought not to be construed so as to deny Russia the frontiers she occupied when Germany attacked her." Hull, however, remained fiercely hostile to the inclusion of territorial provisions in the Anglo-Russian treaty; the American position, Eden noted, "chilled me with Wilsonian memories." Though Stalin complained that it looked "as if the Atlantic Charter was directed against the U.S.S.R.," it was the Russian season of military adversity in the spring of 1942, and he dropped his demands.

He did not, however, change his intentions. A year later Ambassador Standley could cable Washington from Moscow: "In 1918 Western Europe attempted to set up a *cordon sanitaire* to protect it from the influence of bolshevism. Might not now the Kremlin envisage the formation of a belt of pro-Soviet states to protect it from the influences of the West?" It well might; and that purpose became increasingly clear as the war approached its end. Indeed, it derived sustenance from Western policy in the first area of liberation.

The unconditional surrender of Italy in July 1943 created the first major test of the Western devotion to universalism. America and Britain, having won the Italian war, handled the capitulation, keeping Moscow informed at a distance. Stalin complained:

> The United States and Great Britain made agreements but the Soviet Union received information about the results . . . just as a passive third observer. I have to tell you that it is impossible to tolerate the situation any longer. I propose that the [tripartite military-political commission] be established and that Sicily be assigned . . . as its place of residence.

Roosevelt, who had no intention of sharing the control of Italy with the Russians, suavely replied with the suggestion that Stalin send an officer "to General Eisenhower's headquarters in connection with the commission." Unimpressed, Stalin continued to press for a tripartite body; but his Western allies were adamant in keeping the Soviet Union off the Control Commission for Italy, and the Russians in the end had to be satisfied with a seat, along with minor Allied states, on a meaningless Inter-Allied Advisory Council. Their acquiescence in this was doubtless not unconnected with a desire to establish precedents for Eastern Europe.

Teheran in December 1943 marked the high point of three-power collaboration. Still, when Churchill asked about Russian territorial interests, Stalin replied a little ominously, "There is no need to speak at the present time about any Soviet desires, but when the time comes we will speak." In the next weeks, there were increasing indications of a Soviet determination to deal unilaterally with Eastern Europe—so much so that in early February 1944 Hull cabled Harriman in Moscow:

> Matters are rapidly approaching the point where the Soviet Government will have to choose between the development and extension of the foundation of international cooperation as the guiding principle of the postwar world as against the continuance of a unilateral and arbitrary method of dealing with its special problems even though these problems are admittedly of more direct interest to the Soviet Union than to other great powers.

As against this approach, however, Churchill, more tolerant of sphere-of-influence deviations, soon proposed that, with the impending liberation of the Balkans, Russia should run things in Rumania and Britain in Greece. Hull strongly opposed this suggestion but made the mistake of leaving Washington for a few days; and Roosevelt, momentarily free from his Wilsonian conscience, yielded to Churchill's plea for a three-months' trial. Hull resumed the fight on his return, and Churchill postponed the matter.

The Red Army continued its advance into Eastern Europe. In August the Polish Home Army, urged on by Polish-language broadcasts from Moscow, rose up against the Nazis in Warsaw. For 63 terrible days, the Poles fought valiantly on, while the Red Army halted on the banks of the Vistula a few miles away, and in Moscow Stalin for more than half this time declined to cooperate with the Western effort to drop supplies to the Warsaw Resistance. It appeared a calculated Soviet decision to let the Nazis slaughter the anti-Soviet Polish underground; and, indeed, the result was to destroy any substantial alternative to a Soviet solution in Poland. The agony of Warsaw caused the most deep and genuine moral shock in Britain and America and provoked dark forebodings about Soviet postwar purposes.

Again history enjoins the imaginative leap in order to see things for a moment from Moscow's viewpoint. The Polish question, Churchill would say at Yalta, was for Britain a question of honor. "It is not only a question of honor for Russia," Stalin replied, "but one of life and death. . . . Throughout history Poland had been the corridor for attack on Russia." A top postwar priority for any Russian regime must be to close that corridor. The Home Army was led by anti-Communists. It clearly hoped by its action to forestall the Soviet occupation of Warsaw and, in

Russian eyes, to prepare the way for an anti-Russian Poland. In addition, the uprising from a strictly operational viewpoint was premature. The Russians, it is evident in retrospect, had real military problems at the Vistula. The Soviet attempt in September to send Polish units from the Red Army across the river to join forces with the Home Army was a disaster. Heavy German shelling thereafter prevented the ferrying of tanks necessary for an assault on the German position. The Red Army itself did not take Warsaw for another three months. Nonetheless, Stalin's indifference to the human tragedy, his effort to blackmail the London Poles during the ordeal, his sanctimonious opposition during five precious weeks to aerial re-supply, the invariable coldness of his explanations ("the Soviet command has come to the conclusion that it must dissociate itself from the Warsaw adventure"), and the obvious political benefit to the Soviet Union from the destruction of the Home Army—all these had the effect of suddenly dropping the mask of wartime comrade-ship and displaying to the West the hard face of Soviet policy. In now pursuing what he grimly regarded as the minimal requirements for the postwar security of his country, Stalin was inadvertently showing the irreconcilability of both his means and his ends with the Anglo-American conception of the peace.

Meanwhile Eastern Europe presented the Alliance with still another crisis that same September. Bulgaria, which was not at war with Russia, decided to surrender to the Western Allies while it still could; and the English and Americans at Cairo began to discuss armistice terms with Bulgarian envoys. Moscow, challenged by what it plainly saw as a Western intrusion into its own zone of vital interest, promptly declared war on Bulgaria, took over the surrender negotiations and, in-voking the Italian precedent, denied its Western Allies any role in the Bulgarian Control Commission. In a long and thoughtful cable, Ambassador Harriman medi-tated on the problems of communication with the Soviet Union. "Words," he reflected, "have a different connotation to the Soviets than they have to us. When they speak of insisting on 'friendly governments' in their neighboring countries, they have in mind something quite different from what we would mean." The Russians, he surmised, really believed that Washington accepted "their position that although they would keep us informed they had the right to settle their problems with their western neighbors unilaterally." But the Soviet position was still in flux: "the Soviet Government is not one mind." The problem, as Harriman had earlier told Harry Hopkins, was "to strengthen the hands of those around Stalin who want to play the game along our lines." The way to do this, he now told Hull, was to

be understanding of their sensitivity, meet them much more than half way, encourage them and support them wherever we can, and yet oppose them promptly with the greatest of firmness where we see them going wrong. . . . The only way we can eventually come to an understanding with the Soviet Union on the question of non-interference in the internal affairs of other countries is for us to take a definite interest in the solution of the problems of each individual country as they arise.

As against Harriman's sophisticated universalist strategy, however, Churchill, increasingly fearful of the consequences of unrestrained competition in Eastern Europe, decided in earrly October to carry his sphere-of-influence proposal directly to Moscow. Roosevelt was at first content to have Churchill speak for him too and even prepared a cable to that effect. But Hopkins, a more rigorous universalist, took it upon himself to stop the cable and warn Roosevelt of its possible implications. Eventually Roosevelt sent a message to Harriman in Moscow emphasizing that he expected to "retain complete freedom of action after this conference is over." It was now that Churchill quickly proposed—and Stalin as quickly accepted—the celebrated division of southeastern Europe: ending (after further haggling between Eden and Molotov) with 90 per cent Soviet predominance in Rumania, 80 per cent in Bulgaria and Hungary, fifty-fifty in Jugoslavia, 90 per cent British predominance in Greece.

Churchill in discussing this with Harriman used the phrase "spheres of influence." But he insisted that these were only "immediate wartime arrangements" and received a highly general blessing from Roosevelt. Yet, whatever Churchill intended, there is reason to believe that Stalin construed the percentages as an agreement, not a declaration, as practical arithmetic, not algebra. For Stalin, it should be understood, the sphere-of-influence idea did not mean that he would abandon all efforts to spread communism in some other nation's sphere; it did mean that, if he tried this and the other side cracked down, he could not feel he had serious cause for complaint. As Kennan wrote to Harriman at the end of 1944:

> As far as border states are concerned the Soviet government has never ceased to think in terms of spheres of interest. They expect us to support them in whatever action they wish to take in those regions, regardless of whether that action seems to us or to the rest of the world to be right or wrong. . . . I have no doubt that this position is honestly maintained on their part, and that they would be equally prepared to reserve moral judgment on any actions which we might wish to carry out, i.e., in the Caribbean area.

In any case, the matter was already under test a good deal closer to Moscow than the Caribbean. The Communist-dominated resistance movement in Greece was in open revolt against the effort of the Papandreou government to disarm and disband the guerrillas. . . . Churchill now called in British Army units to crush the insurrection. This action produced a storm of criticism in his own country and in the United States; the American Government even publicly dissociated itself from the intervention, thereby emphasizing its detachment from the sphere-of-influence deal.

But Stalin, Churchill later claimed, "adhered strictly and faithfully to our agreement of October, and during all the long weeks of fighting the Communists in the streets of Athens not one word of reproach came from *Pravda* or *Izvestia*," though there is no evidence that he tried to call off the Greek Communists. Still, when the Communist rebellion later broke out again in Greece, Stalin told Kardelj and Djilas of Jugoslavia in 1948, "The uprising in Greece must be stopped, and as quickly as possible."

No one, of course, can know what really was in the minds of the Russian leaders. The Kremlin archives are locked; of the primary actors, only Molotov survives, and he has not yet indicated any desire to collaborate with the Columbia Oral History Project. We do know that Stalin did not wholly surrender to sentimental illusion about his new friends. In June 1944, on the night before the landings in Normandy, he told Djilas that the English "find nothing sweeter than to trick their allies. . . . And Churchill? Churchill is the kind who, if you don't watch him, will slip a kopeck out of your pocket. Yes, a kopeck out of your pocket!. . . . Roosevelt is not like that. He dips in his hand only for bigger coins." But whatever his views of his colleagues it is not unreasonable to suppose that Stalin would have been satisfied at the end of the war to secure what Kennan has called "a protective glacis along Russia's western border," and that, in exchange for a free hand in Eastern Europe, he was prepared to give the British and Americans equally free hands in their zones of vital interest, including in nations as close to Russia as Greece (for the British) and, very probably—or at least so the Jugoslaves believe—China (for the United States). In other words, his initial objectives were very probably not world conquest but Russian security.

It is now pertinent to inquire why the United States rejected the idea of stabilizing the world by division into spheres of influence and insisted on an East European strategy. One should warn against rushing to the conclusion that it was all a row between hard-nosed, balance-of-power realists and starry-eyed Wilsonians. Roosevelt, Hopkins, Welles, Harriman, Bohlen, Berle, Dulles, and other universalists were tough and serious men. Why then did they rebuff the spere-of-influence solution?

The first reason is that they regarded this solution as containing within itself the seeds of a third world war. The balance-of-power idea seemed inherently unstable. It had always broken down in the past. It held out to each power the permanent temptation to try to alter the balance in its own favor, and it built this temptation into the international order. It would turn the great powers of 1945 away from the objective of concerting common policies toward competition for postwar advantage. . . . The Americans were perfectly ready to acknowledge that Russia was entitled to convincing assurance of her national security—but not this way. "I could sympathize fully with Stalin's desire to protect his western borders from future attack," as Hull put it. "But I felt that this security could best be obtained through a strong postwar peace organization."

Hull's remark suggests the second objection: that the sphere-of-influence approach would, in the words of the State Department in 1945, "militate against the establishment and effective functioning of a broader system of general security in which all countries have their part." The United Nations, in short, was seen as the alternative to the balance of power. Nor did the universalists see any necessary incompatibility between the Russian desire for "friendly governments" on its frontier and the American desire for self-determination in Eastern Europe. Before Yalta the State Department judged the general mood of Europe as "to the left and strongly in favor of far-reaching economic and social reforms, but not, however, in favor of a left-wing totalitarian regime to achieve these reforms." Governments in Eastern Europe could be sufficiently to the left "to allay Soviet suspicions" but sufficiently representative "of the center and *petit bourgeois* elements" not to seem a prelude to communist dictatorship. The American criteria were therefore that the government "should be dedicated to the preservation of civil liberties" and "should favor social and economic reforms." A string of New Deal states—of Finlands and Czechoslovakias—seemed a reasonable compromise solution.

Third, the universalists feared that the sphere-of-interest approach would be what Hull termed "a haven for the isolationists," who would advocate America's participation in Western Hemisphere affairs on condition that it did not participate in European or Asian affairs. Hull also feared that spheres of interest would lead to "closed trade areas or discriminatory systems" and thus defeat his cherished dream of a low-tariff, freely trading world.

Fourth, the sphere-of-interest solution meant the betrayal of the principles for which the Second World War was being fought—the Atlantic Charter, the Four Freedoms, the Declaration of the United Nations. Poland summed up the problem. Britain, having gone to war to defend the independence of Poland from the Germans, could not easily conclude the war by surrendering the independence of Poland to the Russians. Thus, as Hopkins told Stalin after Roosevelt's death in 1945, Poland had "become the symbol of our ability to work out problems with the Soviet Union." Nor could American liberals in general watch with equanimity while the police state spread into countries which, if they had mostly not been real democracies, had mostly not been tyrannies either. . . .

Fifth, the sphere-of-influence solution would create difficult domestic problems in American politics. Roosevelt was aware of the six million or more Polish votes in the 1944 election; even more acutely, he was aware of the broader and deeper attack which would follow if, after going to war to stop the Nazi conquest of Europe, he permitted the war to end with the Communist conquest of Eastern Europe. As Archibald MacLeish, then Assistant Secretary of State for Public Affairs, warned in January 1945, "The wave of disillusionment which has distressed us in the last several weeks will be increased if the impression is permitted to get abroad that potentially totalitarian provisional governments are to be set up without adequate safeguards as to the holding of free elections and the realization of the principles of the Atlantic Charter." Roosevelt believed that no administration could survive which did not try everything short of war to save Eastern Europe, and he was the supreme American politician of the century.

Sixth, if the Russians were allowed to overrun Eastern Europe without argument, would that satisfy them? Even Kennan, in a dispatch of May 1944, admitted that the "urge" had dreadful potentialities: "If initially successful, will it know where to stop? Will it not be inexorably carried forward, by its very nature, in a struggle to reach the whole—to attain complete mastery of the shores of the Atlantic and the Pacific?" His own answer was that there were inherent limits to the Russian capacity to expand—"that Russia will not have an easy time in maintaining the power which it has seized over other people in Eastern and Central Europe, unless it receives both moral and material assistance from the West." Subsequent developments have vindicated Kennan's argument. By the late forties, Jugoslavia and Albania, the two East European states farthest from the Soviet Union and the two in which communism was imposed from within rather than from without, had declared their independence of Moscow. But, given Russia's success in maintaining centralized control over the international Communist movement for a quarter of a century, who in 1944 could have had much confidence in the idea of Communist revolts against Moscow?

Most of those involved therefore rejected Kennan's answer and stayed with his question. If the West turned its back on Eastern Europe, the higher probability, in their view, was that the Russians would use their security zone, not just for defensive purposes, but as a springboard from which to mount an attack on Western Europe. . . . If a row with Russia were inevitable, every consideration of prudence dictated that it should take place in Eastern rather than Western Europe.

Thus idealism and realism joined in opposition to the sphere-of-influence solution. The consequence was a determination to assert an American interest in the postwar destiny of all nations, including those of Eastern Europe. In the message which Roosevelt and Hopkins drafted after Hopkins had stopped Roosevelt's initial cable authorizing Churchill to speak for the United States at the Moscow meeting of October 1944, Roosevelt now said, "There is in this global war literally no question, either military or political, in which the United States is not interested. . . .

For better or worse, this was the American position. It is now necessary to attempt the imaginative leap and consider the impact of this position on the leaders of the Soviet Union who, also for better or for worse, had reached the bitter conclusion that the survival of their country depended on their unchallenged control of the corridors through which enemies had so often invaded their homeland. They could claim to have been keeping their own side of the sphere-of-influence bargain. Of course, they were working to capture the resistance movements of Western Europe; indeed, with the appointment of Oumansky as Ambassador to

Mexico they were even beginning to enlarge underground operations in the Western Hemisphere. But, from their viewpoint, if the West permitted this, the more fools they; and, if the West stopped it, it was within their right to do so. In overt political matters the Russians were scrupulously playing the game. They had watched in silence while the British shot down Communists in Greece. In Jugoslavia Stalin was urging Tito (as Djilas later revealed) to keep King Peter. They had not only acknowledged Western preeminence in Italy but had recognized the Badoglio regime; the Italian Communists had even voted (against the Socialists and the Liberals) for the renewal of the Lateran Pacts.

They would not regard anti-Communist action in a Western zone as a *casus belli;* and they expected reciprocal license to assert their own authority in the East. But the principle of self-determination was carrying the United States into a deeper entanglement in Eastern Europe than the Soviet Union claimed as a right (whatever it was doing underground) in the affairs of Italy, Greece or China. When the Russians now exercised in Eastern Europe the same brutal control they were prepared to have Washington exercise in the American sphere of influence, the American protests, given the paranoia produced alike by Russian history and Leninist ideology, no doubt seemed not only an act of hypocrisy but a threat to security. To the Russians, a stroll into the neighborhood easily became a plot to burn down the house: when, for example, damaged American planes made emergency landings in Poland and Hungary, Moscow took this as attempts to organize the local resistance. It is not unusual to suspect one's adversary of doing what one is already doing oneself. At the same time, the cruelty with which the Russians executed their idea of spheres of influence—in a sense, perhaps, an unwitting cruelty, since Stalin treated the East Europeans no worse than he had treated the Russians in the thirties—discouraged the West from accepting the equation (for example, Italy = Rumania) which seemed so self-evident to the Kremlin.

So Moscow very probably, and not unnaturally, perceived the emphasis on self-determination as a systematic and deliberate pressure on Russia's western frontiers. Moreover, the restoration of capitalism to countries freed at frightful cost by the Red Army no doubt struck the Russians as the betrayal of the principles for which *they* were fighting. "That they, the victors," Isaac Deutscher has suggested, "should now preserve an order from which they had experienced nothing but hostility, and could expect nothing but hostility . . . would have been the most miserable anti-climax to their great 'war of liberation.' " By 1944 Poland was the critical issue; Harriman later said that "under instructions from President Roosevelt, I talked about Poland with Stalin more frequently than any other subject." While the West saw the point of Stalin's demand for a "friendly government" in Warsaw, the American insistence on the sovereign virtues of free elections (ironically in the spirit of the 1917 bolshevik decree of peace, which affirmed "the right" of a nation "to decide the forms of its state existence by a free vote, taken after the complete evacuation of the incorporating or, generally, of the stronger nation") created an insoluble problem in those countries, like Poland (and Rumania) where free elections would almost certainly produce anti-Soviet governments.

The Russians thus may well have estimated the Western pressures as calculated to encourage their enemies in Eastern Europe and to defeat their own minimum objective of a protective glacis. Everything still hung, however, on the course of military operations. The wartime collaboration had been created by one thing, and one thing alone: the threat of Nazi victory. So long as this threat was real, so was the collaboration. In late December 1944, von Rundstedt launched his counteroffensive in the Ardennes. A few weeks later, when Roosevelt, Churchill, and Stalin gathered in the Crimea, it was in the shadow of this last considerable explosion of German power. The meeting at Yalta was still dominated by the mood of war.

Yalta remains something of an historical perplexity—less, from the perspective of 1967, because of a mythical American deference to the sphere-of-influence thesis than because of the documentable Russian deference to the universalist thesis. Why should Stalin in 1945 have accepted the Declaration on Liberated Europe and an agreement on Poland pledging that "the three governments will jointly" act to assure "free elections of governments responsive to the will of the people?" There are several probable answers: that the war was not over and the Russians still wanted the Americans to intensify their military effort in the West; that one clause in the Declaration premised action on "the opinion of the three governments" and thus implied a Soviet veto, though the Polish agreement was more definite; most of all that the universalist algebra of the Declaration was plainly in Stalin's mind to be construed in terms of the practical arithmetic of his sphere-of-influence agreement with Churchill the previous October. . . . He could well have been strengthened in this supposition by the fact that *after* Yalta, Churchill himself repeatedly reasserted the terms of the October agreement as if he regarded it, despite Yalta, as controlling.

Harriman still had the feeling before Yalta that the Kremlin had "two approaches to their postwar policies" and that Stalin himself was "of two minds." One approach emphasized the internal reconstruction and development of Russia; the other its external expansion. But in the meantime the fact which dominated all political decisions—that is, the war against Germany—was moving into its final phase. In the weeks after Yalta, the military situation changed with great rapidity. As the Nazi threat declined, so too did the need for cooperation. The Soviet Union, feeling itself menaced by the American idea of self-determination and the borderlands diplomacy to which it was leading, skeptical whether the United Nations would protect its frontiers as reliably as its own domination in Eastern Europe, began to fulfill its security requirements unilaterally.

In March Stalin expressed his evaluation of the United Nations by rejecting Roosevelt's plea that Molotov come to the San Francisco Conference, if only for the opening sessions. In the next weeks the Russians emphatically and crudely worked their will in Eastern Europe, above all in the test country of Poland. They were ignoring the Declaration on Liberated Europe, ignoring the Atlantic Charter, self-determination, human freedom, and everything else the Americans considered essential for a stable peace. "We must clearly recognize," Harriman wired Washington a few days before Roosevelt's death, "that the Soviet program is the establishment of totalitarianism, ending personal liberty and democracy as we know and respect it."

At the same time, the Russians also began to mobilize Communist resources in the United States itself to block American universalism. In April 1945 Jacques Duclos, who had been the Comintern official responsible for the Western communist parties, launched in *Cahiers du Communisme* an uncompromising attack on the policy of the American Communist Party. Duclos sharply condemned the revisionism of Earl Browder, the American Communist leader, as "expressed in the concept of a long-term class peace in the United States, of the possibility of the suppression of the class struggle in the postwar period and of establishment of harmony between labor and capital." Browder was specifically rebuked for favoring the "self-determination" of Europe "west of the Soviet Union" on a bourgeois-democratic basis. The excommunication of Browderism was plainly the Politburo's considered reaction to the impending defeat of Germany; it was a signal to the Communist parties of the West that they should recover their identity; it was Moscow's alert to Communists everywhere that they should prepare for new policies in the postwar world.

The Duclos piece obviously could not have been planned and written much later than the Yalta conference—that is, well before a number of events which revisionists now cite in order to demonstrate American responsibility for the Cold War: before Allen Dulles, for example, began to negotiate the surrender of the German armies in Italy (the episode which provoked Stalin to charge Roosevelt with seeking a separate peace and provoked Roosevelt to denounce the "vile misrepresentations" of Stalin's informants); well before Roosevelt died; many months before the testing of the atomic bomb; even more months before Truman ordered that the bomb be dropped on Japan. William Z. Foster, who soon replaced Browder as the leader of the American Communist Party and embodied the new Moscow line, later boasted of having said in January 1944, "A postwar Roosevelt administration would continue to be, as it is now, an imperialist government." With ancient suspicions revived by the American insistence on universalism, this was no doubt the conclusion which the Russians were reaching at the same time. The Soviet canonization of Roosevelt (like their present-day canonization of Kennedy) took place after the American President's death.

The atmosphere of mutual suspicion was beginning to rise. In January 1945 Molotov formally proposed that the United States grant Russia a $6 billion credit for postwar reconstruction. With characteristic tact he explained that he was doing this as a favor to save America from a postwar depression. The proposal seems to have been diffidently made and diffidently received. Roosevelt requested that the matter "not be pressed further" on the American side until he had a chance to talk with Stalin; but the Russians did not follow it up either at Yalta in February (save for a single glancing reference) or during the Stalin-Hopkins talks in May or at Potsdam. Finally the proposal was renewed in the very different political atmosphere of August. This time Washington inexplicably mislaid the request during the transfer of the records of the Foreign Economic Administration to the State Department. It did not turn up again until March 1946. Of course this was impossible for the Russians to believe; it is hard enough even for those acquainted with the capacity of the American government for incompetence to believe; and it only strengthened Soviet suspicions of American purposes.

The American credit was one conceivable form of Western contribution to Russian reconstruction. Another was lend-lease, and the possibility of reconstruction aid under the lend-lease protocol had already been discussed in 1944. But in May 1945 Russia, like Britain, suffered from Truman's abrupt termination of lend-lease shipments—"unfortunate and even brutal," Stalin told Hopkins, adding that, if it was "designed as pressure on the Russians in order to soften them up, then it was a fundamental mistake." A third form was German reparations. Here Stalin in demanding $10 billion in reparations for the Soviet Union made his strongest fight at Yalta. Roosevelt, while agreeing essentially with Churchill's opposition, tried to postpone the matter by accepting the Soviet figure as a "basis for discussion"—a formula which led to future misunderstanding. In short, the Russian hope for major Western assistance in postwar reconstruction foundered on three events which the Kremlin could well have interpreted respectively as deliberate sabotage (the loan request), blackmail (lend-lease cancellation), and pro-Germanism (reparations).

Actually the American attempt to settle the fourth lend-lease protocol was generous and the Russians for their own reasons declined to come to an agreement. It is not clear, though, that satisfying Moscow on any of these financial scores would have made much essential difference. It might have persuaded some doves in the Kremlin that the U.S. government was genuinely friendly; it might have persuaded some hawks that the American anxiety for Soviet friendship was such that Moscow could do as it wished without inviting challenge from the United States. It would, in short, merely have reinforced both sides of the Kremlin debate; it would hardly have reversed deeper tendencies toward the deterioration of political relationships. Economic deals were surely subordinate to the quality of mutual political confidence; and here, in the months after Yalta, the decay was steady.

The Cold War had now begun. It was the product not of a decision but of a dilemma. Each side felt compelled to adopt policies which the other could not but regard as a threat to the principles of the peace. Each then felt compelled to undertake defensive measures. Thus the Russians saw no choice but to consolidate their security in Eastern Europe. The Americans, regarding Eastern Europe as the first step toward Western Europe, responded by asserting their interest in the zone the Russians deemed vital to their security. The Russians concluded that the West was resuming its old course of capitalist encirclement; that it was purposefully laying the foundation for anti-Soviet regimes in the area defined by the blood of centuries as crucial to Russian survival. Each side believed with passion that future international stability depended on the success of its own conception of world order. Each side, in pursuing its own clearly indicated and deeply cherished principles, was only confirming the fear of the other that it was bent on aggression.

Very soon the process began to acquire a cumulative momentum. The impending collapse of Germany thus provoked new troubles: the Russians, for example, sincerely feared that the West was planning a separate surrender of the German armies in Italy in a way which would release troops for Hitler's eastern front, as they subsequently feared that the Nazis might succeed in surrendering Berlin to the West. This was the context in which the atomic bomb now appeared. Though the revisionist argument that Truman dropped the bomb less to defeat Japan than to intimidate Russia is not convincing, this thought unquestionably appealed to some in Washington as at least an advantageous side effect of Hiroshima.

So the machinery of suspicion and counter suspicion, action, and counter action, was set in motion. But, given relations among traditional national states, there was still no reason, even with all the postwar jostling, why this should not have remained a manageable situation. What made it unmanageable, what caused the rapid escalation of the Cold War and in another two years completed the division of Europe, was a set of considerations which this account has thus far excluded.

Up to this point, the discussion has considered the schism within the wartime coalition as if it were entirely the result of disagreements among national states. Assuming this framework, there was unquestionably a failure of communication between America and Russia, a misperception of signals and, as time went on, a mounting tendency to ascribe ominous motives to the other side. It seems hard, for example, to deny that American postwar policy created genuine difficulties for the Russians and even assumed a threatening aspect for them. All this the revisionists have rightly and usefully emphasized.

But the great omission of the revisionists—and also the fundamental explanation of the speed with which the Cold War escalated—lies precisely in the fact that the Soviet Union was *not* a traditional national state. This is where the "mirror image," invoked by some psychologists, falls down. For the Soviet Union was a phenomenon very different from America or Britain: it was a totalitarian state, endowed with an all-explanatory, all-consuming ideology, committed to the infallibility of government and party, still in a somewhat messianic mood, equating dissent with treason, and ruled by a dictator who, for all his quite extraordinary abilities, had his paranoid moments.

Marxism-Leninism gave the Russian leaders a view of the world according to which all societies were inexorably destined to proceed along appointed roads by appointed stages until they achieved the classless nirvana. Moreover, given the resistance of the capitalists to this development, the existence of any non-communist state was *by definition* a threat to the Soviet Union. "As long as capitalism and socialism exist," Lenin wrote, "we cannot live in peace: in the end, one or the other will triumph—a funeral dirge will be sung either over the Soviet Republic or over world capitalism."

Stalin and his associates, whatever Roosevelt or Truman did or failed to do, were bound to regard the United States as the enemy not because of this deed or that, but because of the primordial fact that America was the leading capitalist power and thus, by Leninist syllogism, unappeasably hostile, driven by the logic of its system to oppose, encircle, and destroy Soviet Russia. Nothing the United States could have done in 1944-1945 would have abolished this mistrust, required and sanctified as it was by Marxist gospel—nothing short of the conversion of the United States into a Stalinist despotism; and even this would not have sufficed, as the experience of Jugoslavia and China soon showed, unless it were accompanied by total subservience to Moscow. So long as the United States remained a capitalist democracy, no American policy, given Moscow's theology, could hope to win basic Soviet confidence, and every American action was poisoned from the source. So long as the Soviet Union remained a messianic state, ideology compelled a steady expansion of Communist power.

It is easy, of course, to exaggerate the capacity of ideology to control events. The tension of acting according to revolutionary abstractions is too much for most nations to sustain over a long period: that is why Mao Tse-tung has launched his Cultural Revolution, hoping thereby to create a permanent revolutionary mood and save Chinese communism from the degeneration which, in his view, has overtaken Russian communism. Still, as any revolution grows older, normal human and social motives will increasingly reassert themselves. In due course, we can be sure, Leninism will be about as effective in governing the daily lives of Russians as Christianity is in governing the daily lives of Americans. Like the Ten Commandments and the Sermon on the Mount, the Leninist verities will increasingly become platitudes for ritual observance, not guides to secular decision. There can be no worse fallacy (even if respectable people practiced it diligently for a season in the United States) than that of drawing from a nation's ideology permanent conclusions about its behavior.

A temporary recession of ideology was already taking place during the Second World War when Stalin, to rally his people against the invader, had to replace the appeal of Marxism by that of nationalism. ("We are under no illusions that they are fighting for us," Stalin once said to Harriman. "They are fighting for Mother Russia.") But this was still taking place within the strictest limitations. The Soviet Union remained as much a police state as ever; the regime was as infallible as ever; foreigners and their ideas were as suspect as ever. "Never, except possibly during my later experience as ambassador in Moscow," Kennan has written, "did the insistence of the Soviet authorities on isolation of the diplomatic corps weigh more heavily on me ... than in these first weeks following my return to Russia in the final months of the war.... [We were] treated as though we were the bearers of some species of the plague"—which, of course, from the Soviet viewpoint, they were: the plague of skepticism.

Paradoxically, of the forces capable of bringing about a modification of ideology, the most practical and effective was the Soviet dictatorship itself. If Stalin was an ideologist, he was also a pragmatist. If he saw everything through the lenses of Marxism-Leninism, he also, as the infallible expositor of the faith, could reinterpret Marxism-Leninism to justify anything he wanted to do at any given moment. No doubt Roosevelt's ignorance of Marxism-Leninism was inexcusable and led to grievous miscalculations. But Roosevelt's efforts to work on and through Stalin were not so hopelessly naive as it used to be fashionable to think. With the extraordinary instinct of a great political leader, Roosevelt intuitively understood that Stalin was the *only* lever available to the West against the Leninist ideology and the Soviet system. If Stalin could be reached, then alone was there a chance of getting the Russians to act contrary to the precriptions of their faith. The best evidence is that Roosevelt retained a certain capacity to influence Stalin to the end; the nominal Soviet acquiescence in American universalism as late as Yalta was perhaps an indication of that. It is in this way that the death of Roosevelt was crucial—not in the vulgar sense that his policy was then reversed by his successor, which did not happen, but in the sense that no other American could hope to have the restraining impact on Stalin which Roosevelt might for a while have had.

Stalin alone could have made any difference. Yet Stalin, in spite of the impression of sobriety and realism he made on Westerners who saw him during the Second World War, was plainly a man of deep and morbid obsessions and compulsions. When he was still a young man, Lenin had criticized his rude and arbitrary ways. A reasonably authoritative observer (N. S. Khrushchev) later commented, "These negative characteristics of his developed steadily and during the last years acquired an absolutely insufferable character." His paranoia, probably set off by the suicide of his wife in 1932, led to the terrible purges of the mid-thirties and the wanton murder of thousands of his Bolshevik comrades. "Everywhere and in everything," Khrushchev says of this period, "he saw 'enemies,' 'double-dealers,' and 'spies.' " The crisis of war evidently steadied him in some way, though Khrushchev speaks of his "nervousness and hysteria ... even after the war began." The madness, so rigidly controlled for a time, burst out with new and shocking intensity in the postwar years. "After the war," Khrushchev testifies,

> the situation became even more complicated. Stalin became even more capricious, irritable and brutal; in particular, his suspicion grew. His persecution mania reached unbelievable dimensions.. . . . He decided everything, without any consideration for anyone or anything.
>
> Stalin's wilfulness showed itself ... also in the international relations of the Soviet Union. ... He had completely lost a sense of reality; he demonstrated his

suspicion and haughtiness not only in relation to individuals in the USSR, but in relation to whole parties and nations.

A revisionist fallacy has been to treat Stalin as just another Real-politik statesman, as Second World War revisionists see Hitler as just another Stresemann or Bismarck. But the record makes it clear that in the end nothing could satisfy Stalin's paranoia. His own associates failed. Why does anyone suppose that any conceivable American policy would have succeeded?

An analysis of the origins of the Cold War which leaves out these factors—the intransigence of Leninist ideology, the sinister dynamics of a totalitarian society and the madness of Stalin—is obviously incomplete. It was these factors which made it hard for the West to. accept the thesis that Russia was moved only by a desire to protect its security and would be satisfied by the control of Eastern Europe; it was these factors which charged the debate between universalism and spheres of influence with apocalyptic potentiality.

Leninism and totalitarianism created a structure of thought and behavior which made postwar collaboration between Russia and America—in any normal sense of civilized intercourse between national states—inherently impossible. The Soviet dictatorship of 1945 simply could not have survived such a collaboration. Indeed, nearly a quarter-century later, the Soviet regime, though it has meanwhile moved a good distance, could still hardly survive it without risking the release inside Russia of energies profoundly opposed to Communist despotism. As for Stalin, he may have represented the only force in 1945 capable of overcoming Stalinism, but the very traits which enabled him to win absolute power expressed terrifying instabilities of mind and temperament and hardly offered a solid foundation for a peaceful world.

The difference between America and Russia in 1945 was that some Americans fundamentally believed that, over a long run, a *modus vivendi* with Russia was possible; while the Russians, so far as one can tell, believed in no more than a short-run *modus vivendi* with the United States.

Harriman and Kennan, this narrative has made clear, took the lead in warning Washington about the difficulties of short-run dealings with the Soviet Union. But both argued that, if the United States developed a rational policy and stuck to it, there would be, after long and rough passages, the prospect of eventual clearing. "I am, as you know," Harriman cabled Washington in early April, "a most earnest advocate of the closest possible understanding with the Soviet Union so that what I am saying relates only to how best to attain such understanding." Kennan has similarly made it clear that the function of his containment policy was "to tide us over a difficult time and bring us to the point where we could discuss effectively with the Russians the dangers and drawbacks this *status quo* involved, and to arrange with them for its peaceful replacement by a better and sounder one." The subsequent careers of both men attest to the honesty of these statements.

There is no corresponding evidence on the Russian side that anyone seriously sought a *modus vivendi* in these terms. Stalin's choice was whether his long-term ideological and national interests would be better served by a short-run truce with the West or by an immediate resumption of pressure. In October 1945 Stalin indicated to Harriman at Sochi that he planned to adopt the second course—that the Soviet Union was going isolationist. No doubt the succession of problems with the United States contributed to this decision, but the basic causes most probably lay elsewhere: in the developing situations in Eastern Europe, in Western Europe, and in the United States.

In Eastern Europe, Stalin was still for a moment experimenting with techniques of control. But he must by now have begun to conclude that he had underestimated the hostility of the people to Russian dominion. The Hungarian elections in November would finally convince him that the Yalta formula was a road to anti-Soviet governments. At the same time, he was feeling more strongly than ever a sense of his opportunities in Western Europe. The other half of the Continent lay unexpectedly before him, politically demoralized, economically prostrate, militarily defenseless. The hunting would be better and safer than he had anticipated. As for the United States, the alacrity of postwar demobilization must have recalled Roosevelt's offhand remark at Yalta that "two years would be the limit" for keeping American troops in Europe. And . . . Marxist theology assured Stalin that the United States was heading into a bitter postwar depression and would be consumed with its own problems. If the condition of Eastern Europe made unilateral action seem essential in the interests of Russian security, the condition of Western Europe and the United States offered new temptations for Communist expansion. The Cold War was now in full swing.

It still had its year of modulations and accommodations. Secretary Byrnes conducted his long and fruitless campaign to persuade the Russians that America only sought governments in Eastern Europe "both friendly to the Soviet Union and representative of all the democratic elements of the country." Crises were surmounted in Trieste and Iran. Secretary Marshall evidently did not give up hope of a *modus vivendi* until the Moscow conference of foreign secretaries of March 1947. Even then, the Soviet Union was invited to participate in the Marshall Plan.

The point of no return came on July 2, 1947, when Molotov, after bringing 89 technical specialists with him to Paris and evincing initial interest in the project for European reconstruction, received the hot flash from the Kremlin, denounced the whole idea and walked out of the conference. For the next fifteen years the Cold War raged unabated, passing out of historical ambiguity into the realm of good versus evil and breeding on both sides simplifications, stereotypes, and self-serving absolutes, often couched in interchangeable phrases. Under the pressure even America, for a deplorable decade, forsook its pragmatic and pluralist traditions, posed as God's appointed messenger to ignorant and sinful man and followed the Soviet example in looking to a world remade in its own image.

In retrospect, if it is impossible to see the Cold War as a case of American aggression and Russian response, it is also hard to see it as a pure case of Russian aggression and American response. "In what is truly tragic," wrote Hegel, "there must be valid moral powers on both the sides which come into collision. . . . Both suffer loss and yet both are mutually justified." In this sense, the Cold War had its tragic elements. The question remains whether it was an instance of Greek tragedy— as Auden has called it, "the tragedy of necessity," where the feeling aroused in the spectator is "What a pity it had to be this way"—or of Christian tragedy, "the tragedy of possibility," where the feeling aroused is "What a pity it was this way when it might have been otherwise."

Once something has happened, the historian is tempted to assume that it had to happen; but this may often be a highly unphilosophical assumption. The Cold War could have been avoided only if the Soviet Union had not been possessed by convictions both of the infallibility of the Communist word and of the inevitability of a Communist world. These convictions transformed an impasse between national states into a religious war, a tragedy of possibility into one of necessity. One might wish that America had preserved the poise and proportion of the first years of the Cold War and had not in time succumbed to its own forms of self-righteousness. But the most rational of American policies could hardly have averted the Cold War. Only today, as Russia begins to recede from its messianic mission and to accept, in practice if not yet in principle, the permanence of the world of diversity, only now can the hope flicker that this long, dreary, costly contest may at last be taking on forms less dramatic, less obsessive and less dangerous to the future of mankind.

Chapter 2 THERE COULD BE NO DEALING WITH COMMUNISTS

A professor of economics at Columbia University during the 1920s, REXFORD G. TUGWELL served in Franklin D. Roosevelt's "Brains Trust" following the 1932 election, and held various government posts during the New Deal years. In 1946 Tugwell supported Henry A. Wallace's bid for the presidency on the Progressive party ticket on the grounds that the Truman administration had deserted Roosevelt's principles in both foreign and domestic policy. In "Off Course: From Truman to Nixon" (1971), Tugwell traces what he believes to be the dire consequences of Cold War policies followed by presidential administrations since FDR's. In what ways do Tugwell and Schlesinger differ over their assessments of Roosevelt's plans for, and likely responses to, the postwar world situation? Over the American attitude towards "spheres of influence"?

First Mistake: The Bomb

...No President ever began with more good wishes than Truman. As he undertook his unaccustomed duties, there was a general realization that he had a very special problem. To succeed such a man as Roosevelt, so long in office, so beloved and so trusted, and especially for one who was relatively unknown and inexperienced, was to undertake something so difficult that all possible allowances must be made and all possible support given. Truman had been Vice-President for only a few months, and it was no secret that he had had no part in wartime decision-making and only the slightest briefing on national affairs or on arrangements for the coming peace. Germany, however, was defeated; and Japan, whose armies were spread throughout

From Rexford G. Tugwell, *Off Course: From Truman to Nixon* (New York: Praeger Publishers, Inc., 1971), pp. 182-198, 203-207, 210-222. Footnotes omitted.

Southeast Asia, was being closed in on and had no chance of defending the home islands successfully; it was a question of time. . . .

Roosevelt's concentration in his last months had been on the coming peace; the strategy of victory was already in the past. He had been failing fast and for some time it had been obvious that he could not go on much longer . . . but he was determined not to recognize that his weakness was permanent. . . .

Roosevelt had felt that his relations with Churchill and Stalin were such that no substitution was possible; and his scheme for the first years of the peace depended on their close collaboration. . . .

There was the consideration also that if Russia and the United States, each dominating a continent, could cooperate, the many dissensions among countries trying for advantage in troubled circumstances could be managed. He quite realistically felt that only he could bring that cooperation into a settled stage. Britain unfortunately did not count much in this. The Empire was falling apart; the war had been fatally impoverishing; and Churchill was vainly trying to arrest the decline. Stalin obviously respected the American President and saw the British situation all too clearly. With Roosevelt gone, the chance that collaboration would be of any use to Russia would be slight.

There had been work going on in Washington to shape an organization for world order. This was Roosevelt's return to the lessons he had learned from Wilson. . . .

He never gave up the hope that an organization would be created that would guarantee the avoidance of further war and would organize cooperation. He had seen Wilson's political errors, and, in the years since, had thought much of ways to avoid making similar ones. Their central cause had been the attempt to enforce the principle of self-determination. There was much remaining sentiment for such an arrangement; it sounded so liberal to speak of independence, of peoples' rights to shape their own government, and to be free of colonial hegemony! Roosevelt understood, however, that only great-power collaboration could prevent the chaos sure to result from the struggle of every ethnic group not only to establish itself as a nation but to take in as many minorities and as much territory as it could grasp. Independence was something to be worked for; but, when minorities demanded what the majority had, it was different. They became rebels; and they must be suppressed to preserve union. He could see chaos in entrusting world order to an assembly of small nations all scrambling for advantage and all having dissident minorities.

The United Nations he visualized, and got agreement from Stalin and Churchill for, was expected to have as its central body a council of the great powers: Russia, the United States, Britain, France, and China—a horrid arrangement to the liberal view; and those who were working on the proposal . . . were unreconstructed Wilsonian liberals. They meant to reconstitute the League of Nations, now dead, in essentially its old form. The United States had never been a member of the League; and Roosevelt had long ago repudiated any intention of re-establishing it. His conception was, in effect, a return to the spheres of influence associated in liberal minds with minorities included in empires who claimed to have been exploited— "oppressed" was the favorite description.

That it was practically impossible to form a nation large enough to survive that did not have uneasy minorities was not a consideration that ever seemed to have weight with the collaborators at Dumbarton Oaks, where the United Nations charter was being drafted. Roosevelt had agreed to an Assembly of nations; but he meant to have the real power rest with the permanent members of the Council. The Assembly might talk but would not be allowed to legislate. This was the essential, the irreducible principle, arrived at, as he thought, by enough, and sufficiently costly, error.

Truman had no sense of these differences and only superficial knowledge of the background Roosevelt was judging from. He was hopelessly unready; but he was suddenly President, and the decisions would be his to make. . . .

For the implementation of Roosevelt's grand postwar design, it was necessary for the five powers to cooperate. In this the lead must be taken by the United States. No other nation had emerged from the war stronger than when it had begun. Productivity was immensely increased; military forces, relatively weak before 1940, and severely set back by Pearl Harbor, had grown to unprecedented size and had reached across both oceans; sharing with the Allies was well organized and was meeting the deficiencies caused by their losses and disorganization since 1939. Russia, in contrast, had been invaded, had been forced to fight mighty last-ditch battles as deep in the heartland as Stalingrad on the Volga. When winter and heroic defense had turned back the invaders, there had been left a lasting expectation of aggression from the west and a deep longing for secure borders. These fears and hopes were not only in Stalin's mind but in that of all those who had suffered through the experience. The Germans, beaten, had to be Germans without power to repeat the outrage.

Less than a month after Roosevelt's death, they surrendered. V-E Day was on May seventh; but less than two weeks after his death American and Russian negotiators (Harriman and Molotov) had fallen out over the regime to be installed in Poland, the staging base for German armies. The question was whether it should be the government in exile, for years headquartered in London, or one chosen by the Russians. The most sensitive element in the situation was that Poland had been conquered with little opposition by Hitler's blitzkrieg (as had France) and had thereafter been helplessly subject to Nazi abuses. Memories of starvation in Leningrad and the costly losses at Stalingrad were mingled with those of massacres as the Germans had crossed the Ukraine. The Russians were determined to prevent another such invasion, and this, for them, meant domination of Eastern Europe all the way to Berlin. They were determined to have buffers.

Roosevelt had understood the Russian trauma. He shared the fear of German recovery and, in another twenty years, the rise of another Hitler. He had allowed the Russians to fight the last battle for Berlin when Eisenhower might have been ordered to take it. He had suggested the four-power occupation, calculated to keep the proven aggressors in disciplined subjection for as long as it might be necessary. Questions having to do with Southeastern Europe, with the Balkan states, Greece, Turkey, Iran, Egypt, and the rest of the Moslem lands remained to be settled; this was the old British and French area of hegemony, monopolizing the warm seas to the south of Russia.

What Roosevelt saw ahead was certainly a difficult time with the suspicious and battered Russians. Their demands for security would clash with the American belief in indiscriminate self-determination. Then too the British had not yet given up in India to the independence movement; and this required control of the passages to the East. He had told Churchill frankly that the empire east of Suez might better be liquidated peaceably and Churchill had been deeply offended, seeing the Russians as threatening what he spoke of as the British lifeline. He meant to follow the traditional policy of blocking that nation at the Dardanelles; and his view of India was well expressed in the books of Henty and Kipling, who had made the Queen's Own Rifles, the Himalayan passes, and resplendent Viceroys items in a romantic drama inviolable to American meddling.

This was not the only issue disagreed on by the two statesmen; but it was the most important. Roosevelt wanted a situation relatively immune to disruption by the pursuit of national interests. For this purpose the British were the worst problem, since the French, whose empire in the East had been almost as extensive, were prostrate and obviously could not recover Indochina. The collapse of 1940 had canceled claims to postwar advantages such as Clemenceau had insisted on in 1919. Italy, as well, was out of consideration. Mussolini's inflated notions about a North African empire had been extinguished. Italy would be lucky to escape heavy reparations.

The two nations with consolidated power were the United States and Russia, the one stronger for the war, the other with territory unimpaired and with a recuperative potential based on solid unity. British control of the seas had kept together many separated territories—so far spread that the sun was never known to set on all of them at once. Without the empire Britain was "a few islands in the northern seas." Churchill would not acknowledge that an end had come to the empire and was furious that Roosevelt should suggest it. With Roosevelt gone, Truman remained to be worked on. How successful Churchill was would be revealed in a famous speech at Westminster College in Missouri. With Truman approving, he invented the metaphor of the iron curtain, and together they welded its parts and extended them around Greece and Turkey, again shutting the Dardanelles to the Russians.

Truman, new in the White House, had many things to consider; and the rescue of the British Empire was not high on the list, if, indeed, he did not share Roosevelt's conviction that it was inconsistent with what must now be done. He might approve the effort to keep Russia out of Europe, but this did not imply a defense of Britain's Far Eastern holdings. Anyway, before the summer was over, Churchill's Conservatives had been defeated, and a Labor government had taken over. It was the new Prime Minister, Atlee, who was to preside over the dissolution of the empire. The changeover took place while the Potsdam conference was in progress (July17-August 2). During that conference, with the least possible emphasis, Stalin was notified that the United States possessed a new weapon of unexampled power and would use it on Japanese targets.

That decision had been made during the preceding weeks after Alamogordo had demonstrated that the bomb was operational. Its existence had been news to Truman, conveyed during his first days in office by Secretary of War Stimson. . . .

It was called the Manhattan Project and had had its first test in a temporary laboratory rigged up under the Stagg Field stands at the University of Chicago. Atom fission was first accomplished there on an occasion all who knew about it saw at once could end conflict as it had been known until then and would begin an era of maneuvering among nations with a fearsome genocidal weapon. At the moment, of course, it was enough that it would finish the Japanese resistance.

Some time after the Chicago success an actual weapon was put together at Los Alamos under the direction of Oppenheimer and others. It was then that the question of its actual use arose. The conflict with Germany had been concluded, and the Japanese had been trying for months to surrender on condition that the Emperor not be deposed (the condition included actually in the terms presented to them later). Nevertheless, for reasons never explained, Stimson convinced Truman that use of the bomb to destroy a city or two in Japan would end the war abruptly and would save the lives of a million Americans who would die in the invasion being prepared.

The argument . . . was sufficient. Its use was ordered; Hiroshima and Nagasaki were pulverized; and the United States was left with the guilt of an unnecessary genocidal attack that had overtones of vast consequences. Was it approved more easily because the Japanese were not white? Was it done to forestall the participation of the Russians in the Japanese defeat? They were getting ready to carry out the pledge exacted of them at Yalta on the insistence of General Marshall. After Hiroshima they were not needed; and the occupation became an exclusive American affair.

After twenty-five years the answers to these questions could only be guessed at; but the suspicions were stronger that issues other than Japanese defeat had entered into the calculations concerning the bomb's use. Whatever they were, they cannot have rested on saving American lives as Truman would persist in saying to the end of his life.

Second Mistake: Disarmament Fumble

Immediately after the war something had to be determined about nuclear weapons. Now that they existed, it seemed obvious that the overwhelming magnitude of their power had made lesser devices obsolete; but on second thought this appeared to be true only in such vast conflicts as had just been finished. In what the military referred to as "brushfire wars" they would be unsuitable. Only a third thought, a somewhat belated one, indicated that they could not be used at all. They were of no use even when they were an American monopoly; the revulsion after Hiroshima ensured that; and when the Russians also had developed similar weapons their use was doubly impossible since it would induce automatic retaliation. Pre-emptive strikes, talked about for some years by xenophobic haters of communism, very quickly faded out of public dialogue.

The simplest policy would be to develop the nuclear potential as an American monopoly and use it for keeping the peace. It was easily assumed that others would trust Americans as its guardian.

When the monopoly was seen to be a fiction, however, a reappraisal of policy was necessary. Others had to be considered as co-possessors of genocidal capability. Somehow the monstrous danger would have to be got under control; and it could only be by mutual agreements. It must be confined, otherwise its destructive power might very possibly destroy the world. This was a new and baffling problem for politicians to confront. They had become addicted to exchanges of bombast whose irresponsibility was relatively safe since threats could not actually be carried out. It had been a heady reliance for those who feared communism that it could be destroyed in one blow. There were unaccustomed silences while reappraisal went on; but there were some outbursts too, and they tended to be taken too seriously abroad. . . .

The monopoly assumption had contributed to division and hostility in the world, making everything more complicated. Nevertheless an agency for its custody had to be devised. A bill sponsored by Senator McMahon finally became law on August 1, 1946. An individual who had survived as long as 1970 could hardly believe his own recollections of the dialogue concerning the bill or of that following its passage. The act was accepted with such reservations on the part of belligerent but confused legislators that it stood in danger of repeal during the year that followed. The commission of five it provided for was appointed by the President only after long delays for consultation, and its members were confirmed after even more protracted hearings. These were accompanied by ignoble political maneuverings and with a legislative history emphasizing bellicose emotions. Ideology overcame practical sense. Communism was still conceived as a monolithic organization directed from Moscow with a totally unrestrained ambition to rule the world. It meant to use the same infiltration by mendacity and subversion abroad that had been used at home. Executions of dissenters by the uncounted millions had been for years in correspondents' accounts.

It was not even considered that Russians might be trusted in international dealings. As allies in the war they had been only as cooperative as they had to be; and there were many who regarded any deal with them as something that must be safeguarded with potential force and policed by American watchers. It was of no importance that Russian interests coincided precisely with those of the United States; at least no use was made of such a perception.

Truman's advisers were among those who were thus affected, and he, himself, if he had more sense of the dangerous forces involved, still had the same convictions about Communists.

There had been, for the past year, a United Nations Commission at work on disarmament with special reference to "the discovery of atomic energy and related matters." To this commission Truman appointed Bernard Baruch as the representative of the United States. The reason for such a selection has never been quite clear; but it may have been the fancied necessity for entrusting such a task to a thoroughly credible representative of the dominant group in American counsels. Baruch was a very wealthy man who had made his fortune in Wall Street, and so was recognized as a member of the group so powerful in policy-making at that time.

In November, 1945, Molotov, the Soviet Foreign Minister, made a pronouncement to a Party Congress denouncing the American "atomic diplomacy" being used to capture world domination. He enlarged bitterly on refusal to recognize Russia's special relationships with the small nations of Eastern Europe. He ridiculed the demand that they be given immediate autonomy, including the right to hold instant elections; that, he said, would mean a return to power of the old capitalist-landlord classes—and orientation toward the West. The Russians had no intention of opening the Balkans to Western intrigue. He made it quite plain that, if Americans approached arrangements with the Soviets guardedly, the Soviets doubly reciprocated. It was basic to their view of the world, one they had impressed on faithful Communists for two decades, that the capitalist-imperialists meant to overthrow the Russian government and impose a decadent democratic regime. American policy was now a confirmation. Baruch was a perfect symbol.

The retort to Molotov was made by Secretary of State James F. Byrnes. It was as vitriolic in denouncing the communist conspiracy as Molotov's was in ridiculing the capitalists' pretensions to the protection of liberty. Exchanges on this model were to proliferate and harden in future years; but the pattern of opposition was set at once. Presently, after an interlude when General Marshall was Secretary, Byrnes was succeeded by Dean Acheson, and that able lawyer would meet the Russians head-on with vituperation worthy of his clientele. That clientele was the business complex grown so powerful during the war and anxious to consolidate that power in the peace. Truman had their representatives in his cabinet; and their sycophants were a

majority in the Congress. Democrats and Republicans alike had accepted the stereo-
type Communist, and this concept was reinforced by domestic events. . . .

An international agreement to limit nuclear weapons was most agreeable to
Truman's circle, especially since an effort to pass what had been called the May-
Johnson bill had failed. This would have consigned the control and development of
nuclear energy to the military. But Senator McMahon, backed by what could only
be described as an uprising by the scientists who had made the bomb, and by a
certain number of liberals, had succeeded in establishing the civilian commission.
This presumably would be interested in peaceful uses of nuclear energy as well as in
its use for warfare. If they could not have it as an exclusive weapon, the military
were agreeable to limiting its use by treaty. But, naturally, that agreement would
recognize the American monopoly and would ensure its perpetuation. This the
conservative politicians heartily applauded.

In this year the Acheson-Lilienthal report was produced at Truman's direction; it
was presumably to guide Baruch as he dealt with the United Nations Commission.
Acheson was not yet Secretary of State but was in Truman's confidence, and
Lilienthal, who had been Chairman of the Board of the Tennessee Valley Authority
was Chairman of the Atomic Energy Commission set up under the McMahon Act.

The report setting out American proposals recognized that a small object with
paralyzing effectiveness could only be controlled under certain conditions. There
must be revolutionary modification of national attitudes; and it must go to the
extent of mutual cooperation, if not trust. How could this come about with the
Americans still having a monopoly of the weapon? In spite of this absurdity—as the
Russians saw it—there was proposed a Development Authority to be entrusted with
"all phases of the development and use of atomic energy, starting with the raw
materials and including:

1. Managerial control or ownership of all atomic energy activities potentially dangerous to world security;
2. Power to control, inspect and license all other atomic activities;
3. The duty of fostering the beneficial uses of atomic energy;
4. Research and development responsibilities of an affirmative character intended
   to put the Authority in the forefront of atomic knowledge and thus enable it to
   comprehend and therefore to detect misuse of atomic energy. . . ."

This seemed at first reading to be generous; but accompanying the list of objectives
there was disclosed the price for surrendering the existing monopoly: the Security
Council must give up the veto power accorded its members in the U.N. charter; also
there must be assurances of safety—"a guarantee . . . not only against offenders in
the atomic area, but against illegal uses of other weapons—bacterial, biological,
gas—perhaps, and why not—against war itself."

To the embattled, but still hopeful, nuclear scientists these initiatives seemed the realization of their desire to escape the heavy guilt they bore for their part in the creation of the genocidal weapon—one already used to exterminate two whole cities. Naturally the Russian response was awaited with anxiety. Perhaps the proposal was only intended to establish a bargaining position; but it could have been accepted only if the Russians agreed to American custody of nuclear weaponry. That custody was a fact, whether or not it was agreed to, and giving it up without guarantees would have been an unnecessary and unreasonable sacrifice—so it was argued. The reply, however, was a counterproposal. It came on June 19, 1946. Gromyko, for the Russians, offered:

> . . . a study of the conclusion of international agreements forbidding the production and use of weapons based upon the use of atomic energy for the purposes of mass destruction. The purpose of such an agreement should be to forbid the production and use of atomic weapons, the destruction of existing stocks of atomic weapons, and the punishment of all activities undertaken with a view to violation of such agreements.

The Russians saw in the Baruch proposal an attempt to establish American domination and to smother their communist ideology. While the international organization was being set up the Americans would keep control until satisfied that the Soviets had stopped all attempts to spread their philosophy—and this undoubtedly meant independence for their buffer states in Eastern Europe. They saw themselves caught in an intimate embrace with an enemy whose intention was to strangle them or, at least, to confine them, powerless, within their old, insecure borders. What they demanded was that the United States voluntarily divest itself of this power by getting rid, entirely, of all nuclear weapons—at once. That this would leave Russia with the advantage of vast manpower reserves and the huge armies they were maintaining on the borders of Europe was quite obvious; but also they demanded that the agreement be enforced by each nation *on itself.*

This last was recognizably the result of Russian suspicions. An inspection system had been part of the American plan to prevent violations. As they saw it this would amount to foreign outposts inside Russia; and, having given up their veto power in the Security Council, they could not prevent extensions of this espionage. The secretive Russians, who knew what Westerners thought of their government, their ideology, and their methods of maintaining discipline, were outraged by such a suggestion. Control from outside while disarmament was going on meant that the Communists would be helpless.

The Americans were surprised, or at least, disappointed, that the power of nuclear weaponry should not be acknowledged by a willingness to accept conditions for its gradual diminution until it no longer existed. Each nation was bargaining for an advantage the other would not grant; and unless some mutual giving way could be arranged there could be no agreement. In this the Americans could have afforded to be the more generous; but acrimonies reached irreversible offensiveness and no concessions were made.

The opportunity was wasted. Guarantees were demanded that the Russians would rather perish than give; the proposal was put to them by a representative of the hard-core capitalists they believed meant to destroy their system; and, even in the interest of future security, consent was not given to the abolition of nuclear weaponry. There were no mortal risks in this; the Russians were as yet years from capability; and they might never have developed it if the Americans had given up theirs.

So the moment passed when the nuclear threat might have been contained. It was judged by Truman that the positions were too far apart for further useful bargaining, and, so, it was not seriously pursued. Presently Baruch resigned, and the United Nations Commission faded into obscurity. That the Russians would presently have produced a nuclear weapon themselves, and in a quarter-century would have at least an equality with the United States was not a consideration among the policy-makers of 1946. They simply could not believe it. They went on holding to the fantasy that the secrets of the bomb's production could be monopolized. If they could, it was confidently concluded, the United States would be secure and dominant in the world.

In 1946, policies being shaped by misconceptions and emotional politics would persist through succeeding administrations. Then Nixon, who had based his career on the hardening of suspicions and the acerbation of relations, would find himself obliged to retreat. Only then would accommodation seriously be sought.

The interlude seemed the more foolish, looking back, because by then it was clear that the Russians had assessed quite accurately the effect of Hiroshima on the American conscience. Since they believed it would never be used again, the bomb was not really a threat; and they could go on developing their own with no concern whatever for belligerent speeches. Failure to understand this, and still to go on making threats, was, however inexcusable, the basis for a quarter-century of diplomacy.

Opportunity for a mistake of this colossal size is not given to many men. It was given to Truman, and it must be said that he made the most of it.

Third Mistake: Containment

... The first President after Truman policies were clearly exposed as bankrupt would have to abandon the whole undertaking and do the best he could to create a new strategy. It had taken only two years after Roosevelt's death, and with Truman's management, to turn two great victorious allied powers into aggressive enemies. Russia and China would, in future, far overbalance the United States in population—in 1970 about a billion to two hundred million. Neither would be so productive per person, but neither would be in danger of starvation. Each would have drawn the United States into futile containment activities—the two together costing annually more than half the total expenditures of the federal government.

Could the situation have been avoided? To conclude that it could have been, it has only to be assumed that the Soviet Union and China might have been induced to remain American allies for the purposes of peace as they had been for the purposes of war. This would have required consent to the extension of Russia's sphere of influence into Eastern Europe short of Germany but with the Germans under compulsion not to rearm. For China it would have required recognition that the time had come to rid the nation of the reactionary—and corrupt—regime of Chiang Kai-shek, and bring that vast country into the twentieth century. Neither of these policies was tolerable to those in charge of American foreign relations; and in disregard of all reason they undertook the impossible.

The two most praised initiatives in the years immediately following Roosevelt's death were the Truman Doctrine and the Marshall Plan. Both were part of the general containment policy—the one to shut Russia off from the Mediterranean and the other to set up opposition to supposed communist designs on Western Europe.

The exclusion from the seas to the south had two obvious motives. One was to protect the British lifeline to the east; the other was to ensure that oil from Arabia would continue to be an exclusive Western resource. In spite of the enormous expenditures for these purposes the whole area had by 1970 fallen into Russian hegemony. The British had been forced to liquidate their imperial interests beyond the Red Sea, and so had no further use for a lifeline, and the oil for Europe was at such risk that new sources were being sought with frantic intensity. Both were therefore mistaken efforts. If they had never been undertaken the result would not have been much different; it might even have been more favorable. The Russians had no need for Arabian oil, having plenty of their own, and they might well have agreed to a sharing arrangement; the Suez Canal might have been open, and shipping not diverted to the tedious route around South Africa.

After years of effort neither Russia nor China would be contained. It would not be fair to blame Truman alone for these vast misfortunes. Only their beginnings and their early phases, when allies, were turned into enemies and enemies into allies, are chargeable to him. That, however, may be the most serious criticism that can be made of any American President except Buchanan, who allowed the Civil War to develop. Even then it has to be recalled how many collaborators and what almost universal support Truman had. Still, he was the President who kept on his desk that inscribed motto saying "the buck stops here." He cannot be exonerated; nor, to do him justice, would he want to be.

The policy once begun, wars with communists on the Asian mainland were inevitable. Confrontation with Russia having been undertaken, it proved difficult for Truman's successors to abandon it. Instead, the confrontation was enlarged, and this would go on until Johnson faced failure in 1968 and Nixon, because of Johnson's forced abdication, was obliged to find means for liquidation. Seldom had people paid a higher price in dissension at home and opportunity abroad for decisions made in pursuit of futile aims.

It is impossible to exonerate Dean Acheson from a large part of the responsibility for these results. He was Assistant Secretary of State from 1941 to 1945, when Roosevelt was busy with the war, and he had much to do with drafting a United Nations charter that Roosevelt did not approve but thought could be modified. He was then Undersecretary from 1945 to 1947 and was Secretary from 1949 to 1953. He was the proximate author of the Truman Doctrine and of the Marshall Plan. His assistants in the Department included Rusk and Rostow, who went on after he left until Johnson was through. His influence was pervasive all this time. He persisted into the Nixon age in defending his part in making policy during the Truman years. Throughout his service, and even later, he continued to identify Russian communism with imperialism and to claim that the measures of those years were no more than an essential defense of the "free" world.

A necessary part of that defense gradually became the insistence that all disturbances, especially revolutionary ones, were instances of communist aggression and that they must be met everywhere with military opposition. This was true in Germany, in Persia, in Greece, in Asia, and in the Near East. This came to be called the domino theory and was used effectively to justify intervention in Southeast Asia.

George Kennan, who was ambassador to Russia in 1946, was the author of the "X" article in *Foreign Affairs* that first outlined the containment doctrine. In dispatches to the Department he spoke of the "Kremlin's neurotic view of world affairs." The Russians meant, he said, to "infiltrate, divide and weaken the West." Kennan, however, offered various proposals for accord with the Russians. These, Acheson rejected as useless. Kennan afterward said in his *Memoirs* (Boston: Atlantic, Little, Brown, 1967) that they failed because no other way to deal with the Russians was found than military opposition. There should have been a political solution. He said, also, looking back, that there had been a faulty interpretation of the North Korean attack on the South as inspired by Russia; actually the Russians had tried to stop it. This was an example of failure

... to take advantage of the opportunities for useful political discussion, when, in later years, such opportunities began to open up, and exerted itself, in its military preoccupations, to seal and perpetuate the very divisions of Europe which it should have been concerned to remove. ...

The author of containment lived to regret the rationale he provided for the politicians who had their own reasons for exaggerating his warnings about Russian intentions.

Fourth Mistake: Korea

... The "settlements" of the postwar years were these: the communists had expelled Chiang Kai-shek, Kennan had written his famous dispatch from Moscow, and Harriman had reported from Paris that there was in progress "a new barbarian invasion of Europe." In August, 1947, a naval task force had been sent to the Mediterranean, and it would still be there, as the seventh fleet, in 1970. Britain had given up in Greece and Turkey, and the United States had taken over. Marshall had made his speech at Harvard and the famous plan had been accepted by sixteen nations—but not by the wary Russians. Bevin, the Labor government's Foreign Minister, had proposed defense treaties, and the Brussels Pact had been signed, to be followed by the North Atlantic Treaty with its military establishment in Europe....

In June of 1950 the North Koreans invaded South Korea in an attempt to overrun the country before a defense could be organized. Truman reacted at once and, with the United Nations backing (the Russians having some time before boycotted the Security Council), entrusted the joint command to MacArthur. A combat team opposed itself to the full force of the invaders and delayed them until two divisions stationed in Japan could arrive and begin effective defense.

There was something curious about the immediate undertaking to defend South Korea. It followed almost at once on the expulsion from China of Chiang Kai-shek and was, therefore, on the border of a hostile nation. It was assumed that the attack was inspired by Russia, although this assumption later appeared to have been false. Truman treated it as a provocation and met it as such even though there had been no promise of defense and American forces had been diminished. It had been omitted by Acheson himself when he had defined the defense perimeter of the United States in a policy statement; in April, 1948, he had said unequivocally that the nation should not become so involved in the Korean situation that an action taken by any faction in Korea or by any other power could be considered a *casus belli*. ...

The defense of Korea was, then, a reversal, undertaken as a riposte to what was supposed to be a Russian thrust outward. It was unjustified either by the supposition supporting it or by the defense of any American interest. ...

The Korean conflict was still going on, but was somewhat stabilized, when Truman announced his intention not to run again. The Democrats nominated Adlai Stevenson—although Truman preferred his cold war assistant, Averell Harriman. Stevenson made a brave try but was defeated in a hopeless contest with General Eisenhower, who, in the multifarious troubles besetting the nation, appeared as a father figure who would become the stabilizer everyone was longing for. He had made that unfortunate statement about soldiers sticking to soldiering; but he allowed himself to be persuaded that a crusade to save America must be undertaken—and that only he could undertake it. His winning promise was that he would end the now unpopular war in Korea—and, because he was a victorious general, he was believed.

Truman retired to Independence, Missouri, having been President for nearly eight years. During that time the world had been divided with such zeal on both sides that Churchill's iron curtain speech was accepted as an inspiration. The acceptance of this view continued to be practically unanimous; and Truman, in retirement, was a statesman who had held off evil forces and deserved well of his countrymen.

What must be said about these strategic decisions at the opening of the nuclear age is this: there is a choice between two views. Either there were colossal misjudgments or what happened was inevitable because of Russian intractability. What there is no doubt about is that the communists came out ahead. By 1970 that was what the inheritor of Truman's policies had to face. Nixon had to escape a dilemma that ought somehow never to have happened. This was ironic, since he had been, as a member of the Congress, and as Vice-President, one of the most active xenophobes. Because of his record it was fair that he should have to deal with the consequences. Only occasionally does a politician find himself thus confronted with his past; he can usually blur the record in some way; but Nixon had built his career on the exposure of a communist conspiracy. He had won his congressional campaigns on this issue; and he had been the most prominent figure in the immolation of Alger Hiss as a conspirator. But for these activities he would never have come prominently into notice and been found acceptable as a running mate for Eisenhower.

There are these questions: would the Russians have been able to establish satellites in Eastern Europe and dominate the Mediterranean and the passages to the East, if they had been more sensitively dealt with? If the United States had not used its monopoly to demand that in return for eventual disarmament the communists must accept surveillance as force was reduced, would they have consented to an arrangement for coexistence? Could mutual interests have been made to prevail then and there?

It is arguable that Roosevelt might have been able to do it. Truman did not—and all his life was proud that he had not conceded anything. So, in fact, was Acheson. His *Present at the Creation* was one long rooster-crow over the results of his hard-line policy. It had cost by 1970 a hundred thousand American lives and well over a hundred billion dollars. It is hard to assess the result achieved as worth all that, especially if it is suspected that Roosevelt—or other American statesmen—might have made it unnecessary.

There is a caveat to be entered here. The faults were not all American. The

Russians were intractable, unreliable, ill-mannered, and inscrutable. It required patience and almost saintly forbearance to deal with them in decent exchanges. Such virtues, however, ought to have been easier to cultivate for the representatives of the one nation in the world possessed of absolute power. The United States in those years could have forced Russia into submission. It would have required a holocaust to do it; but a holocaust was available. The difficulty was the Russians correctly calculated the Americans' adherence to an ethic that would not allow the genocidal weapon to be utilized. They therefore felt free to act as though it did not exist.

All through the fruitless exchanges between Molotov, Vishinsky, Gromyko, and other Russians and the various American negotiators, the Americans were unable to understand why their monopoly of force was not recognized. They were obviously dealing with an inferior power; but its representatives refused to behave as they should; and the Americans never reached such an understanding as would have permitted the concessions to the Russians' surly suspicions needed for an approach to mutual conciliation. Negotiators from the American elite, with a background of deomocratic experience, cannot really be forgiven for allowing the time to pass when invective should have given way to forbearance. If the Russians had been allowed their overbearing pride and their brutal denunciations and if their affronts had been met with patient silence, the outcome might have been different. There was nothing to lose by such a policy except face. Words could not change the fact of power. But it was not done. American manners tended to match those of the Russians, and there were no agreements.

There is something else; if the invasion of South Korea was not what it was assumed to be in Washington, then it ought not to have roused American emotions as it did. There seems to have been faulty intelligence in this as in so much else having to do with that crisis. MacArthur, it will be recalled, was quite certain that China would not meet him at the Yalu with overwhelming force appearing out of nowhere.

Korea, therefore, was a strategic mistake, ending in an occupation to be maintained for years. If it was not one of those Russian attempts to challenge the United States on the periphery of the American sphere of influence that became a fixed point of departure for American policy, then it was undertaken under a misapprehension still being paid for in 1970.

Fifth Mistake: Assisting the French in Indo-China

As the Japanese retreated from their conquered territories, Roosevelt had tried to persuade the colonial powers that they must divest themselves of their Southeast Asia holdings or be expelled. The British recognized the inevitable; the French and the Dutch had to be forced out. The general result, after years of turmoil, was that several small nations emerged whose borders defied all geographic sense. This would seem to have been in accord with the ideal of self-determination, so much prized by American progressives; but it must be recalled that, at the same time, Roosevelt was trying to negotiate the acceptance of world order to be maintained by those who had the capability of repressing aggression. Since he relied on accord among the great powers to keep the smaller nations from squabbling among themselves and drawing the big ones into taking sides with the hope of gaining some advantage—access to resources, perhaps, or the extension of an ideology—the postwar arrangements among the victorious allies whould have been made with this in mind. The moment for persuasion was then, before opportunities for making trouble had arisen.

Self-determination was not, in his view, a wholly unworkable principle; but once a people had agreed to live together as a nation, minorities with grievances, whether ethnic or economic, ought not to further break down the arrangement into progressively smaller national units. If every minority could make itself into a nation the world would become impossibly fractionalized. Such disaffected minorities would not be able to establish viable states, and their attempt to maintain the posture of nationhood would inevitably fail, with just such spreading disturbance as had happened repeatedly in Eastern Europe. Consolidations by the colonial powers were in this sense a more efficient arrangement; but some of the associated peoples simply would not live together if separatism was a possibility. Subsequent troubles in India showed how difficult it was; those in Indo-China were even more illuminating; and Africa illustrated the consequences of tribalism transformed into nationalism.

The demand for independence would obviously have to be satisfied whenever it was possible; but it would need a strong organization of the great powers to prevent further rebellions so serious as to engage the powers themselves in defense of dissidents and perhaps in competition with each other.

It was Roosevelt's intention that small nations should be allowed autonomy unless they threatened the disruption of world order; but if they caused serious trouble the great powers must enforce settlements. This should not be done, however, by each separately, but by all in concert. This was not a proposal to divide the world into areas where one or another of the great powers would be recognized as dominant by the others and expected to exploit it as seemed best. On the contrary, no power would have authority beyond its own borders or would try to extend them. The third world would be collectively overseen by the Security Council, where the great powers met.

This was the essential scheme of Roosevelt's United Nations. The Assembly of that body would be able to debate and recommend; but only the Security Council would be able to act, and every action must be unanimous. That is to say, no member would be able to discipline small nations or dissident minorities by itself, only when the others agreed that it was necessary; then all would act together, presumably having as their agents a United Nations conciliation service and such a neutral police force as might be necessary. . . .

Truman did not explicitly abandon the Roosevelt conception; he simply never attempted to effectuate it. Perhaps he did not understand it; or, if he did, he considered that close association with the Russians would be an ideological impossibility. At any rate, almost at once he exhibited an implacable hostility; and this became the central principle of American policy in direct contravention of the Roosevelt strategy he professed to be following.

A national policy may be allowed to die, or it may be reversed. The first is a mild kind of change, the other an aggressive one. Truman did not merely stop cooperating with the Russians; he became their enemy. He would say—did say—that it was all the Russians' fault. No one could deny that they were exasperating; the manners of their representatives were boorish; and they never spoke of the United States without using the clichés of communist intercourse with others—sometimes very hard to bear. It would have required a stopping of speechmaking for political effect to have made possible calmer consideration of mutual interests. This was not done; conciliation was not attempted; and presently the situation had got beyond the possibility of reversal.

There is no evidence that any effort was made on the American side. The guiding notion was that there could be no dealing with communists. They were liars and cheats. No doubt they were; but they were still immensely powerful, and American interests required that ways should be found to reach reasonable exchanges. Interests, however, were less important than emotions.

The abandonment of Roosevelt's conception emerged eventually into perilous situations all around the world—in Germany, the Mideast, Southeast Asia, and in Africa—of the kind he had anticipated and hoped to prevent. In Asia it began by, of all things, assisting the French, who were trying to re-establish their colonial power in Indo-China as the Japanese withdrew. This was about as complete a reversal as could possibly be imagined. Truman was quoted in a Department of State Bulletin on July 3, 1950, as saying:

> The attack upon Korea makes it plain beyond all doubt that communism has passed beyond the use of subversion to conquer independent nations and will now use armed invasion and war. . . . Accordingly . . . I have directed acceleration in the furnishing of military assistance to the forces of France and the Associated States in Indochina and the dispatch of a military mission to provide close working relations with those forces . . .

There thus began an involvement that would reach a nearly complete American takeover of the anticommunist war on the Asian mainland in 1965 and would have gone on from there to vaster efforts if the American public had not by then begun to question the necessity for protecting a population with no very strong wish to be protected. That this last was true was recognized by Acheson himself in 1952. He advised the incoming Eisenhower administration:

... The central problem in Indochina was fence-sitting by the population. They would never come down on one side or another until they had reasonable assurance of who would be the victor ...

He went on to inform his successor:

We are helping France to the extent of carrying between one-third and one-half of the financial burden. . . .

It was not until years later that it became apparent on what flimsy foundations the assumption was made that the Russians instigated the North Korean or the North Vietnamese invasion of the southern halves of those countries.

Lackadaisical self-defense on the part of the South Vietnamese, and, earlier, the South Koreans, was the reason why, once begun, their defense became so largely an American enterprise; but this did not explain the strategy. This, of course, rested on the conviction that the communists meant to dominate Southeast Asia and that, if they did, American interests would be so seriously injured that it must be stopped at all costs. These costs were not known at first, but not counting them was deliberate. Whatever it required was to be invested. When, however, it ran to half a million men and perhaps one-third of the national budget, there was general insistence that the costs *should* be counted and that they should be weighed against the possible gains. The discrepancy was appalling.

These were perfect illustrations of the danger Roosevelt had anticipated. The Russians, as well as the Chinese, were drawn into support of satellite communists against other great powers—except that the Russians always managed to let someone else do the fighting, a lesson learned also by the Chinese after Korea. They only furnished the munitions and the rhetoric.

It has to be said for Truman that the earliest involvement in Southeast Asia was urged on him by all those around him. There must have been practical unanimity among the White House coterie that the Russians were attempting the sort of thrust assumed in the accepted theory of aggressive expansionism. That the Chinese did help the North Koreans, and that the Russians stood aloof, was considered to be no more than a typical wily maneuver of Stalin. The Chinese and Russians were not differentiated then as they came to be later; they were both communists, and communists were assumed to be a unified horde committed to world conquest; and they had to be stopped at the beginning. Containment was the rubric.

That Truman accepted this general conviction and its policy implications is not strange considering his origins and experiences—but he was President and, so, responsible, as others were not. There must have been intelligence available to him showing at least the beginning of what became so significant within a short time; that the Russians and Chinese were dividing in what seemed on the surface merely ideological differences, but actually were geopolitical grounds. They had the longest mutual border in the world, and Chinese maps showed extensive territories now occupied by the Russians.

The Truman decisions, from using the bomb on live targets in Japan, to supporting the French in Indo-China, were thus preceded by what later would seem either shallow explorations or faulty intelligence, as well as failure to evaluate future consequences in any significant depth. His advice came from those who were biased in these ways; but frequently, he needed none. Someone must have told him, or he must have read—he was an assiduous student of American history and often expressed admiration for James K. Polk—that strong Presidents acted decisively. They were responsible; they made up their minds; they must not appear to have doubts. It was better to make mistakes than to hesitate and give the impression of uncertainty.

Or, perhaps, it was just Truman's nature. After ten years in the Senate, after being a county official, he had power to dispose of. It was a heady possession. He used it freely.

Oppenheimer might agonize over the dead Japanese at Hiroshima and Nagasaki, but Truman never agonized over anything. He had no afterthoughts and no regrets. If that is not the careful weighing process expected of one entrusted with decision-making for a great power, it was the method of the American President who presided over the war's end and the arrangements for what was to follow. . . .

Chapter 3   THE LOYALTY PROGRAM, CIVIL LIBERTIES, AND McCARTHYISM

ATHAN THEOHARIS, *currently teaching history at Marquette University, has written "Seeds of Repression: Harry S. Truman and the Origins of McCarthyism" (1971). The article that follows summarizes the main arguments and conclusions presented more fully in this book. Unlike most students of McCarthyism, who portray Truman as a defender of civil liberties against the McCarthyite onslaught, Theoharis contends that the President's zealous promotion of anti-Communism, on behalf of his own foreign and domestic policies, helped pave the way for the hysteria upon which the Wisconsin senator capitalized. Does Theoharis give sufficient weight to the existence of undoubted Soviet espionage activities in the immediate postwar years? To pressures from the political Right, which contended at the time that the administration was "soft on Communism"?*

With the emergence of the Cold War, the Truman administration sought to protect the nation from what the President defined as the serious menace of subversion. To achieve that objective, his administration developed procedures intended to avert an internal security threat, whether in the form of sabotage, espionage, or "subversive" political activities. The goal was absolute security: the operational premise was preventative, not corrective—i.e., to avert any possible (and not necessarily imminent) threat of subversion. These priorities were basic to what became a permanent federal employee loyalty program directed to prevent "communist" infiltration of the federal government.

In establishing the program, a second and no less important motivation was

From Athan Theoharis, "The Escalation of the Loyalty Program," reprinted by permission of Quadrangle Books from *Politics and Policies of the Truman Administration*, edited by Barton J. Bernstein, copyright ©1970 by Quadrangle Books, Inc., pp. 242-268. Footnotes omitted.

President Truman's interest in foreclosing Republican use of the issue of anti-communism, either criticizing his administration's surveillance of communist activities or charging that previous Democratic administrations (the New Deal) had "coddled" communists or were sympathetic to communism. Truman in his own right was a militant anti-communist and he distrusted political radicalism, specifically the American Communist party. His commitment was intensified by the criticisms of former New Dealers (particularly Harold Ickes, Henry Wallace, and Rexford Guy Tugwell) that the Truman administration had repudiated or betrayed the principles of Roosevelt's foreign and domestic policies, and by the 1948 Progressive party campaign aimed at denying Truman and the Democrats electoral success.

These factors explain Truman's support for a federal employee loyalty program. Initially he sought to balance anti-subversive procedures with safeguards to minimize the effect of the program on individual liberties. But this balancing act failed. Instead, the administration established a far-ranging loyalty program which extended beyond simple considerations of national security. Intended safeguards for individual rights were subverted or abandoned. And the federal program served to legitimize state and private loyalty investigations. The nature of the administration's leadership and policy priorities, moreover, intensified public fears, contributed to a more repressive political atmosphere, and eventually led to a real obsession with loyalty that culminated in the rise of Senator Joseph McCarthy and "McCarthyism."

The loyalty program, moreover, altered national politics by redefining national priorities and recasting the domestic political debate. At the same time, the bureaucracy that was established to administer the program, because it was committed to establishing its expertise and perpetuation, insured a preference for administrative efficiency over individual rights.

With the passage of time, procedures which in 1945 would have been bitterly renounced on constitutional or civil libertarian grounds were accepted because they appeard to advance the loyalty program's objectives. These procedures, by further altering the program's priorities, in turn served to support demands for additional, essentially repressive "corrective" revisions. The movement was gradual, but the shift away from individual liberties was significant.

The groundwork for the loyalty program had been laid even before World War II—a fear that the United States might suffer the same fascist and communist subversion that plagued Europe in the 1930s, as dramatized in Czechoslovakia, Austria, and France. Congress assumed a central role in establishing safeguards against such activities, at times independent of or in opposition to Roosevelt's efforts. Only over the question of wiretapping did Congress, both in 1940 and 1941, reject Roosevelt's request for legislative authority in cases affecting the national security. Otherwise, in 1939, Congress forbade federal employment to any member of an organization advocating the overthrow of "our constitutional government." In 1940 it ceded to the armed services the right of summary dismissal of "suspect" employees, and during World War II it significantly extended this authority by empowering the Civil Service Commission to dismiss suspect employees in either the civil or military services. In 1941 special appropriations of $100,000 authorized the Department of Justice to investigate federal employees suspected of belonging to "subversive organizations." Subsequently Congress voted an additional $200,000 for these investigations. And in 1943 congressional conservatives sought to force the dismissal of certain "suspect" individuals already in government employ. The House, in fact, designated a subcommittee of the Appropriations Committee, the Kerr Committee, to investigate all charges of "subversive tendencies" of federal employees. This committee recommended and the House formally stipulated that no money be spent for the salaries of three particular employees.

World War II provided the impetus for these congressional actions. Although their stated purpose was anti-subversion, they were frequently applied to political radicalism. Cognizant of this possibility and of conservative attempts to hamstring the New Deal, President Roosevelt, in establishing guidelines for a wartime anti-espionage program, tried to insure that investigatory procedures would distinguish between radical politics and espionage. The President imposed definite restraints and required proof of overt action as the basis for dismissing a federal employee for security reasons.

In an August 1940 order, Roosevelt stipulated that the FBI could initiate investigations of incumbent employees only upon the request of the individual's department head. By placing responsibility and initiative within the department, Roosevelt's order limited the FBI's investigatory role. A year later, on October 22, 1941, Attorney General Francis Biddle countermanded this protection when he authorized the FBI to investigate "subversive" activities of federal employees. Biddle directed the FBI, however, to submit its findings to the head of the appropriate department, and he did not require the head to act on the report.

This procedure created administrative problems, complicated by the heightened security concern which came with American involvement in World War II. In response to the situation, the President, on the advice of the Attorney General, established a special Interdepartmental Committee. This committee was intended to provide an expert, independent service to inexperienced department heads who lacked competence or confidence in their ability to evaluate the FBI reports. Again, the department head was not required to act on the committee's recommendation. And the committee's actions were limited to the "credible evidence" standards established by the Hatch Act (party membership or present advocacy of revolution) and not mere suspicion.

Thus Roosevelt's internal security program restricted the scope of FBI investigations and insured that dismissals would be based on documented charges. Inevitably, violations of individual rights occurred, but they were limited by the program's temporary duration, the emphasis on departmental responsibility, the refusal to delegate authority to investigating agencies, and the fact that a permanent loyalty bureaucracy had not been established. Because of its war orientation, the program presumably would end with the surrender of Germany and Japan.

The limited character of this program was affirmed by Roosevelt's Attorney General Biddle. Shortly before the end of the war (March 19, 1945) he introduced and recommended congressional action on legislation dealing with sabotage. Biddle specifically warned against repression, declaring that "the crime of sabotage should be comprehensively defined and should include conspiracies to commit the offense." Seeking to limit legislative restrictions on civil liberties, the Attorney General stressed the effectiveness of the administration's wartime internal security program with its commitment to civil liberties.

No action was taken on Biddle's proposals, for a new administration under Harry S. Truman was soon inaugurated. Truman responded to the tensions in U.S.-Soviet relations and continued the wartime program. A marked change in focus now occurred, however: the Truman administration's program was directed not only at the activities of "subversive" agents who might be spies but also at the open political activism and involvement of the American Communist party in the labor and civil rights (anti-segregation) movements. Truman's priorities increased the influence of hard-liners in the Congress and in the Justice Department, particularly that of his appointee as Attorney General, Tom Clark.

Clark had a broader view than Biddle of what constituted threats to internal security. Specifically, by relying on postwar developments Clark pressed Truman to revise existing procedures and allow the FBI greater investigative leeway. Soon after acceding to the Attorney Generalship, Clark urged the President to order the repatriation of "alien enemies" who seriously endangered the safety of the United States because of their adherence to foreign governments or to the "principles" of such governments.

At the same time Clark enhanced the FBI's investigatory authority. Despite the formal restrictions of Roosevelt's directives, during the war the FBI had exceeded those limits and had even acted contrary to constitutional safeguards. In fact, FBI agents had, as the *Amerasia* case subsequently disclosed, resorted to wiretapping and had unlawfully entered and searched private offices and homes of suspect individuals. Although its investigations did not result in conviction (for procedural reasons), the FBI did uncover evidence confirming that foreign service personnel had pilfered government documents for the use of *Amerasia* editors. The *Amerasia* case, although technically not involving espionage (the documents were published and not passed on to foreign agents), contributed to a heightened concern over subversion. A Royal Canadian Commission report of 1946, disclosing Soviet atomic espionage efforts during the war, added to this fear and provided important leverage for congressional internal security proponents. These congressmen pressed the administration for action in the internal security field. Related to this purpose, during the late 1945 and 1946 a subcommittee of the House Committee on Civil

Service conducted hearings investigating federal employee loyalty. After these hearings, the subcommittee recommended that Congress establish a special commission composed exclusively of individuals having an investigative background, to study existing laws, standards, and procedures and ascertain whether the government was effectively protected from individuals not "primarily loyal" to the United States. The subcommittee further recommended that the Congress appropriate sufficient funds to fingerprint all federal employees.

Truman encountered relentless pressure from the chairman of the parent committee, Jennings Randolph, from Civil Service Commissioner Arthur Flemming (and his successor Harry Mitchell), and from Attorney General Tom Clark, to establish the proposed commission. Though he never expressed opposition to the commission and investigation, Truman did not act immediately upon the suggestion. Until the November 1946 congressional elections, the President simply kept the proposal under study.

The Republicans' dramatic victory in the 1946 elections forced Truman to act. After November he could no longer ignore the possibility that a congressional loyalty investigation, relying on the impact of the Canadian Royal Commission disclosure of Soviet espionage, would institute a conservative investigation of the entire New Deal. On November 25 the President established by executive order a Temporary Commission on Employee Loyalty to review existing programs, standards, and procedures. Composed of representatives of executive departments involved in investigative activities, the commission was directed to evaluate the adequacy of existing security measures in protecting the government from "disloyal or subversive" employees. The commission was further directed to report back to the President no later than February 1, 1947, and to recommend specifically whether any agency (or agencies) should be given responsibility for prescribing and supervising the implementation of security procedures.

The wording of the executive order, the composition of the Temporary Commission (solely of individuals with investigative experience), and the letters of the commission chairman (A. Devitt Vanech of the Justice Department) to department heads and intelligence agencies, asking their recommendations and advice, reflected the predilections of the investigation. Truman had decided that unquestionably a loyalty program and more effective safeguards were needed to protect the national security. Through the commission he intended to establish the limits and requirements for an effective but fairly administered program.

The timing of the order, as well as the stipulation that the commission report back no later than February 1, also reflected Truman's desire to avert congressional action and preclude Republican efforts to monopolize the anti-communist issue. In part his haste was laudable, for Truman sought to remove loyalty from partisan politics and protect individual rights against the danger of loyalty investigations. Nonetheless, the haste and sense of expediency that led to the establishment of the program, in addition to the priorities basic to the approach, effectively outweighed this limited gain. By his action Truman in effect bowed to the pressures of conservative, anti-New Dealers in Congress and indirectly legitimized their concerns and procedures.

The commission witnesses generally emphasized that in the absence of a loyalty program the national security was gravely threatened. Stressing the need for loyalty safeguards, they affirmed that "even one" disloyal federal employee was a "serious" threat to the national security. Ostensibly their testimony emphasized the need for safeguards against sabotage or espionage. Their concern centered, however, not only on overt acts but on potential "subversion" as reflected in an individual's political radicalism. Distinctly conservative, the witnesses maintained that only individuals with correct and patriotic ideas should obtain federal employment, for it offered the opportunity to shape domestic and foreign policy.

The testimony of FBI Director Hoover dramatized the main priorities. He listed espionage as one of five potential dangers that the employment of a "subversive or disloyal person" posed for the federal government. He then enumerated the other four dangers, indicating his anti-reformist concern:

b. Influencing the formation of policies of the United States Government either domestic or foreign so that those policies will either favor the foreign country of their ideological choice or will weaken the United States Government domestically or abroad to the ultimate advantage of the above indicated foreign power.

c. Influencing the execution of the foreign or domestic policies of the United States Government or the policies of the Federal agency with which the employee is connected . . .

d. The spreading by the employee within his particular agency of the Federal service of propaganda favorable to the foreign country of his ideological choice in such a way as to influence other personnel of the agency and the expression of such propaganda to non-employees in such a way as to create an impression of official sanction to such propaganda.

e. Recruiting of other individuals, either federal workers or non-Government employees, for membership in the subversive or disloyal group which the employee represents.

The conclusions of the commission's final report were shaped by the emphasis of Hoover's testimony (as that of the other witnesses), the investigatory orientation of commission members, and the President's initial directive. The commission concluded that existing standards and procedures would not effectively safeguard the national security from internal threats, and that a loyalty program, administered by the executive branch and requiring the screening and surveillance of federal employees, was needed. The commission admitted, however, that it had not uncovered conclusive evidence to support these recommendations.

In an executive order of March 22, 1947, President Truman adopted these recommendations and established a Federal Employee Loyalty Program. The President's order sought to balance internal security and civil libertarian considerations. The procedures outlined were designed to insure the government against the employment of disloyal individuals without violating due process of law or individual rights, or simply dismissing an individual because of his political ideas or activities. Loyalty procedures, accordingly, were standardized; a hierarchical system of review boards in each department, under the supervision of a Loyalty Review Board, was established to conduct investigations and hearings. The order, like the commission's report, was inadvertently vague in defining "loyalty," "disloyalty," "serious" threats, or "subversion." And the thrust of the program was that dismissal or denial of clearance need not be limited to overt acts confirming disloyalty or treason but included a review of the employee's subversive proclivities, hence his ideas and associations.

To limit abuses, the order established two standards. First, it provided that past political associations (particularly membership in organizations listed by the Attorney General as subversive) would not *ipso facto* justify an adverse loyalty decision. The standard for dismissal stipulated that "on all the evidence, reasonable grounds exist for the belief that the person involved is disloyal to the Government of the United States." This standard, though vague, required proof, not mere suspicion, of disloyalty. In addition, the order, by establishing a hierarchical review procedure, enabled the accused employee to appeal an adverse ruling and to refute unsubstantiated charges.

As a second safeguard, Truman limited the investigatory roles of the FBI and the Loyalty Review Board (established to coordinate and provide an impartial overview for an agency-centered program). The FBI was strictly limited to gathering information about incumbent employees; agencies were not required to use its investigative services. The commission had intentionally recommended restricting the role of the FBI in order to allay suspicions of a program based on the Bureau's investigations. Truman's executive order, moreover, delegated to the Civil Service Commission supervisory responsibility over both the investigative and review (through the Loyalty Review Board) phases of the program. At the same time, agency heads were designated as the final authority for dismissing an employee and developing procedures for the operation of the program. (The Loyalty Review Board's decisions were to be only advisory, not binding, recommendations.) If any agency lacked investigative means, its director could rely either on the services of the Civil Service Commission or on the FBI.

These intended safeguards did not work. Instead, the desire for efficiency in administering the program superseded the concern for individual rights; investigation and prosecution objectives became primary considerations. The independence of departments, the standard for dismissal, and the functions of the FBI and the Loyalty Review Board were subsequently altered to reflect this desire. Operating on the premise that federal employment was a privilege and not a right, the program subordinated individual rights to the quest for absolute security against potential subversion.

The first major shift, in essence contradicting the provisions of the President's executive order, concerned the FBI's investigatory role. Whereas the order stringently restricted the functions of the FBI to securing information when requested by the Civil Service, the Bureau, aided by Attorney General Clark, pressed for unlimited jurisdiction over investigations. The shift was related to budgetary considerations. Existing budgeted appropriations for 1947 did not cover expenses for administering loyalty investigations of present or potential employees. The proposed special supplemental appropriations, which the administration requested, provided for a substantial increase only for the FBI and thus insured its sway over investigations. . . .

This preference for effective prosecution underlay a related decision by the Truman administration to insure the confidentiality of FBI investigative reports. The March executive order had directed investigating agencies to make available to department heads "all investigative material and information" concerning the designated employee. The investigating agency was allowed to refuse to disclose the names of confidential informants if it provided sufficient background information about such informants to permit an adequate evaluation of the charges, and if it established "in writing" the necessity of confidentiality for "the protection of the informants or . . . the investigation of other cases." The order further stipulated that "Investigating agencies shall not use this discretion to decline to reveal sources of information where such action is not essential." The intent was to insure maximum information, to protect the accused employee from unfounded charges, and to avert the possibility that resort to confidentiality might become a ruse for refusing disclosure. The investigating agency would have to justify its resort to confidentiality, and this action was clearly to be the exception.

After 1947, however, a procedure evolved to insure the complete confidentiality of the FBI investigative reports. This development resulted from the administration's partisanship and commitment to expediting prosecution and aiding the FBI. Initially (as in the 1947-1948 House Appropriations Subcommittee investigation of the State Department) the administration had cooperated with Congress to permit committee access to departmental loyalty files. Truman, in March 1948, reversed this procedure to require prior presidential approval of all nonexecutive requests for loyalty records. By this order the President sought to thwart Republican attempts to discredit the Roosevelt-Truman administrations and to deny the Congress, particularly the Republican leadership, access to the FBI's investigatory record. In 1950 Truman reaffirmed this order, rejecting demands raised by Senator McCarthy and other conservatives for the end of this executive restriction. Confidentiality,

Truman then asserted, was essential to insure the effective operation of FBI investigations (safeguarding potential and actual sources) and to protect innocent employees from the publicity of unfounded accusations. . . .

The same subordination of individual rights to administrative requirements evolved from the operational role of the Loyalty Review Board. Initially it had been given limited review responsibility over adverse (dismissal) decisions of department loyalty boards. Its recommendations were advisory, intended to safeguard the individual employee from unfair departmental investigators. In time, however, the board's presumably advisory recommendations became binding on agency heads. In December 1951 the Loyalty Review Board assumed the right to review *any* decision of a lower review board, even in cases where the individual had been cleared, if the board felt that the case might affect the national security. Thereby the board attempted to impose on other federal agencies its definition of what constituted loyalty or threats to the national security. A procedure originally intended to preclude departmental abuses of individual rights and to insure uniformity and fairness in the operation of the loyalty program, had resulted in the emergence of a self-appointed, all-encompassing central authority.

The Loyalty Review Board consistently sought to avert any civil-libertarian criticisms of the loyalty program and, at the same time, to insure the program's continuance. The original loyalty program, as established in 1947, had not been considered permanent or perfect. The Temporary Commission and the White House staff had recognized that the operation of the program might disclose the need for minor or radical revisions, or even that time would diminish the need for such a program. Once established, however, the program was accepted as a permanent and necessary protection. More significantly, after 1947 the only changes seriously considered by the administration were intended to insure efficiency or prosecution. The Loyalty Review Board thereby assumed a central role. From 1948 through 1950 the board publicly denounced protests by civil-libertarians, whether Congresswoman Helen Douglas, the Americans for Democratic Action, the American Civil Liberties Union, the NAACP, or the White House staff, that the program violated individual rights. These protests, the board affirmed, were unwarranted; the demands for an impartial review of loyalty procedures were unnecessary and harmful. . . .

In 1950 the operation of the program was again challenged. Senator McCarthy's charges of "communists in government," and the Tydings Committee's unconvincing rebuttal of his "81 cases," provided the opportunity for liberals to pressure the President to appoint an impartial commission to review existing loyalty procedures. In discussions on this proposal, the Loyalty Review Board and the Justice Department, joined by Democratic congressional leaders, opposed an independent review of the program. The congressional leaders questioned the efficacy of an outside investigation and feared that it might simply tend to support McCarthy. The board and the Justice Department opposed any interference with existing arrangements. Defending existing procedures and denying that the McCarthyites' criticisms were justified, the board chairman, Seth Richardson, impugned the patriotism of those demanding a review. He suggested that only individuals who opposed a loyalty program would support a review of existing procedures. The independent administration of the program and the continued confidentiality of the loyalty records, Richardson affirmed, were necessary to safeguard the national security and the reputations of unfairly accused employees. The Justice Department's and the board's concern for civil liberties was more rhetorical than central: by this time both were pressing for approval of a proposed bill providing for the summary dismissal of "suspect" civilian employees.

While the Loyalty Review Board and the Justice Department opposed suggestions that restricted the operation of the program, they argued for administrative reforms which would close loopholes and prevent the employment of individuals of "doubtful" loyalty "potentially" dangerous to the national security. The implication was that existing procedures reflected an excessive concern with individual rights. Attorney General J. Howard McGrath, Clark's successor, forthrightly expressed this view in averring that

> the Basic Loyalty Program . . . is quite satisfactory . . . there are no sound grounds for criticizing its findings. Therefore, I believe the question as to whether the basic program should be re-examined at this time should be answered in the negative. However, experience gained in operating the program through the past two and one-half years has demonstrated . . . the desirability of an administrative review of the organizational structure . . . as well as some of the regulations and procedures which have been adopted. . . .I believe that such review should be made by you in consultation with persons in this Department and the Civil Service Commission who have been connected directly with the Loyalty Program.

In a 1949 report on the operation of the loyalty program, the board urged revision of the standard for dismissal. The board objected to the requirement that loyalty officers interpret this standard—namely, "on all the evidence, reasonable *grounds* exist for the belief that the person involved is *disloyal* to the Government of the United States"—to mean that an incumbent employee "is at present disloyal." Individuals "who are *potentially* disloyal or who are bad security risks," the board protested, had thus been able to secure clearance. The board recommended instead that clearance be denied "if there is a reasonable *doubt* as to their [the applicants'] *loyalty* to the Government of the United States."

Although the board's recommendation originally was to be limited to applicants for federal employment, by 1950 it sought to secure adoption of this standard for the loyalty program as a whole. Senator McCarthy's dramatic accusations, the crisis of the Korean War, the resulting public concern over administration priorities, and the passage (in 1950) of the McCarran Internal Security Act provided new impetus for a more "effective" program. These developments enabled the board in early 1951 to renew pressure on the administration for a revised standard. The board wanted to replace "reasonable *grounds* exist for the belief that the persons involved is *disloyal*" with "reasonable *doubt* exists as to the *loyalty* of the person involved."

The proposed change was a complete reversal of the burden of proof. Sweeping in scope and intent, this standard resolved doubts about an individual's loyalty in favor of the loyalty officers, thereby expediting dismissal or the denial of clearance. Mere suspicion, as opposed to tangible evidence, became enough for a dismissal or refusal to grant clearance. Inevitably, this revised standard placed greater emphasis on the individual's political beliefs and associations, for it involved a judgment of his proclivities for subversions. . . .

Hiram Bingham, chairman of the board, offered his recommendation at a time when Truman had established a special commission to investigate the adequacy of existing loyalty procedures and legislation. Truman directed the commission to settle on procedures for an effective loyalty program to protect the national security without transgressing individual rights.

Bingham immediately pressured the new commission, headed by former Admiral Chester Nimitz, to consider the recommended revision of the standard for dismissal. Emphasizing the board's heavy work load and the perils of delay, Bingham (with support from the Department of Justice) urged the commission to render an "early" decision approving the new standard. The commission, however, was then unprepared to act, having as yet not resolved organizational or operational problems. It was waiting for Congress to approve special enabling legislation waiving the conflict-of-interest requirement for commission employees. Despite Senator Pat McCarran's opposition, it appeared that the commission might gain congressional approval of this legislation. Given the situation, the President required the Loyalty Review Board to defer any changes in the operation of the loyalty program unless approved or considered by the commission.

As congressional opposition to waiving the conflict of interest requirement hardened, the commission was not able to organize itself. President Truman was soon faced with the decision either to await congressional approval of special legislation, with the prospect of a long delay, or to bypass the commission and implement the board's request. At issue was a choice between administrative expediency and individual rights. Ostensibly, Truman had appointed the Nimitz Commission to insure an impartial judgment of existing procedures and legislation, intended to strengthen both security safeguards and individual liberties. That impartial judgment was never made. In April 1951 Truman, unwilling to wait until the commission became operative, approved the new standard.

The Loyalty Review Board and the Department of Justice immediately sought to exploit this executive decision. In May the board ordered all department loyalty boards to apply the new standard to the 565 cases then under consideration and, in addition, to review the cases of those federal employees who had been dismissed but later cleared on appeal to a higher loyalty board. Agency heads were further directed to review any case (even if the individual in question had previously been cleared) if there was reasonable doubt as to the employee's loyalty, and then to inform the Loyalty Review Board of all favorable decisions so that these cases could be post-audited. Extending the procedure in December, the board announced its intention to review periodically "as it deems necessary" any agency decision, even in cases where no appeal had been made.

In substance the board assumed ultimate jurisdiction over the loyalty program and attempted to achieve absolute security. The board viewed its recommendations as binding, not advisory, and sought to remove any doubt concerning the program's efficacy in confronting the "communist menace." Thus the board recommended and secured the dismissal of John Stewart Service (who earlier had been thrice reviewed and cleared). The government, board chairman Bingham noted, could not take "unnecessary chances" with federal employees of "doubtful loyalty" and, regardless of outside protests, ought to be the "sole" judge of employee loyalty. At the same time, Bingham warned against the "potential danger" of an undue concern over laxity. An effective program could not simply be judged by the number of dismissals, he said, because communists would be discouraged from seeking federal employment. . . .

On a different plane, the Truman administration acted to extend the scope of the loyalty program. In part the administration hoped to establish its unquestioned anti-communism, the vigilance of its methods, and the correctness of its approach, thereby discrediting McCarthyite attacks. The new procedures instituted in 1951 were not simply intended to deal with new contingencies or threats. Rather, they reflected a cautious policy designed to avoid cases which the McCarthyites might exploit.

The original review procedure of the loyalty program had not covered presidential appointments to advisory or consultative commissions. In 1952, at the behest of the loyalty agencies, the question of such exclusion came under White House review. The White House staff supported only a limited investigative program (simply to be on the safe side), consisting of a pre-appointment check. In contrast, the Civil Service Commission, the Loyalty Review Board, the Department of Justice, and the FBI recommended doing away with this exclusion so that all federal employees and applicants would be covered by the loyalty program (the Civil Service Commissioner even insisted that ambassadorial appointments be included). Hiram Bingham, chairman of the Loyalty Review Board, pointedly asserted that

consultants who have any contact with policy-making or with scientific or technical studies having any relationship to the national defense should not be excluded from the investigative requirements of the Loyalty program.

The proponents of extended coverage won. The priorities basic to this new procedure effectively stifled dissent. As one result, simple opposition to existing "national security" policies (whether the loyalty program's procedures or the containment of communism throughout the world) raised doubts about an individual employee's loyalty; the individual's policy recommendations became one basis for a denial of clearance.

This obsession similarly lent support to demands for restrictions on the news media's access to federal information. In 1951 the White House, after reviewing existing policy, extended classified or security coverage (formerly confined to defense and foreign policy agencies) to civilian agencies of the federal government. Truman defended this extension on national security grounds, arguing that it had become necessary to "strengthen our safeguards against divulging to potential enemies information harmful to the security of the United States." The President denied that this decision would result in censorship, the concealing of mistakes, or the denial of legitimate information to the public. . . .

Despite the President's denial, his order did impose definite restrictions on the divulgence of information. A federal employee naturally would hesitate to release information that had a possible bearing on national security. Inevitably the news media protested the order, arguing that it unduly restricted access to necessary information. Specifically, the Associated Press Managing Editors' Association assailed the standard's vagueness, its lack of clear-cut definitions of security-related information, and its failure to provide a review procedure concerning classification. The editors also denied any immediate necessity for the issuance of the order. Accordingly, they urged the President to rescind it and instead establish an impartial (non-administration) commission to review the operations of civilian agencies and determine the need for new security safeguards consistent with the public's right to full information about the government.

In reply, administration spokesmen reaffirmed the need for the order and disparaged these criticisms as irresponsible. Too much security information, Secretary of Commerce Charles Sawyer noted, had already been released. The Secretary argued that "Our object should be not only the utmost freedom consistent with safety, but the utmost safety consistent with freedom." And the President admonished the newspaper editors for standing on the outside and carp[ing] and criticiz-[ing] without being at all helpful." The editors, Truman observed, had not taken up his offer of cooperation to improve the order but had "passed up this opportunity to serve the cause of freedom of information in the dangerous days ahead when the safety of our country and the freedom for which it stands are in peril. . . . We can only win in the present struggle if we all work together."

This portrayal of opposition to "national security" restrictions as unpatriotic had by this time become the norm for the administration's defense of the loyalty program. The administration demanded an unquestioned acceptance of existing procedures and dismissed criticisms of the program (whether protesting excess or adequacy) as somehow disloyal, partisan, or unpatriotic. As defined by the government, legitimate and responsible criticisms were limited to positive suggestions that "perfected" existing procedures. . . .

By 1952 the earlier (whether in 1945 or 1947) concern over the effect of administrative procedures on civil liberties had been subordinated to the goal of insuring potential loyalty or expediting prosecution of "suspect" employees. At the same time, the administration, by releasing for publication the number of suspect employees denied clearance or dismissed, sought to dramatize its vigilant anti-communism. By 1952 the administration supported the loyalty program in part to preclude disloyal acts, in part to undercut the McCarthyite protest and to legitimize an anti-communist policy. The process, not policy or principle, had become controlling.

In essence, the establishment of the loyalty program altered national priorities. First, a review of the political beliefs and associations of federal employees (and indirectly of private citizens) had been legitimized. A program ostensibly aimed at safeguarding the national security from subversive threats established standards that reviewed individual loyalty not on the basis of overt actions or proven offenses but on the basis of suspicions and doubts. Standards that would have been rejected in 1945 or 1947 as repressive and unfair—reasonable doubt as to loyalty, or restrictions on civilian agency information—were accepted by 1951.

Second, the establishment of the Loyalty Review Board, intended originally to coordinate matters and insure fairness to the individual, actually increased pressures to extend the program. The board used its supervisory status to insure its dominance over, and the continued existence of, the program. The duration of the program established, at least in the public mind, the "expertise" of board members. Their parochial view of loyalty became the program's operational norm. At the same time, this direction effectively discounted civil libertarian protests over administrative procedures or recommendations. As a result, the Loyalty Review Board successfully monopolized control over, while extending the scope of, the program by: (1) revising the loyalty standard to permit the dismissal of suspicious employees without having to secure documented evidence; (2) assuming determinative, not advisory, jurisdiction over the program; and (3) identifying criticisms of the program as irresponsible if not treasonous.

Finally, the loyalty program legitimized the tactics of McCarthy and similar procedures by state and local governments and private industry. The result was a plethora of loyalty oath crusades, loyalty programs, loyalty investigations—all seeking the total, unremitting loyalty of the individual. Emotional patriotism displaced critical reasoning; an assessment of issues became secondary to proven anti-communism; dissent and criticism were discredited. The climate and tone of the American political debate were significantly altered. A conservative concern for order and conformity was sustained. And the Attorney General's list, established without due process or the right to review, and based on the political biases of FBI agents or Attorneys General Tom Clark and J. Howard McGrath, became the litmus test for distinguishing between loyal and disloyal organizations and individuals. These consequences were neither inherent in nor intended by the original loyalty program. But the very establishment of the program and the Truman administration's hesitant, appeasing responses contributed to an escalatory process which could not be reversed.

Part Two

THE FAIR DEAL: ECONOMIC, SOCIAL, AND CIVIL RIGHTS POLICIES

Chapter 4 EXTENDING THE HORIZONS OF DEMOCRATIC LIBERALISM

Professor of Government and Director of the Institute of Politics in the John F. Kennedy School of Government at Harvard University, RICHARD E. NEUSTADT *has written "Presidential Power: The Politics of Leadership" (1960), among other works. In the following article Neustadt assesses the legislative achievements and failures of the Truman administration's Fair Deal program, indicating a number of factors that helped account for the outcome of the president's encounters with Congress on domestic issues. In general, the article arrives at a favorable view of the Fair Deal's accomplishments both in its own time, and as a signpost for liberals in the years that followed. Written in 1954, it conveys attitudes that helped begin the resuscitation of President Truman's reputation soon after he left office.*

On September 6, 1945, three weeks after V-J Day, Harry S. Truman sent to Congress a twenty-one point program of domestic legislation—his first comprehensive venture in home affairs since Franklin Roosevelt's death five months before. This marked the beginning of a long series of Presidential proposals for Congressional action in the fields of economic development and social welfare; proposals which steamed out of the White House for nearly seven years, from the first session of the 79th Congress through the second session of the 82nd; a legislative program which became each year more comprehensive, more organized, more definite, receiving after 1948, the distinction of a label: The Fair Deal.

Looking back upon this enterprise, this Fair Deal program and its fortunes in

From Richard E. Neustadt, "Congress and the Fair Deal: A Legislative Balance Sheet," *Public Policy*, Vol. V (1954), ed. by Carl Friedrich and John Galbraith, pp. 351-381. Footnotes omitted.

those years, no less an observer than Elmer Davis has ventured the following verdict:

All in all, in domestic affairs, Mr. Truman was an unsuccessful President. [He] presented . . . a liberal program which was coherent and logical as the New Deal had never been. Congress, not being liberal, refused to take it; yet every year he persisted in offering it all to them again and they still wouldn't take it . . . Truman kept asking for all of it and getting none of it.

This retrospective vision of the President who never changed his pace and of the Congress never altering in opposition is no doubt widely shared these days. No doubt, there is an element of reality behind it. Certainly, President Truman held out for more than he could reasonably hope to gain; certainly his four Congresses persisted in frustrating many of his aims.

Yet in its bold relief and simple black and white, this vision of the Truman record misses much light and shadow in a very complex situation. And by virtue of its very sharpness and simplicity, it becomes a stumbling block to understanding and appraisal. Students of post-war politics and of the Presidency, and Congress, have need to start their march through Truman's years with a more elaborate guide to the terrain than this quick characterization can supply.

It is much too soon, of course, for the definitive appraisal of the Fair Deal legislative program, its fundamental emphasis and purposes, its ultimate success or failure. But it is not too soon to go behind neat generalizations and draw a balance on the record as it stood when Truman left the White House. What was attempted, what accomplished, what lost? And more important still, what seem now, at this reading, to have been the underlying motivations, the determinative circumstances? These are the questions to which this essay is addressed.

A General Note on Congress—1945 To 1952

Before turning to the Fair Deal, as such, something need be said by way of background about the work load and the composition of the four Congresses which Truman faced as President.

These were the Congresses of post-war reconstruction and cold war and Korea. For seven successive years their sessions tackled and put through an extraordinary series of Administration measures in the fields of international cooperation, collective security and national defense; a series which for scope and scale and continuity has no precedent in our history.

On no previous occasion has American foreign policy required—much less received—comparable Congressional participation for such a span of time. Rarely before, save at the onset of our greatest wars, has the Congress broken so much new and unfamiliar ground; rarely, if ever, has momentum been so long sustained.

One thinks of Franklin Roosevelt's first four years, and the legislative breakthrough into broad new areas of Federal action here at home. We look back on that as a revolution—a stunning departure from the traditional limitations of pre-depression years. So, too, were these post-war programs revolutionary—shattering all manner of shibboleths and precedents, in the international sphere untouchable right up to World War II. And what stands out historically is a record of immense accomplishment, in legislative terms, both for the Administration that framed the measures and for the Congresses that put them through.

The record becomes still more impressive when one recalls that President Truman never did command a "safe" working majority of the rank and file in either House of Congress. His "honeymoon" did not outlast the war. There was no bloc of "Truman men," sufficient for his purposes, on which he could rely to follow through, without cavil, whatever leads he gave. Rather, the thing was done through that extraordinary phenomenon, postwar "bipartisanship," a carefully conceived and executed coalition launched by Roosevelt, husbanded by Truman, actively furthered by effective leadership in the Congressional power centers of both parties.

This enterprise was in its way as distinctive an achievement, for both President and Congress, as the roster of enactments which it helped to frame and legislate. Of course, the idyl of bipartisanship did not last forever. But even in 1952, the "internationalist" alignment, though reduced in strength by mass Republican defections—and some Democratic backsliding as well—remained a strong bi-factional, if not bipartisan reality, producing—in support of foreign policy—majorities, however bare, which could not have been mustered for a moment behind most Fair Deal domestic programs.

This raises a crucial point: the internationalist coalition, which supported Truman's foreign policy, existed, cheek by jowl, with a "conservative" coalition, which opposed Administration policies at home. What's more, the two most vital elements in the conservative alignment, were also chief participants in the internationalist bloc—the "moderates" of both parties; the Vandenberg Midwest Republicans and the Russell Southern Democrats.

These were the swing groups, joining the "Fair Dealers" to beat off the "extremists" of both parties in their raids on foreign programs; joining the extremists in opposition to most of the Fair Dealers' pet proposals at home. Internationalism combined with conservatism was the formula which kept two coalitions going, side by side, through issue after issue, Congress after Congress.

A great deal happened after 1949, to sap the strength of the internationalist coalition. On the personality side, of course, came Vandenberg's illness and death, Connally's advancing age, Acheson's unpopularity. Deeper down were the accumulating frustrations of twenty Democratic years, capped with "Communism, Corruption, Korea"—and China; mercilessly exploited by Congressional Republicans made desperate after 1948 and cured, thereby, of any faith in "high level" politics, or the "me-too" approach. In addition, after 1950, after Korea, came a development which threatened the whole basis of compatability between internationalism and conservatism: the full cost of our commitments in the world—in dollars and in human terms as well—took on a new and frightening dimension. Conservatism and internationalism began to come unstuck, to war with one another. And if the Democratic "moderates"—taken as a whole—did not react as sharply or as soon as the Republicans who buried Vandenberg, this may be taken, partly, as a tribute to party loyalties and hopes for 1952.

Taking Truman's four Congresses together, in all these terms of work load and alignment, three further observations are in order. First, had no more been attempted or accomplished, by way of major, controversial, forward measures, than the great landmarks in the international and mobilization fields alone, we would still have to grant, in retrospect, that these were busy and productive years of legislation for the Congress—outstanding years, by pre-war standards.

Moreover, whatever else might have been tried, on the domestic front, there was no time, from 1945 to 1952, when Truman's Administration—could afford to trade a major objective in the foreign field for some advantage in the domestic. Consistently, it was, and had to be, the other way around.

Finally, considering the integral relationships between the "internationalist" coalition which supported Truman and the conservative coalition which opposed him, every major venture in home affairs was bound to complicate the progress, endanger the timetable of those all-important measures in his foreign policy. From his first days in office, when he reaffirmed Roosevelt's arrangements for Republican participation in the San Francisco Conference, Truman acknowledged his dependence, in the foreign field, on elements of the anti-New Deal coalition—an enterprise which, always potent after 1937, had spent the wartime "truce" maturing its relations, building its lines and thwarting FDR on secondary issues.

Why, then, did Truman press a host of "hot" Fair Deal domestic issues, sure to arouse the wrath of this entrenched conservative alignment? To this question there is no single, easy answer, but rather a whole series, arising out of motivations and responses which varied with circumstance, over the years. To get at these we need now turn to straight, historical review, beginning with the first Truman "inventory" of legislative needs in home affairs—the twenty-one point program of 1945.

To Reaffirm the Roosevelt Purpose: 1945-46

The original "twenty-one point" program went to Congress by special message on September 6, 1945. Then, within a ten-week span, the President sent Congress six more special messages, each adding a major new proposal to the September list. In January 1946, Truman again presented a "twenty-one point" program, in a radio appeal to the country, reiterated three weeks later in his annual message to the Congress. This second listing was somewhat different from the first. Most of September's minor points had been removed from the enumeration to make room, among the twenty-one, for measures recommended in October and November. And in the annual message there was discussion of additional proposals—over and above the list of twenty-one—which had not previously been mentioned at all.

In summarizing the domestic program which Truman set forth after V-J Day, it makes no sense at all to attach significance to order or to timing of particular proposals in this confusing sequence. Obviously some things were ready, came to mind, or got approval earlier than others. Obviously, also, these were the days of scatter-shot approach, when everything was put on record fast, in a sort of laundry-listing of post-war requirements with little indication of priority or emphasis.

What counts, here, is that between September 1945 and January 1946, Truman staked out for himself and his Administration, a sweeping legislative program in the fields of social welfare and economic development, embracing, in essential outline if not in all details, the whole range of measures we now identify with the Fair Deal.

Nearly everything was there, though later formulations were to alter some specifics. Among September's numbered "points" were full employment legislation, expanded unemployment compensation, the permanent FEPC, an increased minimum wage, comprehensive housing legislation, a National Science Foundation, grants for hospital construction, permanent farm price supports, and—less specifically—protection and assistance for small business and expanded public works for resource conservation and development.

To these, the "points" of January's message added a comprehensive health program—including health insurance—nationalization of atomic energy and development of the St. Lawrence project. In addition, the message stressed, though it did not number, a "thorough-going reconsideration of our social security laws"; financial aid "to assist the states in assuring more nearly equal opportunities for . . . education"; an emergency veterans housing program "now under preparation"; and various kind words for statehood or self-government in the territories and insular possessions and the District of Columbia. Finally, of course, there were appropriate exhortations about extending price and rent controls.

This was the program Truman threw at Congress, the moment the war was won. Roosevelt had supplanted "Dr. New Deal" with "Dr. Win-the-War." Why then did Truman hurry so to call the old physician in again?

Look back two years, to January 1944, and part of the answer becomes plain. Remember Roosevelt's "Economic Bill of Rights," with which he opened that election year, the year of hoped-for victory in Europe and feared post-war depression here at home:

The right to a useful and remunerative job. . . .
The right to earn enough., . . .
The right of every farmer to . . . a decent living.
The right of every businessman . . . to trade in . . . freedom from unfair competition. . . .

The right of every family to a decent home.

The right to adequate medical care. . . .

The right to adequate protection from . . . fears of old age, sickness, accident and unemployment.

The right to a good education.

All these rights spell security. And after the war is won, we must be prepared to move forward in the implementation of these rights. . . .

Truman was thus reasserting Roosevelt's stated purpose; not in so many words, not necessarily in Roosevelt's way, or with his means, or his specifics—or his men—but consciously and definitely this was for Truman an affirmation of fidelity to the cause and the direction of liberal Democracy; rekindling the social outlook of the New Deal, if not, precisely, of the New Dealers.

The legislative program of 1945 was a reminder to the Democratic party, to the Congress, to the country, that there was continuity between the new national leadership and the old—and not merely in war policy, but in peace policy as well; not only overseas, but here at home.

Beyond this, the new President had a very personal stake in his September message: reaffirmation of his own philosophy, his own commitments, his own social outlook; denial of the complacent understandings, the comfortable assertions that now, with "That Man" gone, the White House would be "reasonable," "sound" and "safe." Harry Truman wanted, as he used to say, to separate the "men" from the "boys" among his summertime supporters. V-J Day brought him his first real chance to think or act in terms of home affairs, and he lost no time in straightening out the record on who he was and what he stood for.

Some of the New Dealers may not have been convinced; conservatives, however, were quick to understand that here, at least on paper, was a mortal challenge. Editors glowered; so did Congressmen. And one of the President's "soundest" advisers, who ornamented the Administration in that capacity from first to last, fought to the point of threatened resignation against sending that "socialistic" message to the Congress.[1]

Here, then, is explanation for the character and over-all direction of Truman's program. But what of its specific scope and range? Granting all this, why was so much territory covered all at once; why so many points; why, in fields like health and housing, go "all out" in a single bite?

Most commentators have seen these things simply as errors in tactics and judgment, charging them off to personal idiosyncrasy, or inexperience. Other Presidents, it is said, would never have concocted so diverse a program, or asked, indiscriminately, for everything at once. But something more was operating here than just the human factor, however significant that may have been. We have no means of knowing what Roosevelt would have done, after the war. But we do know that he had made the "Economic Bill of Rights" an issue in the 1944 campaign—with

Truman as his running mate. And in one of his last major campaign addresses, Roosevelt came out strongly, if in general terms, for most of the controversial measures Truman, a year later, urged on Congress.

We also know that in the post-war period, a Democratic President was bound to face a fundamentally different situation, a different set of popular alignments and demands than Roosevelt dealt with in the thirties. Then, the New Deal pioneered, releasing a flood of ideas and impulses for reform that had been dammed up since Wilson's time. And every effort in those years, each new program, every experiment, set into motion a widening circle of needs and expectations for governmental action—and of organized interest groups to defend the gains and voice the new requirements.

The first Roosevelt Administration broke into virgin territory; the Truman administration had to deal with the demand for its consolidation and development. Clearly, Roosevelt was aware of this in 1944. Clearly, Truman's sweeping program in 1945 was conceived as a response. And not alone in 1945; from first to last, the Fair Deal legislative program sought to express the vastly heightened expectations of those groups of Americans on which the liberal cause depended for support.

For all these reasons, then, the 79th Congress found itself encumbered with a great, diverse collection of proposals from the President. And what did Congress do? Not very much. This was the Congress elected with the Roosevelt-Truman ticket in 1944. But even before Roosevelt's death, it had shown little disposition to follow the White House lead in home affairs. At the very start of the first session, the conservative coalition got the bit between its teeth and almost overturned Henry Wallace's appointment as Secretary of Commerce. From then on, the coalition remained a power to be reckoned with, its temper not improved by Truman's exhortations, its influence culminating, finally, in emasculation of the price control extender, during the summer of 1946.

From the confusions, irritations and forebodings of defeat, which marked the whole course of its second session, the 79th Congress did produce a number of the major measures Truman had proposed—most notably the Employment Act, the Atomic Energy Act, the Hospital Construction Act and the Veterans Emergency Housing Act. The Congress was not ungenerous in authorizing and appropriating funds for reclamation, flood control, power and soil conservation; these also raised some landmarks on the Fair Deal road. But for the rest, at least in terms of final action, Congress stood still, or even "backslid" here and there—as with the Russell Amendment eliminating the wartime FEPC.

Perhaps, if experience over the months had not dispelled the spectre of post-war unemployment, much more might have been done with Truman's program of September, 1945. But as it was, this turned out to be the least of worries for most Congressmen and their constituents back home. Not job shortages, but strikes, not pay envelopes but price regulations bothered both. The country, like the Congress, far from rallying to Presidential visions of a better future, reacted negatively against the irritations of the present, and punished Truman's party with its worst Congressional defeat in eighteen years.

To Pillory the Opposition: 1947-48

To gauge the impact of the 1946 election on the attitude and outlook of the Truman Administration, one merely has to contrast the President's address to the incoming 80th Congress, with his wide-ranging message and radio appeal of the preceding year.

The change in tone was very marked. In the annual messages of 1947 domestic affairs were relatively played down; domestic recommendations limited to a few specifics and some gently-phrased, general remarks. In his State of the Union Message, Truman gave more emphasis to budget balancing (e.g., no tax relief) than to any "welfare" measure, save the comprehensive housing program—which had Senator Taft among its sponsors. He also did "urge" action on the balance of his 1945 health program, but not under the heading of "major policies requiring the attention of the Congress.[2] And while brief mention was made of social security, minimum wages and resource development, it is clear from the context that these, too, were relegated to some secondary category.[3]

This was the comparatively mild and qualified domestic program which the President presented to a supremely confident opposition Congress, where he was generally regarded—on both sides of the aisle—as an historical curiosity, a holdover, a mere chair warmer by accident of constitution, for two more years. The view was widely shared. Inside the Administration, many, perhaps most, of Truman's advisers were persuaded, if not that all was over, at least that the post-war reaffirmation of the liberal cause had been a crashing failure at the polls—out of fashion with the public, out of date for officeholders.

The counsels of caution and conservatism within the President's own entourage, muffled somewhat since the fall of 1945, were now heard everywhere, voiced by almost everybody. Whatever Truman's own views may have been, the course of his Administration through much of 1947 seemed to display real hesitancy, real indecisiveness about further assertion of the cause he had so vigorously espoused a year before.

It is true that as the spring wore on, the White House sent up certain special messages along reminiscent lines. In May, another health message repeated the proposals of 1945—but the tone was mild and the issue, then, by no means so inflammable as it was to become in later years. In June, the President vigorously protested inadequacies in the rent control extender and called again for a comprehensive housing program—but this included specific indorsement for Senator Taft's own bill.

Lump these reminders in with the rest, and Truman's domestic program in the spring of 1947 still remains a very consiliatory version of what had gone before. Under the intitial impact of defeat, the Administration, clearly, had fallen way back to regroup. And with the Truman Doctrine to be implemented that same spring, by that same opposition Congress, it is no wonder there was hesitation and divided counsel about where to take a stand and when, if ever, to resume the forward march.

Yet, scarcely a year later, Harry Truman was back at the old stand, once again, raising old banners, rubbing salt in old wounds, firing broadsides at Congress more aggressively than ever. What happened here? Wherefore the change from the conciliatory tone of 1947 to the uncompromising challenge of 1948? Obviously, somewhere along the line, the President became convinced that his initial impulse had been correct, that he was right in 1945—that the New Deal tradition, brought up to date, remained good policy—and good politics—despite the set back of 1946. In this decision, Truman's temperament, his social outlook, all sorts of subjective factors, no doubt played a part. But also, in the course of 1947 there appeared some perfectly objective indications that a renewed offensive would be not merely "natural" but rational.

Twice, in the early summer of 1947, Truman vetoed tax reductions voted by the Congress. Both times he charged that the reductions were inequitable and ill-timed; that they relieved only upper income groups, and would add new burdens of inflation for the rest to bear. Both times there was some stirring of approval and response around the country—both times his veto was sustained.

In point of fact, these vetoes were no new departure. They had been foreshadowed from the first by warnings in the annual messages. But the actuality of veto, and the words in which expressed, did convey a fresh impression: the vision of a sturdy President—courageous even in the face of lower taxes—defending the "national" interest and the "poor," against a heartless (Republican) Congress mindful only of the "rich." This was a new note—and it did not go badly.

Four days after his first tax veto, Truman vetoed the Taft-Hartley Act. To the general public, the measure was chiefly notable, then and since, because it did something about work stoppages in "national emergency" disputes—an issue the President himself had recognized in prior messages to Congress. But to the spokesmen for organized labor the act was shot full of unwarrantable interferences with basic union rights which had been guaranteed, by law, for half a generation.

And when Truman struck out against these interferences—in the strongest language he had yet addressed to the 80th Congress—he evoked a warm response from a part of the public whose apathy, in 1946, had prominently helped defeat his party and his post-war cause. The quick Congressional override of Truman's veto merely heightened this response from those who felt themselves despoiled—and further dramatized, for them, the vision of the Presidential "tribune" standing up against the onslaughts of a rapacious (Republican) Congress.

Here, in the summer of 1947, were some straws in the wind. Their meaning was confirmed for the Administration, even enlarged upon, at the special session in the fall.

When Truman called the Congress back to Washington, the principal emergency was international—with the economies of Western Europe verging on collapse. But in his address to the special session, Truman asked not only for interim aid abroad—pending completion of the European Recovery Program—but also for a ten-point program against inflation, billed as an equal emergency at home. And the tenth point of this domestic plan was nothing less than selective restoration of price and wage controls.

This was the first occasion when Truman made an all-out public effort to revive and dramatize an issue which had failed him in 1946, capitalizing on a measure which—as everybody knew—was still anathema to the majority in Congress. This was the first occasion, too, since the election of 1946, when the President presumed to give so controversial a domestic issue equal billing with an essential aspect of his foreign policy.

The program for the 1947 special session was, no doubt, a trial run, in a sense. Had the result been very bad, the President might perhaps have stayed his hand in 1948. In the event, however, the majority in Congress found it expedient to enact something called an "anti-inflation" bill, a most limited measure but indicating that times—and prices—had changed since 1946. Moreover, despite the patent irritations which the price issue aroused, interim aid for Europe went through Congress without a hitch, and just before adjournment, the European Recovery Program was sent up and well received.

By January, 1948, the President had obviously read the signs and portents of the half year before, and put out of mind the memory of defeat in 1946, with all the cautious counsels it provoked. Truman's address to the new session was confident and sharp, evoking all the liberal issues half suppressed a year before. His presentation was much more coherent than it had been in 1945 or 1946, the language tighter, the focus sharper, the follow-up firmer. But nothing was omitted from the original post-war program and in a number of respects Truman went beyond any earlier commitments.

This was the message which set forth goals for the decade ahead. This was the message which proposed a new, "anti-inflationary" tax program: credits for low income groups to offset the cost of living, with revenues to be recouped by increased levies on corporate profits.

And as Truman began, so he continued through the spring, with "a message a week," to keep Congress off balance their protection in demands on Congress for actions it could not, or would not, take. If the record of Congress could be turned against the opposition, then the President would make that record, not on performance, but on non-performance, not on the opposition's issues but on his issues—those liberal measures which, perhaps, had not gone out of fashion after all.

And as Truman began, so he continued through the spring, with "a message a week," to keep Congress off balance and the spotlight on. In this series there was but one great new formulation—the civil rights message of February, 1948. The legislative program it set forth incorporated most of the proposals of the President's Committee on Civil Rights, which had reported in December 1947. . . .

Of all Truman's proposals through eight years in office, these were, perhaps, the most controversial. That they loosed a lasting political storm, everyone knows; that they had special political significance in early 1948—appearing just as Henry Wallace made his break to the Progressive Party—is certainly no secret. But there was much more than politics in this. The Civil Rights Committee had originally been established out of genuine concern lest there be repeated in the post-war years, the rioting and retrogression which followed World War. I. Congressional indifference had been made manifest in 1946—hence the turn to prominent outsiders. Once having set these people to their task, on problems so potentially explosive, it is hardly credible that Truman could have ignored their report, no matter what the politics of his own situation.

Nothing else, half so dramatic, was unveiled by the President in 1948. But all the older measures were furbished up and trotted out anew. And as the months wore on, Truman's tone to Congress grew steadily more vigorous. He began by lambasting in January, and ended by lampooning in July.

His last address to the 80th Congress was the nearest thing to an outright campaign speech that he—or probably any other President—ever made before the assembled Houses.[4] Opening the post-convention special session, he first demanded action to stop inflation and start more houses—the ostensible purpose for which Congress had been recalled. He then proceeded to list nine other measures which he thought the Congress might be able to enact without delaying the two primary items. Finally he listed every other major proposal advanced since 1945, commenting: ". . . If this Congress finds time to act on any of them now, the country will greatly benefit. Certainly, the next Congress should take them up immediately."

Of course, that hapless session accomplished precisely nothing, in any of these categories. And Truman proceeded to pillory the 80th Congress at every whistle stop across the country, working his way to victory in the Presidential election of 1948.

Toward a Liberal Majority: 1949-50

The legislative program Harry Truman presented in 1949, to the new Congress which had shared his victory, reflected all the Fair Deal commitments of the 1948 campaign. "Certainly, the next Congress should take them up immediately," he had proclaimed to the Republicans in July. And he could do no less in January than spread them out—all of them—before his brand-new Democratic majorities.

All interest groups and sponsoring politicians understood the "law of honeymoon"; none was prepared to stand aside, leaving a pet proposal for some later, less naturally advantageous date. All civil rights groups, and most politicians North and South, knew very well that only the extra leverage of an early log jam would suffice, in time, to shut off debate. All trade union spokesmen were agreed that there could be no compromise on Taft-Hartley "repeal" and no delay on any part of it. And so it went, group after group, issue after issue.

Both President and Congress were thus prisoners, in a sense, of the election and the way it had been won. It was one thing to throw a host of highly controversial measures at an opposition Congress which could—and did—reject most of them out of hand. It was quite another thing to throw the same load on a relatively receptive Congress, prepared to make a try at action on them all. Action is much harder than inaction; action on this scale, of this variety, an almost intolerable burden on the complex machinery of the legislative process—and on a President's capacity to focus attention, to rally support.

Despite this hadicap, the 81st Congress, be it said, turned out more New Deal-Fair Deal measures than any of its predecessors after 1938 . . . becoming, on its record, the most liberal Congress in the last fifteen years.

This was the Congress that enacted the comprehensive housing program, providing generously for slum clearance, urban redevelopment and public housing; the Congress that put through the major revision of social security, doubling insurance and assistance benefits and greatly—though not universally—extending coverage. This was the Congress that reformed the Displaced Persons Act, increased the minimum wage, doubled the hospital construction program, authorized the National Science Foundation and the rural telephone program, suspended the "sliding scale" on price supports, extended the soil conservation program, provided new grants for planning state and local public works and plugged the long-standing merger loophole in the Clayton Act. And it was principally this Congress that financed Truman's last expansions of flood control, rural electrification, reclamation, public power and transmission lines.

But this record of domestic accomplishment was obscured for commentators, public and Administration by a series of failures on the most dramatic and most dramatized of 1948's great expectations. In the first session of the 81st Congress—the last full session before Korea—aid to education, health insurance, FEPC and Taft-Hartley repeal were taken up, debated, fought over and either stalled or killed outright somewhere along the line.

General aid to education—that is, maintenance and operation funds for state school systems—had won Senate approval in 1948, in a form that represented careful compromise among religious interests and between the richer and the poorer states. Reintroduced in 1949, the same measure speedily received Senate approval once again. But as the year wore on, these compromises started to unravel; various groups and individuals took second looks, had second thoughts. The whole basis of agreement fell apart before the Senate bill had cleared the House Committee. There the bill remained, unreported at the session's end, eight months after Senate passage. There the second session found it—and left it.

The story on health is similar in some respects. The interest groups supporting Truman's health program and its Congressional sponsors did not seriously hope for early victory on compulsory health insurance. But they—and the Administration— saw this issue as a stick with which to beat the Congress into passing other major aspects of the program—increased hospital construction and research, aid to medical education and grants to local public health units; all obvious and necessary preliminaries to effective operation of any general insurance scheme. In the Senate, all four of these secondary measures were approved by early fall of 1949. Hospital construction and research grants—both expansions of existing programs—also fared well in the House. But the medical education and local health bills never got to the House floor. They were smothered to death in committee by a resurgent opposition—medical and other—which seized the stick of health insurance and used it to inflict increasing punishment, not only on these bills, their sponsors and supporters, but on the whole Administration and the Democratic Party.

In the case of civil rights, Truman's program was not merely stalled but buried during 1949. At the session's start, the interest groups—supported by the leadership in Congress and Administration—would stand for nothing but a test on the most controversial measure of them all: compulsory FEPC. The measure's proponents were perfectly aware they could not gain compulsion from the House, nor cloture from the Senate, without a major showing of Republican support. This was not forthcoming; the test proved that at any rate. It also helped Democrats, Southern as well as Northern, discharge some pressing obligations toward constituents. But the long filibuster of 1949 was all the Senate could endure. None of its leaders was prepared to face another bloodletting in 1950.

The Congressional failure on Taft-Hartley repeal was just as conclusive as that on civil rights and much more surprising to Administration, press and public. In 1949, the struggle in both Houses was intense, but save for the injunction in emergency disputes—the one feature opponents of repeal could press home to the general public—the advocates of a new law probably would have had their way. The interest groups could not, or would not give on this; the Administration could not, or would not impel them—so everything was lost; lost in 1949 and left, then, to await a new test in a new Congress. A decisive beating in the first session might be compromised in the second, but hardly reversed. And trade union leadership was in no mood for compromise.

Nor was the President. His response to each of these defeats in 1949—and other, lesser scars sustained that year—was a renewed recommendation in 1950. His January messages to the second session of the 81st Congress included virtually all proposals still outstanding, that he had listed to the first session in his moment of honeymoon a year before.

Clearly, there was little hope, in 1950, for much of what he asked. Yet the 81st

Congress, as Truman was to say that spring, had "already reversed" its predecessor's backward "trend." And if the "trend" now ran the Fair Deal's way, perhaps what this Congress withheld, would be forthcoming from the next—the 82nd Congress to be elected in November.

Not since 1934, had the Democratic Party increased its majorities in a mid-term election; breaking into new terrain in North and West. Yet that, and nothing less, was surely Truman's goal for 1950. "I hope," remarked the President, "that by next January, some of the obstructionists will be removed." And not content with pressing, once again, all the remaining issues of 1948, he urged on Congress three further measures each of which, if it appealed at all, would tap new sources of support, beyond the groups and areas where Democratic power was presumably entrenched.

One of these measures involved a new departure for the President on farm legislation. His 1950 State of the Union Message was the occasion for Truman's first formal use of the magic words connoting "Brannan Plan."[5] There he first attached the adjective "mandatory" to price supports, first urged "a system of production payments," first declared, "as a matter of national policy," that "safeguards must be maintained against slumps in farm prices," in order to support "farm income at fair levels."

To the uninitiate these words may look very little different from their counterparts in prior Presidential messages. But in the language of farm bureaucrats and organizations, these were magic words indeed, fighting words, emphasizing finally and officially, a sharp turn in Truman's agriculture policy—a turn which had begun in 1948, progressively distinguishing Democratic from Republican farm programs, and bringing the Administration now to ground where the Republicans in Congress—not to speak of many Democrats—could not or would not follow.[6]

By the time Truman spoke in January 1950, the more far-reaching measures his words implied had already been rebuffed at the preceding session of the Congress— and the "Brannan Plan" had already become a scare word, rivalling "socialized medicine" in the campaign arsenal the Republicans were readying. Yet by his endorsement Truman seemed to say that scare word or no, here was an issue to cement for Democrats the farm support which he had gained so providentially in 1948.

The second new measure to be proposed in the State of the Union message for 1950, concerned the housing shortage "for middle-income groups, especially in large metropolitan areas." The Housing Act of 1949 had granted more aids for private home financing which swelled the flood of relatively high priced houses. The Act also had promised more public housing, with subsidized rentals for people in the lowest income brackets. Between these two types of housing was a gap, affecting mainly urban and suburban "middle" groups of white collar and blue collar families; swing groups politically, as time would show. For them, in 1950, the President proposed "new legislation authorizing a vigorous program to help cooperatives and other non-profit groups build housing which these families could afford."

The third of 1950's new proposals was billed as a mere promissory note in the State of the Union message. "I hope," said Truman, "to transmit to the Congress a series of proposals to . . . assist small business and to encourage the growth of new enterprises." As such, this was no more concrete than the benign expressions in many earlier messages and party platforms. But in the spring of 1950, the President kept his promise and put meat on these old bones with a comprehensive small business program far more elaborate than anything advanced since the emergency legislation of the early thirties.[6] The immediate reaction, in Congress and out, was very favorable. A leading spokesman for "big" business called the Truman message "tempered, reasoned, non-political." Small business groups expressed great interest; even some bankers had kind words to say.

The President's small business program went to Congress as he entrained for the Far West, on his "non-political" tour of May, 1950. The Fair Deal's prospects were then enticing numbers of Administration stalwarts to leave their safe House seats and campaign for the Senate. Many signs encouraged them. The country was prosperous, recession ending; the Presidential program popular, to all appearances, attracting interest in useful quarters and stirring overt opposition only where most expected and least feared. Foreign policy was costly but not noticeably burdensome, defense pared down, the budget coming into balance.

Yet on the other side were signs of change, foretastes of things to come, making 1950 a very special year, a year of sharp transition, in retrospect a great divide. The preceding winter saw the last of Chinese Nationalist resistance on the Asian mainland. In January Alger Hiss was convicted in his second trial—and Secretary Acheson quoted from the Scriptures. In February, Senator McCarthy first shared with the public his discovery of Communism's menace here at home. In May, Senator Kefauver's committee began televised crime hearings, exposing criminal connections of political machines in some of the nation's largest cities—where, as it happened, the Democratic Party had been long in control.

And on the twenty-fifth of June, the North Korean Communists invaded the Republic of Korea.

Korea: The Great Divide

In legislative terms, the initial impact of Korea on the Fair Deal is symbolized by the collapse of Truman's small business program. Senate hearings had just got under way when the fighting began. They terminated quickly in the first days of July. The Senate committee which had started down this track enthusiastically, turned off to tackle the Defense Production Act—controls for the new, part-way war economy.

All along the line, Fair Deal proposals were permanently shelved or set aside, as Congress worked on measures for defense. And on one of these measures, price controls, which had long been identified with the Fair Deal, not the President but Congress forced the issue—never again was Truman able to resurrect it as his own. . . .

Apart from price controls, the conflict in Korea drew Congressional—and national—attention away from the traditional Fair Deal issues. As election time approached, in 1950, there was no backdrop of recent, relevant Congressional debate to liven up these issues, stressing their affirmative appeal. Instead, the opposition had a field day with the negative refrain of "socialism"—or worse—invoking spectres of the "Brannan Plan," "socialized medicine," and Alger Hiss, to unnerve a public preoccupied with sacrifices in a far-off peninsula, nervous over rumors about "Chinese volunteers."

In the first week of November, the electorate—far from increasing Democratic power—reduced to a bare minimum the Democratic Party's lead in both Houses of Congress, abruptly closing the careers of some very senior Senators and some very staunch Administration Congressmen. And in the last week of November the full-scale Chinese intervention in Korea turned virtual victory into disastrous retreat, confronting the Administration and the country with a "new" war, a most uncertain future, and endless possibilities of worse to come.

Mobilization and Reluctant Retreat: 1951-52

On December 15, 1950, the President proclaimed a National Emergency. Three weeks later, in January, 1951, the 82nd Congress assembled to hear, in virtual silence, what Truman had to say.

His State of the Union Message was somewhat reminiscent, in its tight organization and sharp phrasing, of the fighting address of 1948. But in tone and content it was, by far, the most conciliatory annual message since 1947.

The entire address was devoted to events abroad and mobilization at home. Its ten-point legislative program was couched in emergency terms. Among the ten points only one Fair Deal item remained in its entirety—aid for medical education, now billed as a means of "increasing the supply of doctors . . . critically needed for defense. . . ." Two other pillars of the Fair Deal program were included in qualified form. General aid to education was requested, "to meet . . . most urgent needs . . . ," with the proviso that "some of our plans will have to be deferred. . . ." And while there was no specific mention of Taft-Hartley, or its repeal, the President did ask "improvement of our labor laws to help provide stable . . . relations and . . . steady production in this emergency."

Aside from a bland and wholly unspecific reference to "improvements in our agriculture laws," an opening for subsequent proposals never made, these were the only references to Fair Deal measures in the Presidential list of "subjects on which legislation will be needed. . . . " They were almost the only references in the entire message; but not quite. After his ten-point enumeration, Truman remarked "the government must give priority to activities that are urgent," and offered "power development" as an example. Then he added, "Many of the things we would normally do . . . must be curtailed or postponed . . . "; the door was finally closing, but—the Congress should give continuing attention ". . . to measures . . . for the long pull." There followed four brief and unelaborated but unmistakable references to increased unemployment and old age insurance, disability and health insurance and civil rights.

As in 1947, so in 1951, the President was shifting emphasis, relegating most welfare measures to some secondary order of priority, without quite ceasing to be their advocate. It was too subtle a performance for the press; the distinctions much too fine for headlines or wide public notice—though not, perhaps, for Congressmen to grasp. Yet in its way, this message represented Truman's recognition of the fundamental change in his circumstances and the Nation's; his nearest approach to Roosevelt's sharp, dramatic switch, a decade earlier, from "Dr. New Deal" to "Dr. Win-the-War."

And unlike 1947, this mild beginning, in January 1951, heralded a more conciliatory tone, an increased interest in negotiation, on some of the Fair Deal's most striking programs. As the year wore on, Truman gradually changed tactics on at least three fronts, seeking different ground from that staked out in pre-Korean years.

The first of these shifts came in the field of health. There the Administration was hopelessly on the defensive by 1951. The vocal presence of an aroused and potent medical opposition, victorious in trials of strength at 1950's elections, sufficed to make most Congressmen suspect and fear a taint of "socialized medicine" in any Truman health measure, however limited its purpose or narrow its scope. The President had barely raised the health insurance issue in January, 1951, but its mere invocation was now enough to halt all legislation in the field. So far had the opposition come, from its days on the defensive, back in 1949.

Finally, Truman voiced his recognition of the situation: "I am not clinging to any particular plan," he told an audience in June. This was followed, six months later, by appointment of the President's Commission on the Health Needs of the Nation, charged with surveying, from the ground up, all problems and proposals in the field.[8] In January 1952, addressing the second session of the 82nd Congress, the President remarked of health insurance, "So far as I know it is still the best way. If there are . . . better answers I hope this Commission will find them."

A second change in tactics during 1951 came on the issue of Taft-Hartley. Senator Taft's triumphant re-election, the preceding autumn, had symbolized how futile were the hopes of 1949 for a renewal, in a "better" Congress, of that year's stalled attack. In Truman's January messages of 1951 there was no mention of "repeal." The following October, his first address at a trade-union affair, that year, was notable for subdued treatment of the issue. "We want a law . . . that will be fair . . .," he said, "and . . . we will have that kind of law, in the long run . . ." and that was all. Two months later, the President enlarged upon this theme, telling the Congress, "we need ... to improve our labor law ... even the sponsors ... admit it needs to be changed. ...." The issue of "repeal" was dormant, so Truman seemed to say. Amendment, even perhaps piecemeal amendment—anathema in 1949—now measured the ambitions of his Administration.

The President's third shift in emphasis came on his agriculture program. Since the Korean outbreak, farm prices had soared, along with the demand for food and fibre. There was little in the current situation to promote wide interest in Brannan's innovations, or counteract the socialistic spectres that his "plan" invoked. In January 1951, the President had no specific comment on the ideas he had endorsed a year before. By January 1952, Truman was prepared with some specifics, but on much narrower ground. That year, his State of the Union message asked—and Congress shortly granted—renewed suspension of the "sliding scale" on price supports, which otherwise would have become effective at the end of 1952. For the rest, he simply remarked that there was "need to find ... a less costly method for supporting perishable commodities than the law now provides"—a plug for "production payments," surely, but in a fashion that softpedalled the far-reaching overtones of 1950.

The year of 1951 turned out to be a hard and unrewarding time for the Administration; a year marked by MacArthur's firing, by strenuous debates on foreign policy and on controls, by blighted hopes for quick truce in Korea, by snowballing complaints of government corruption—and by prolonged Congressional indifference to the welfare measures on the trimmed-down Truman list.

The State of the Union message in January, 1951, was less incisive than its predecessor—so was the emergency—but hardly less moderate in its approach on home affairs. Besides the new departures on health insurance, labor laws and farm legislation, the President appealed again for aid to education and the supplementary health bills of a year before. Again he mentioned power needs. Again he raised, briefly and generally, the issues of civil rights. Otherwise, in only two respects did he go beyond specifics urged in 1951—asking cost-of-living increases for social security recipients and readjustment benefits for Korean veterans.

These two requests were granted rather promptly, giving Truman his last minor successes. But in the spring of 1952, the second session of the 82nd Congress was interested less in legislating than investigating; less concerned with pending measures than with Administration struggles over corruption—and the steel dispute; preoccupied above all else with the coming Presidential nominations and the campaign to follow in the fall. The session's main contribution to the Fair Deal program was not positive, but negative, rousing one last Truman proposal in opposition to the McCarran Act; creating one more Fair Deal issue; liberalization of the immigration laws.[9]

In this fashion, Truman's last Congress slowed to a close. And in Chicago, that July, appeared a final summary of Fair Deal business left undone—the Democratic Platform of 1952.

What Truman had played down, in his last annual messages, the platform now set forth in some detail. It called for action on the civil rights program, avoiding retrogression by a hair; pledged still more improvement in the social insurance laws; promised more resource conservation and development, including public power; urged Federal help for schools, this time stressing construction along with "general" aid; called for a firm stand on public housing and revived the "middle income" issue of two years before; spoke feelingly of protection and assistance for small business, hinting at specifics unmentioned since Korea; adopted Truman's formula on health, with kind words for the President's Commission; followed him also on farm price supports, on immigration and on a host of lesser issues, long the stock-in-trade of Democratic documents.

At one point only did the platform diverge sharply from the President's more recent formulations. On Taft-Hartley it abandoned his new stand, reverting to the cliche of "repeal." The Democratic candidate was put to some trouble by this change, but it cannot be said to have much mattered to the voters.

It had been seven years since Harry Truman, reaffirming Roosevelt's purpose, first charted the Fair Deal in his twenty-one point program of 1945. Now it received its last expression in his party's platform for 1952. This remains the final statement. In January 1953, Truman and his party yielded office to the first Republican Administration in twenty years.

A Fair Deal Balance Sheet

Set the platform of 1952 alongside the program of 1945, allow for changing circumstances and particulars, then run a quick calculation on the Fair Deal legislative program. What did Truman gain in seven years from his four Congresses? What came of all the trials and tribulations recorded in this essay?

In the first place, it is clear that Truman managed to obtain from Congress means for modernizing, bringing up to date, a number of outstanding New Deal landmarks in social welfare and economic development among them: social security, minimum wages, public health and housing; farm price supports, rural electrification, soil conservation, reclamation, flood control and public power. Not all of these were strictly New Deal innovations, but all gained either life or impetus from Roosevelt in the thirties. And in the new circumstances of the post-war forties they were renewed, elaborated, enlarged upon, by legislative action urged in Truman's Fair Deal program; even their underlying rationale nailed down in law by the Employment Act of 1946.

This is significant, and not alone by virtue of particulars attained. A generation earlier, the very spirit of Wilsonian New Freedom had been buried deep in the debris of reaction following world war. Not so with the New Deal.

As a consolidator, as a builder on foundations, Truman left an impressive legislative record; the greater part achieved, of course, in less than two year's time, and by a single Congress. Moreover as protector, as defender, wielder of the veto against encroachments on the liberal preserve, Truman left a record of considerable success—an aspect of the Fair Deal not to be discounted. He could not always hold his ground, sustained some major losses, but in the process managed to inflict much punishment on his opponents.

The greater Truman vetoes pretty well define what might be called the legislative program of the conservative coalition in his time. On many of these measures he made his veto stick, as with the offshore oil bills in 1946 and 1952, or natural gas and basing points in 1950. . . . On a few—especially the two already noted—Congress overrode him, and the ground once lost was not made up in Truman's time: the Taft-Hartley Act in 1947 and the McCarran Act in 1952.

Besides these, Truman asked of Congress four main things which were denied him: aid to education, health insurance, civil rights and—for want of better shorthand—"Brannan Plan." On the outstanding features of these four, he got no satisfaction: no general grants for all school systems; no national prepayment plan for medical care; no FEPC, or anti-poll tax or anti-lynching laws; no wholesale renovation of price supports to insure good returns from general farm production. Here, if anywhere, does Elmer Davis' refrain approach reality: "Truman kept asking for all of it and getting none of it."

Why did he keep asking? From 1945 to 1950, one may concede that year by year there always seemed to be good reason to press on: reason to hope and plan for action, if not in one session then the next, reason to believe the very chance for future action might depend on present advocacy. But after 1950, after Korea, faced with a dozen hard new issues, on the defensive all the way from "Communism to corruption," what then explains the Truman course? He must have known, his actions show awareness, that there had come a real sea change in his affairs and in the country's. Why move so slowly towards a bare minimum of reappraisal, readjustment?

Perhaps the answers lie, in part, in Truman's temperament; partly in his concept of the Presidency. Unquestionably he thought these measures right for the country; hence proper for the President to advocate, regardless of their chances in Congress. He had assumed responsibility as keeper of the country's conscience on these issues; as its awakener, as well, by virtue of stands taken far ahead of the procession. For civil rights, especially, Truman could claim—like Roosevelt after the court fight of 1937—that while he may have lost a legislative battle, the forcing of the issue helped to win a larger war. "There has been a great awakening of the American conscience on the issue of civil rights," he was to say in his farewell report to

Congress, "all across the nation ... the barriers are coming down." This was happening; by his demands for legislation he conceived that he helped make it happen. On that promise, he was bound not to abandon his position, no matter what the legislative outcome, present or prospective.

Even in strictly legislative terms there was, perhaps, much to be gained by standing firm. Were not some of the fights that failed a vital stimulus to others that succeeded? Were not some votes against a measure such as health insurance, repaid by other votes in favor of reciprocal trade renewal, say? Was not a total Presidential program basically advantaged if it overshot the limits of assured Congressional response? There are no ready measurements providing certain answers to these questions. But Presidents must seek them all the same. And on his record there is little doubt what answers Truman found.

For Truman then, each of his great outstanding issues had value as a legislative stalking horse, if nothing more. But that is not to say he saw no more in them. On the contrary, had he not thought many things attainable, still actionable in the not too distant future—still meaningful, therefore, in rallying political support—he scarcely would have bothered, during 1951, to cleanse his farm and health programs—much less Taft-Hartley—of the worst taints absorbed in the campaign of 1950, thus rendering them useable for 1952.

Those changes in approach were hardly aimed at Congress—not, anyway, the current Congress. Rather, the President was preparing new positions for his party, shifting to ground on which it could afford to stand with him and to uphold, if in adjusted guise, the Fair Deal label and the Truman cause.

Right to the last, then, Truman was persuaded that those Fair Deal issues touched felt needs, roused real response among Americans; no longer viable objectives for his time in office, but crucial undertakings in his party's future.

Notes

1. This is indicative of a sharp cleavage of opinion in the circle of advisers immediately around the President, involving much argumentation against the proposed post V-J Day program.

2. The five items under this heading, in addition to the budget and housing, included generalizations about farm welfare and competitive enterprise along with specific proposals for a study of labor-management relations and for limited changes in the Wagner Act.

3. The Economic Report lumped these and other matters into a "long-range" program. Its "short-range" recommendations included only one new item besides the five "major policies" in the earlier message: namely, cost-of-living increases for social security beneficiaries.

4. The "Turnip Day" address, July 27, 1948, delivered two weeks after Truman's nomination by the Democratic Convention.

5. In May 1949, the Secretary of Agriculture, Charles Brannan, set before the Congressional Agriculture Committees, a complicated series of proposals, and suggestions—which, to his chagrin, an alert opposition promptly labelled "The (Socialistic) Brannan Plan." The complex

and controversial specifics Brannan then advanced were intended to make price supports more nearly serve the purpose of maintaining high-level farm income under conditions of increasing total production and consumption, with subsidies ("production payments") to bridge the gap between an adequate return to the producer and an inviting price to the consumer on perishable commodities.

6. The Agriculture Act of 1948, the so-called Hope-Aiken Bill, passed by the Republican 80th Congress, had emphasized "flexibility," its mechanism the "sliding scale," its underlying philosophy not maintenance of high income, but prevention of excessive loss. Brannan's proposals represented a sharply different philosophy about the purposes of Federal action, let alone specifics. But the first session of the 81st Congress went with him only a small part of the way. His more striking innovations were side-tracked during 1949.

7. The program was contained in a special message dated May 5, 1950. Five points were included: (1) insurance of small bank loans, (2) provisions to encourage equity investment, (3) broadened lending powers for RFC, (4) strengthened managerial and technoligical aids, and (5) consolidation of all assistance programs under the Secretary of Commerce.

8. The Commission, chaired by Dr. Paul Magnuson, was established December 29, 1951, and given a free hand. It reported, a year later, December 18, 1952, recommending, among many other things, various forms of public subsidy for private health insurance plans to meet the high cost of medical care—the problem to which Truman's governmental health insurance proposal had been addressed.

9. Truman vetoed the McCarran Act, June 25, 1952, urging instead his emergency immigration program of March 24, 1952, together with a general long-range study. Congress promptly overrode the veto. Thereupon, on September 4, 1952, Truman established a President's Commission on Immigration and Naturalization which reported January 1, 1953. Its report generally confirmed the President's objections and recommended many changes in the law. These were, of course, no longer actionable, as far as Truman was concerned, but formed the base for a continuing agitation by some Democrats. . . .

Chapter 5 THE LIMITATIONS OF THE LIBERAL VISION

Now teaching American history at Stanford University, BARTON J. BERNSTEIN *specializes in the New Deal and Fair Deal periods. Frequently identified with the New Left group of historians, he has edited "Towards a New Past: Dissenting Essays in American History" (1967). In an article he prepared for that volume, and reprinted here, Bernstein takes a critical look from the New Left position at the alleged failures of American liberalism, especially on domestic issues, during the wartime and postwar era. What are the implications of the fact that the Neustadt article appeared in 1954, while Bernstein wrote in 1967? To what extent can President Truman be held responsible for what Bernstein obviously regards as defects of the American liberal tradition in general?*

The domestic events of the war and postwar years have failed to attract as much scholarly effort as have the few years of the New Deal. The reforms of the thirties and the struggle against depression have captured the enthusiasm of many liberal historians and have constituted the major themes shaping their interpretations. Compared with the excitement of the New Deal years, the events at home during the next decade seem less interesting, certainly less dramatic.

The issues of these years also seem less clear, perhaps because the period lacks the restrictive unity imposed upon the New Deal. Despite the fragmentary scholarship, however, the major issues are definable: economic policies,[1] civil rights and civil liberties,[2] and social welfare policies.[3] The continued dominance by big busi-

"America in War and Peace: The Test of Liberalism," by Barton J. Bernstein. From *Towards a New Past*, edited by Barton J. Bernstein. Copyright © 1967, 1968 by Random House, Inc. Reprinted by permission of the publisher.

ness, the consolidation of other groups within the economy, the challenge of racial inequality—these are the themes of the wartime Roosevelt administration. Toward the end of Roosevelt's years, they are joined by another concern, the quest for social reform, and in Truman's years by such themes as economic readjustment, the renewed struggle against inflation, and the fear of disloyalty and communism. These problems are largely the legacy of the New Deal: the extension of its limited achievements, the response to its shortcomings, the criticism of its liberalism.

It was during the war years that the nation climbed out of depression, that big business regained admiration and increased its power, and that other interests became effective partners in the political economy of large-scale corporate capitalism. While the major interests focused on foreign policy and on domestic economic problems—on mobilization and stabilization, later on reconversion and inflation— liberal democracy was revealing serious weaknesses. Opposing fascism abroad as a threat to democratic values, the nation remained generally insensitive to the plight of its citizens who suffered indignity or injury because of their color. Violating liberal values in the process of saving American democracy, Roosevelt's government, swept along by a wave of racism, victimized Japanese-Americans. Uncommitted to advancing the Negroes' cause, the war government resisted their demands for full participation in democracy and prosperity, and grudgingly extended to them only limited rights.

Though the New Deal had gone intellectually bankrupt long before Pearl Harbor and reform energies were submerged during most of the war, they reappeared in the last years of the conflict. Reviving the reform spirit in 1944, Roosevelt called for an "Economic Bill of Rights" for post-war America. In his last year, however, he was unable to achieve his goals, and Truman's efforts were usually too weak to overcome the conservative coalition blocking his expanded reform program. Mobilized by apprehension, liberals wrongly believed that the conservative bloc wished to destroy unions, to reorganize the corporate economy, and to leave the nation without protection from depression. But as unions endured and the economy grew, the fears and energies of liberals wanted. Exaggerating the accomplishments of past reforms and believing that widespread prosperity had been achieved, they lost much of their social vision: they came to praise big business, to celebrate pluralism, to ignore poverty. Yet to their surprise they fell under vigorous attack from the right, in a new assault on civil liberties. In viewing McCarthyism as an attack upon the reform tradition, however, liberals failed to understand that they and the Democratic administration, as zealous anticommunists, also shared responsibility for the "red scare."

I

During the war and postwar years, big business regained national admiration and received lavish praise for contributing to victory over fascism. Yet few realized that business had not initially been an enthusiastic participant in the "arsenal of democracy." Such firms as Standard Oil of New Jersey, Dow Chemical, United States Steel, Dupont, General Motors, and the Aluminum Company of America had assisted the growth of Nazi industry and delayed America's preparation for war. Even after most Americans had come to condemn fascism, these corporations had collaborated with German business, sharing patents and often blocking production of defense materials in America.[4] The general ideology of these firms was probably best expressed by Alfred Sloan, Jr., the chairman of the General Motors board, when he replied to a stockholder: ". . . an international business operating throughout the world should conduct its operations in strictly business terms without regard to the political beliefs in its management, or the political beliefs of the country in which it is operating."[5]

In the two years before Pearl Harbor, major industries were also reluctant to prepare for defense. Though the aircraft industry ended its "sit-down" strike after the government had relaxed profit restrictions and improved terms for amortization,[6] other industries continued to resist expansion and production for defense. Sharing the common opinion that American intervention was unlikely, and painfully recalled the glutted markets of the depression decade, the steel industry and the aluminum monopoly (Alcoa) opposed growth, which might endanger profits. Nor were the automobile makers and larger producers of consumer durables willing to take defense contracts which would convert assembly lines from profitable, peacetime goods to preparation for a war that many believed, and President Roosevelt seemed to promise, America would never enter.[7]

Fearful of bad publicity, the leaders of these industries never challenged the administration nor demanded a clear statement of their responsibility. They avoided a dialogue on the basic issues. Still suffering from the opprobrium of the depression, industrialists would not deny corporate responsibility to the nation. Though privately concerned about the welfare of their companies, industrialists never argued that they owed primary responsibility to their stockholders. Fearful of jeopardizing their firms' well-being, company officials did not publicly express their doubts. Yet they could have objected publicly to executive suasion and contended that the issues were so grave that a Congressional mandate was necessary. Instead, they publicly accepted their obligation to risk profits for American defense, but in practice they continued to avoid such risks. Often they made promises they did not fulfill, and when they resisted administration policy, they took refuge in evasion. They restricted the dialogue to matters of feasibility and tactics—that expansion in steel and aluminum was unnecessary, that partial conversion was impossible, and that available tools could not produce defense goods.

The government also avoided opening the dialogue. The prewar mobilization agencies, administered largely by dollar-a-year men, did not seek to embarrass or coerce recalcitrant industries. Protecting business from public censure, the directors of mobilization—such men as William Knudsen of General Motors and Edward

Stettinius of United States Steel—resisted the efforts of other government officials to force prompt expansion and conversion. In effect, Knudsen, Stettinius, and their cohorts acted as protectors of "business as usual." Despite the protests of the service secretaries, Roosevelt permitted the businessmen in government to move slowly. Though he encouraged some assistants to prod business, and occasionally spurred the dollar-a-year men, he avoided exerting direct pressure on big business.

The President was following the strategy of caution. Reluctant to encourage public criticism of, or even debate on, his foreign policy, he maneuvered to avoid conflict or challenge. Because the nation respected big businessmen, he chose them to direct mobilization. He too had faith in their ability, and he hoped to win cooperation from the suspicious business community by selecting its leaders as his agents.

While many liberals criticized Roosevelt's reliance upon big business, the most direct, public challenge to business power came from Walter Reuther, vice-president of the recently formed United Automobile Workers, and from Philip Murray, president of the CIO and the United Steel Workers.[8] Criticizing "business as usual" policies, they proposed a labor-management council to guide industry during war. The plan shocked industrialists. It was radicalism, an invasion of management's prerogatives, a threat to private enterprise, asserted business leaders.[9] They would not share power or sanction a redefinition of private property. Having grudgingly recognized industrial unions shortly before the war, they remained suspicious of organized labor and were unwilling to invite its leaders into the industrial councils of decision making.[10]

Despite these suspicions, the administration called upon labor leaders and their organizations for cooperation in the war effort. Needing their support, Roosevelt appointed union chiefs to positions in the stabilization and mobilization agencies, and thus bestowed prestige upon organized labor. Calling for a labor-management partnership, he secured a wartime no-strike pledge.[11] As junior partners in the controlled economy, labor leaders generally kept the pledge.[12] Cooperating with business leaders in the defense effort, union representatives, by their actions, convinced many businessmen that organized labor did not threaten large-scale corporate capitalism.[13] By encouraging labor-management cooperation, the war years, then, provided a necessary respite between the industrial violence of the thirties and sustained collective bargaining, and speeded the consolidation of the new organization of the American economy.

It was within a government-controlled economy (dominated by business) that the major interests struggled for economic advantages. Farmers, rescued from the depression by enlarged demand, initially battled price controls but soon acceded to them and tried simply to use political power to increase their benefits. Also reaping the gains of war, workers received higher incomes but bitterly criticized the tight restraints on hourly wage increases. Business, also recovering from the depression, complained about price controls, which indirectly limited profits. Though all interests chafed under the restraints, none disputed in principle the need for government-imposed restraints on wages and prices: all agreed that a free price system during war, when civilian demand greatly outstripped consumer goods, would have created inequity and chaos.[14]

Despite price restrictions and the excess-profits tax, the major corporations prospered, benefiting from cost-plus contracts and the five-year amortization plan (which made the new plants partial gifts from the government).[15] As dollar-a-year men poured into Washington, big firms gained influence and contracts. Smaller businessmen, unable to match the influence and mistrusted by procurement officers, declined in importance. In a nation that prized the large corporation, few had confidence in small business. Even the creation of a government agency to protect small business failed to increase significantly its share in the war economy.[16]

The interests of big business were defended and advanced by the dollar-a-year men, and particularly by those on the War Production Board (WPB), the agency controlling resources. In many wartime Washington agencies, and especially on the WPB, the leaders of big business and the military served together and learned to cooperate. Burying earlier differences about preparation for war, they developed similar views of the national interest and identified it with the goals of their own groups. The reconversion controversy of 1944, which C. Wright Mills views as the beginning of the military-industrial alliance,[17] is the outstanding example of this coalition of interests.

In early 1944, big business was experiencing large military cutbacks and withdrawing subcontracts from smaller firms, often leaving them idle. Temporarily proponents of strong controls, most of the WPB executives from industry and finance would not allow these smaller firms to return to consumer goods. They collaborated with representatives of the military to block the reconversion program. Desiring control of the wartime economy, such military leaders as Robert P. Patterson, Under Secretary of War, James Forrestal, Under Secretary of the Navy, and Major General Lucius Clay, Assistant Chief of Staff for Matériel, feared that reconversion would siphon off scarce labor and disrupt vital production. Joining them were such WPB executives as Charles E. Wilson, president of General Electric, Lemuel Boulware, a Celotex executive and later a General Electric vice-president, and financiers Arthur H. Bunker of Lehman Brothers and Sidney Weinberg of Goldman, Sachs. Sympathetic to military demands, they were also afraid that the earlier return of small producers to consumer markets would injure big business. While some may have acted to protect their own companies, most were simply operating in a value system that could not accept a policy which seemed to threaten big business. Through cunning maneuvering, these military and industrial leaders acted to protect the prewar oligopolistic structure of the American economy.[18]

The war, while creating the limited prosperity that the New Deal had failed to create, did not disrupt the economic distribution of power. Nor did the extension of the wartime income tax significantly reallocate income and wealth, for the Congress even rebuffed Roosevelt's effort to limit the war incomes of the wealthy. Though the wartime measures and not the New Deal increased the tax burden on the upper-income groups, "the major weight," emphasizes Gabriel Kolko, "fell on income groups that had never before been subjected to the income tax."[19]

II

Failing to limit business power or to reallocate wealth, the wartime government was more active in other areas. Yielding to pressures, Roosevelt slightly advanced the welfare of the Negro, but the President also bowed to illiberal pressures and dealt a terrible blow to civil liberties when he authorized the forced evacuation of 110,000 loyal Americans of Japanese descent.

It was the "worst single wholesale violation of civil rights" in American history, judged the American Civil Liberties Union.[20] Succumbing to the anti-Japanese hysteria of Westerners (including the pleas of California Attorney-General Earl Warren and the Pacific coast congressional delegation under Senator Hiram Johnson) and the demands of the military commander on the coast, the President empowered the Army to remove the Japanese-Americans.[21] ("He was never theoretical about things. What must be done to defend the country must be done," Roosevelt believed, later wrote Francis Biddle, his Attorney-General.)[22] "Japanese raids on the west coast seemed not only possible but probable in the first months of war, and it was quite impossible to be sure that the raiders would not receive important help from individuals of Japanese origin," was the explanation later endorsed by Secretary of War Henry Stimson.[23]

Privately Stimson called the episode a "tragedy," but he supported it as War Department policy.[24] Opposing the decision, Biddle could not weaken the resolve of Roosevelt. Though liberals protested the action, the Supreme Court later upheld Roosevelt and the War Department.[25] "The meaning of the decision," concludes Arthur Link, "was clear and foreboding: in future emergencies no American citizen would have any rights that the President and the army were bound to respect when, *in their judgment,* the emergency justified drastic denial of civil rights."[26]

Though anti-Japanese feeling was most virulent on the Pacific coast, racism was not restricted to any part of America. In most of America, Negroes had long been the victims of hatred. Frequently lacking effective legal protection in the South, Negroes also encountered prejudice, fear, and hatred in the North. During the war there were racial clashes in Northern cities. New York narrowly averted a major riot. In Los Angeles whites attacked Negroes and Mexicans, and in Detroit whites invaded the Negro sector and pillaged and killed.[27]

Despite the evidence of deep racism, liberal historians have usually avoided focusing upon the hatred in white America and the resort to violence.[28] Curiously, though emphasizing the disorganization of the Negro community, they have also neglected the scattered protests by organized Negroes—boycotts of white-owned stores in Negro areas of Memphis and Houston when they would not hire Negroes, a sit-in in a public library in Alexandria, Virginia, a Harlem boycott of a bus line to compel the hiring of Negro drivers.[29]

Condemned to inferiority in nearly all sectors of American life, Negroes did not share in the benefits of the early defense economy.[30] Denied jobs in many industries, they also met discrimination by the military. The Air Corps barred them, the Navy segregated them to the mess corps, and the Army held them to a small quota, generally restricting them to menial tasks.[31] During the 1940 campaign, Negro leaders attacked the administration for permitting segregation and discrimination, and demanded the broadening of opportunity in the military. It is not "a fight merely to wear a uniform," explained *Crisis* (the NAACP publication). "This is a struggle for status, a struggle to take democracy off a parchment and give it life."[32]

Negroes gained admission to the Air Corps when it yielded under White House pressure, but they failed to gain congressional support for wider participation in the military. At Roosevelt's direction the War Department did raise its quota of Negroes—to their proportion in the population. But the Army remained segregated. Though unwilling to challenge segregation, the administration still courted Negro leaders and the black vote. Rather than bestowing benefits upon the masses, Roosevelt maintained their allegiance by offering symbolic recognition: Colonel Benjamin O. Davis, the Army's highest ranking Negro, was promoted to Brigadier General, and some prominent Negroes were appointed as advisers to the Secretary of War and the Director of Selective Service.[33] ("We asked Mr. Roosevelt to change the rules of the game and he countered by giving us some new uniforms," complained the editors of the *Baltimore Afro-American*. "That is what it amounts to and we have called it appeasement."[34])

As the nation headed toward war, Negroes struggled to wring other concessions from a president who never enlisted in their cause and would not risk antagonizing powerful Southerners. Discriminated against by federal agencies during the depression and denied an equal share of defense prosperity, Negroes were unwilling to acquiesce before continued injustice. In some industrial areas the NAACP and *ad hoc* groups organized local protests. After numerous unsuccessful appeals to the President, Negro leaders planned more dramatic action—a march on Washington.[35]

Demanding "the right to work and fight for our country," the leaders of the March on Washington Movement—A. Philip Randolph, head of the Brotherhood of Sleeping Car Porters, Walter White, executive secretary of the NAACP, and Lester Granger, executive secretary of the Urban League—publicly requested executive orders ending racial discrimination in federal agencies, the military and defense employment.[36] In private correspondence with the President they sought more: the end of segregation in these areas. So bold were their goals that some still have not been enforced by the government, and it is unlikely that Negro leaders expected to secure them.[37]

Refusing to give up the march for the promise of negotiations, Negro leaders escaped the politics of accommodation. Though white liberals urged Randolph and his cohorts to call off the march, they would not yield.[38] Applying pressure on an uncomfortable administration, they ultimately settled for less than they had requested (and perhaps less than they had anticipated[39])—an executive order barring discrimination in defense work and creating a Federal Employment Practices Committee (FEPC). Meager as the order was, it was the greatest achievement in American history for organized Negro action.[40]

FEPC did not contribute significantly to the wartime advancement of the Negro. His gains were less the results of federal efforts than of the labor shortage. Undoubtedly, the committee would have been more effective if Roosevelt had provided it with a larger budget, but the Negro's cause never commanded the President's enthusiasm. Yet he did protect FEPC from its enemies, and by maintaining the agency, stressed its symbolic importance.[41]

It affirmed the rights of Negroes to jobs and focused attention on the power of the federal government to advance the interests of its black citizens. It did not smash the walls of prejudices; it only removed a few bricks. FEPC, concludes Louis Ruchames, "brought hope and a new confidence into their [Negro] lives. It gave them cause to believe in democracy and in America. It made them feel that in answering the call to their country's colors, they were defending, not the oppression and degradation, to which they were accustomed, but democracy, equality of opportunity, and a better world for themselves and their children."[42]

Still relegated to second-class citizenship, Negroes had found new dignity and new opportunity during the war. Loyal followers of Roosevelt, loving him for the few benefits his government had extended, black Americans had become important members of the shifting Democratic coalition. By their presence in Northern cities, they would also become a new political force.[43] For the Democratic party and the nation, their expectations and needs would constitute a moral and political challenge. By its response, white America would test the promise of liberal democracy.

III

When the nation joined the Allies, Roosevelt had explained that "Dr. Win-the-War" was taking over from "Dr. New Deal," and there were few liberal legislative achievements during the war years. Those benefits that disadvantaged groups did receive were usually a direct result of the labor shortage and the flourishing economy, not of liberal politics. By 1944, however, Roosevelt was prepared to revive the reform spirit, and he revealed his liberal vision for the postwar years. Announcing an "Economic Bill of Rights," he outlined "a new basis for security and prosperity": the right to a job, adequate food, clothing, and recreation, a decent home, a good education, adequate medical care, and protection against sickness and unemployment.[44]

Noble as was his vision of the future society, Roosevelt was still unprepared to move far beyond rhetoric, and the Congress was unsympathetic to his program.[45] While approving the GI Bill of Rights,[46] including educational benefits and extended unemployment pay, Congress resisted most liberal programs during the war. Asserting its independence of the executive, the war Congress also thwarted Roosevelt in other ways—by rejecting a large tax bill designed to spread the cost of war and to reduce inflationary pressures[47] and by liquidating the National Resources Planning Board, which had originated the "second bill of rights" and also studied postwar economic planning.[48]

By its opposition to planning and social reform, Congress increased the anxieties of labor and liberals about the postwar years and left the new Truman administration poorly prepared for the difficult transition to a peacetime economy when the war suddenly ended.[49] Fearing the depression that most economists forecast, the administration did, however, propose a tax cut of $5 billion. While removing many low-income recipients from the tax rolls, the law was also of great benefit to large corporations. Charging inequity, organized labor found little support in Congress or the executive, for the government was relying upon business activity, rather than on consumer purchasing power, to soften the economic decline. Significantly, despite the anticipated $30 billion deficit (plus the $5 billion tax), no congressman expressed any fear of an unbalanced budget. Clearly fiscal orthodoxy did not occupy a very high place in the scale of values of congressional conservatives, and they accepted in practice the necessity of an unbalanced budget.[50]

Before the tax bill passed, the wartime harmony of the major interest groups had crumbled: each struggled to consolidate its gains and advance its welfare before the anticipated economic collapse. Chafing under the no-strike pledge and restrictions on wage raises, organized labor compelled the administration to relax its policy and free unions to bargain collectively.[51] Farmers, fearful of depression, demanded the withdrawal of subsidies which artificially depressed prices.[52] Big business, despite anticipated shortages, secured the removal of most controls on the allocation of resources.[53]

As the economic forecasts shifted in late autumn, the administration discovered belatedly that inflation, not depression, was the immediate economic danger. The President acted sporadically to restrain inflationary pressures, but his efforts to resist the demands of interest groups and the actions of his own subordinates.[54]

Beset by factionalism and staffed often by men of limited ability, Truman's early government floundered. By adopting the practice of cabinet responsibility and delegating excessive authority to department chiefs, Truman created a structure that left him uninformed: problems frequently developed unnoticed until they had swelled to crises, and the choice then was often between undesirable alternatives. Operating in a new politics, in the politics of inflation, he confronted problems requiring greater tactical skill than those Roosevelt had confronted. Seeking to maintain economic controls, and compelled to deny the rising expectations of major interest groups, his administration found it difficult to avoid antagonizing the rival groups. In the politics of depression, the Roosevelt administration could frequently maintain political support by bestowing specific advantages on groups, but in the politics of inflation the major interest groups came to seek freedom from restrictive federal controls.[55]

So difficult were the problems facing Truman that even a more experienced and skilled president would have encountered great difficulty. Inheriting the hostile Congress that had resisted occasional wartime attempts at social reform, Truman lacked the skill or leverage to guide a legislature seeking to assert its independence of the executive. Unable to halt fragmentation of the Democratic coalition, and incapable of ending dissension in his government, he also found that conservative subordinates undercut his occasional liberalism. Though he had gone on record early in endorsing a reform program[56] ("a declaration of independence" from congressional conservatives, he called it),[57] he had been unsuccessful in securing most of the legislation—a higher minimum wage, public housing, expanded unemployment benefits, and FEPC. Even the employment act was little more, as one congressman said, than a license to look for a job.[58] The President, through ineptitude or lack of commitment, often chose not to struggle for his program. Unable to dramatize the issues or to command enthusiasm, he was an ineffectual leader.[59]

So unsuccessful was his government that voters began jibing, "To err is Truman." Despairing of a resurgence of liberalism under Truman, New Dealers left the government in droves. By the fall of 1946, none of Roosevelt's associates was left in a prominent position. So disgruntled were many liberals about Truman and his advisers, about his unwillingness to fight for price controls, housing, benefits for labor, and civil rights, that some turned briefly to serious consideration of a new party.[60]

IV

Achieving few reforms during his White House years, Truman, with the notable exception of civil rights, never moved significantly beyond Roosevelt. The Fair Deal was largely an extension of earlier Democratic liberalism,[61] but Truman's new vigor and fierce partisanship ultimately made him more attractive to liberals who despairingly watched the GOP-dominated Eightieth Congress and feared a repeal of the New Deal.

Their fears were unwarranted, as was their enthusiasm for the Fair Deal program. In practice it proved very limited—the housing program only provided for 810,000 units in six years of which only 60,000 were constructed;[62] social security benefits were extended to ten million[63] and increased by about 75 percent, and the minimum wage was increased to 75 cents, but coverage was reduced by nearly a million.[64] But even had all of the Fair Deal been enacted, liberal reform would have left many millions beyond the benefits of government. The very poor, the marginal men, those neglected but acknowledged by the New Deal, went ultimately unnoticed by the Fair Deal.[65]

While liberals frequently chafed under Truman's leadership and questioned his commitment, they failed generally to recognize how shallow were his reforms. As the nation escaped a postwar depression, American liberals gained new faith in the American economy. Expressing their enthusiasm, they came to extoll big business for its contributions. Believing firmly in the success of progressive taxation, they exaggerated its effects, and congratulated themselves on the redistribution of income and the virtual abolition of poverty. Praising the economic system, they accepted big agriculture and big labor as evidence of healthy pluralism that protected freedom and guaranteed an equitable distribution of resources.[66]

Despite the haggling over details and the liberals' occasional dismay at Truman's style, he expressed many of their values. Like Roosevelt, Truman never challenged big business, never endangered large-scale capitalism. Indeed, his efforts as well as theirs were directed largely to maintaining and adjusting the powers of the major economic groups.

Fearing that organized labor was threatened with destruction, Truman, along with the liberals, had been sincerely frightened by the postwar rancor toward labor.[67] What they failed to understand was that most Americans had accepted unions as part of the political economy. Certainly most major industrialists had accepted organized labor, though smaller businessmen were often hostile.[68] Despite the overwrought rhetoric of debates, Congress did not actually menace labor. It was not seeking to destroy labor, only to restrict its power.

Many Americans did believe that the Wagner Act had unduly favored labor and was creating unions indifferent to the public welfare and hostile to corporate power. Capitalizing on this exaggerated fear of excessive union power, and the resentment from the postwar strikes, businessmen secured the Taft-Hartley Act.[69] Designed to weaken organized labor, it tried but failed to protect the membership from leaders; it did not effectively challenge the power of established unions. However, labor chiefs, recalling the bitter industrial warfare of the thirties, were still uneasy in their new positions. Condemning the legislation as a "slave-labor" act, they responded with fear, assailed the Congress, and declared that Taft-Hartley was the major political issue.[70]

Within a few years, when unions discovered that they were safe, Taft-Hartley faded as an issue. But in 1948 it served Truman well by establishing the GOP's hostility to labor and casting it back into the Democratic ranks. Both the President and union chiefs conveniently neglected his own kindling of antilabor passions (as when he had tried to draft strikers).[71] Exploiting Taft-Hartley as part of his strategy of patching the tattered Democratic coalition, Truman tied repeal of the "slave-labor" law to price controls, farm benefits, anticommunism, and civil rights in the campaign which won his election in his own right.

V

In courting the Negro the Truman administration in 1948 made greater promises to black citizens than had any previous federal government in American history. Yet, like many Americans, Truman as a senator had regarded the Negro's plight as peripheral to his interests, and with many of his generation he believed that equality was compatible with segregation.[72] As President, however, he found himself slowly prodded by conscience and pushed by politics. He moved cautiously at first and endorsed only measures affirming legal equality and protecting Negroes from violence.

Reluctant to fragment the crumbling Democratic coalition, Truman, in his first year, had seemed to avoid taking positions on civil rights which might upset the delicate balance between Northern and Southern Democrats. While he endorsed legislation for a statutory FEPC that the Congress would not grant, his efforts on behalf of the temporary FEPC (created by Roosevelt's executive order) were weaker. Having already weakened the power of the temporary agency, he also acquiesced in the legislative decision to kill it.[73] Despite the fears of Negro leaders that the death of FEPC would leave Negroes virtually unprotected from discrimination in the postwar job market, Truman would not even issue an order requiring nondiscrimination in the federal service and by government contractors.[74]

Though Truman was unwilling to use the prestige or power of his great office significantly on behalf of Negroes, he did assist their cause. While sidestepping political conflict, he occasionally supported FEPC and abolition of the poll tax. When Negroes were attacked, he did condemn the racial violence.[75] Though generally reluctant to move beyond rhetoric during his early years, Truman, shortly before the 1946 election, found conscience and politics demanding more. So distressed was he by racial violence that when Walter White of the NAACP and a group of white liberals urged him to assist the Negro, he promised to create a committee to study civil rights.[76]

The promise of a committee could have been a device to resist pressures, to delay the matter until after the election. And Truman could have appointed a group of politically safe men of limited reputation—men he could control. But instead, after the election, perhaps in an effort to mobilize the liberals for 1948, he appointed a committee of prominent men sympathetic to civil rights. They were men he could not control and did not seek to control.[77]

The committee's report, undoubtedly far bolder than Truman's expectations,[78] confirmed charges that America treated its Negroes as second-class citizens. It called for FEPC, an antilynching law, an anti-poll tax measure, abolition of segregation in interstate transportation, and the end of discrimination and segregation in federal agencies and the military. By attacking Jim Crow, the committee had moved to a redefinition of equality and interpreted segregation as incompatible with equality.[79]

Forced by the report to take a position, he no longer could easily remain an ally of Southern Democrats and maintain the wary allegiance of Negro leaders and urban liberals. Compelled earlier to yield to demands for advancement of the Negro, pressures which he did not wish fully to resist, Truman had encouraged these forces and they were moving beyond his control. On his decision, his political future might precariously rest. Threatened by Henry Wallace's candidacy on a third-party ticket, Truman had to take a bold position on civil rights or risk losing the important votes of urban Negroes. Though he might antagonize Southern voters, he foresaw no risk of losing Southern Democrats, no possibility of a bolt by dissidents, and the mild Southern response to the Civil Rights Report seemed to confirm this judgment.[80]

On February 2, 1948, Truman asked the Congress to enact most of the recommendations of his Civil Rights Committee (except most of those attacking segregation). Rather than using his executive powers, as the committee had urged, to end segregation in federal employment or to abolish segregation and discrimination in the military, he *promised* only to issue orders ending discrimination (but not specifying segregation) in the military and in federal agencies.[81] Retreating to moderation, the administration did not submit any of the legislation, nor did Truman issue the promised executive orders. "The strategy," an assistant later explained, "was to start with a bold measure and then temporize to pick up the right-wing forces. Simply stated, backtrack after the bang."[82]

Truman sought to ease Southern doubts by inserting in the 1948 platform the party's moderate 1944 plank on civil rights. Most Negro leaders, fearing the taint of Wallace and unwilling to return to the GOP, appeared stuck with Truman and they praised him. Though they desired a stronger plank, they would not abandon him at the convention, for his advocacy of rights for Negroes was unmatched by any twentieth-century president. To turn their backs on him in this time of need, most Negroes feared, would be injuring their own cause. But others prepared to struggle for a stronger plank. Urban bosses, persuaded that Truman would lose, hoped to save their local tickets, and prominent white liberals sought power and principle. Triumphing at the convention, they secured a stronger plank, but it did not promise social equality. By promising equality when it was still regarded as compatible with segregation they were offering far less than the "walk forthrightly into the bright sunshine of human rights," which Hubert Humphrey, then mayor of Minneapolis, had pledged in leading the liberal effort.[83]

When some of the Southerners bolted and formed the States Rights party, Truman was freed of any need for tender courtship of the South. He had to capture the Northern vote. Quickly he issued the long-delayed executive orders, which established a federal antidiscrimination board, declared a policy of equal opportunity in the armed forces, and established a committee to end military discrimination and segregation. (In doing so, Truman courted Negro voters and halted the efforts of A. Philip Randolph to lead a Negro revolt against the draft unless the military was integrated.[84] Playing politics carefully during the campaign, Truman generally stayed away from civil rights and concentrated on inflation, public housing, and Taft-Hartley.

In the new Democratic Congress Truman could not secure the civil rights program, and a coalition of Southern Democrats and Northern Republicans blocked his efforts. Though liberals were unhappy with his leadership, they did not question his proposed legislation. All agreed on the emphasis on social change through legislation and judicial decisions. The liberal way was the legal way, and it seldom acknowledged the depth of American racism or even considered the possibility of bold new tactics. Only occasionally—in the threatened March on Washington in 1941, in some ride-ins in 1947,[85] and in the campaign of civil disobedience against the draft in 1948—had there been bolder means. In each case Negroes had devised and carried out these tactics. But generally they relied upon more traditional means: they expected white America to yield to political pressure and subscribe to the dictates of American democracy. By relying upon legal change, however, and by emphasizing measures to restore a *modicum* of human dignity, Negroes and whites did not confront the deeper problems of race relations which they failed to understand.[86]

Struggling for moderate institutional changes, liberals were disappointed by Truman's frequent unwillingness to use his executive powers in behalf of the cause he claimed to espouse. Only after considerable pressure did he create a FEPC-type agency during the Korean War.[87] His loyalty-and-security program, in its operation, discriminated against Negroes, and federal investigators, despite protests to Truman, apparently continued to inquire into attitudes of interracial sympathy as evidence relevant to a determination of disloyalty.[88] He was also slow to require the Federal Housing Administration to stop issuing mortgages on property with restrictive covenants, and it continued, by its policies, to protect residential segregation.[89]

Yet his government was not without significant achievements in civil rights. His special committee had quietly acted to integrate the armed forces,[90] and even the recalcitrant Army had abolished racial quotas when the President secretly promised their restoration if the racial imbalance became severe.[91] And the Department of Justice, despite Truman's apparent indifference,[92] had been an active warrior in the battle against Jim Crow. Entering cases as an *amicus curiae,* Justice had submitted briefs arguing the unconstitutionality of enforcing restrictive covenants and of requiring separate-but-equal facilities in interstate transportation and in higher education.[93] During the summer of 1952, the Solicitor-General's Office even won the administration's approval for a brief directly challenging segregated primary education.[94]

The accomplishments of the Truman years were moderate, and the shortcomings left the nation with a great burden of unresolved problems. Viewed from the perspective of today, Truman's own views seem unduly mild and his government excessively cautious; viewed even by his own time he was a reluctant liberal, troubled by terror and eager to establish limited equality. He was ahead of public opinion in his legislative requests, but not usually in his actions. By his occasional advocacy, he educated the nation and held high the promise of equality. By kindling hope, he also may have prevented rebellion and restrained or delayed impulses to work outside of the system. But he also unleashed expectations he could not foresee, and forces which future governments would not be able to restrain.

VI

Never as committed to civil rights as he was opposed to communism at home and abroad, Truman ultimately became a victim of his own loyalty-and-security policies. . . .

In their own activities, many liberals were busy combatting domestic communism. Taking up the cudgels, the liberal Americans for Democratic Action (ADA) came often to define its purpose by its anticommunism. As an enemy of those liberals who would not renounce association with Communists, and, hence, as vigorous foes of the Progressive party, the ADA was prepared to do battle. Following Truman's strategy, ADA members assailed Wallace and his supporters as Communists, dupes of the Communists, and fellow travelers. To publicize its case the ADA even relied upon the tactic of guilt by association and paid for advertisements listing the Progressive party's major donors and the organizations on the Attorney-General's list with which they were or had been affiliated.[95] (Truman himself also red-baited. "I do not want and will not accept the political support of Henry Wallace and his Communists. . . . These are days of high prices for everything, but any price for Wallace and his Communists is too much for me to pay.")[96] In the labor movement liberals like the Reuther brothers led anticommunist crusades, and the CIO ultimately expelled its Communist-led unions. ("Granting the desirability of eliminating Communist influence from the trade union movement," later wrote Irving Howe and Louis Coser, "one might still have argued that mass expulsions were not only a poor way of achieving this end but constituted a threat to democratic values and procedures.")[97]

Expressing the administration's position, Attorney-General J. Howard McGrath proclaimed a "struggle against pagan communist philosophies that seek to enslave the world." "There are today many Communists in America," he warned. "They are everywhere—in factories, offices, butcher stores, on street corners, in private business. And each carries in himself the death of society."[98] (I don't think anybody ought to be employed as instructors [sic] for the young people of this country who believes in the destruction of our form of government," declared Truman.)[99]

Calling for a crusade against evil, viewing communism as a virulent poison, the administration continued to emphasize the need for *absolute* protection, for *absolute* security. By creating such high standards and considering their fulfillment easy, by making success evidence of will and resolution, the administration risked assaults if its loyalty-and-security program was proved imperfect. To discredit the administration, all that was needed was the discovery of some red "spies," and after 1948 the evidence seemed abundant—Alger Hiss, William Remington, Judith Coplon, Julius and Ethel Rosenberg.[100]

In foreign policy, too, Truman, though emphasizing the danger of communism, had promised success. Containment could stop the spread of communism: military expansion could be restrained and revolutions prevented. Since revolutions, by liberal definition, were imposed on innocent people by a small minority, a vigilant American government could block them. By his rhetoric, he encouraged American innocence and left many citizens little choice but to believe in their own government's failure when America could not thwart revolution—when the Chinese Communists triumphed. If only resolute will was necessary, as the administration suggested, then what could citizens believe about America's failure? Was it simply bungling? Or treason and betrayal?[101]

By his rhetoric and action, Truman had contributed to the loss of public confidence and set the scene in which Joseph McCarthy could flourish. Rather than resisting the early movement of anticommunism, he had acted energetically to become a leader, and ultimately contributed to its transformation into a crusade which threatened his administration. But the President could never understand his own responsibility, and his failure handicapped him. Because he had a record of vigorous anticommunism, Truman was ill-prepared to respond to McCarthy's charges. At first the President could not foresee any danger and tried to dispense with McCarthy as "the greatest asset the Kremlin has."[102] And later, as the Senator terrorized the government, Truman was so puzzled and pained that he retreated from the conflict and sought to starve McCarthy without publicity. Rather than responding directly to charges, the President tried instead to tighten his program. But he could not understand that such efforts (for example, revising the loyalty standard to "reasonable doubt as to the loyalty of the individual")[103] could not protect the administration from charges of being soft on communism. He only encouraged these charges by seeming to yield to criticism, admitting that the earlier program was unnecessarily lax.

The President was a victim of his own policies and tactics. But bristling anticommunism was not simply Truman's way, but often the liberal way.[104] And the use of guilt by association, the discrediting of dissent, the intemperate rhetoric—these, too, were not simply the tactics of the Truman administration. The rancor and wrath of these years were not new to American politics, nor to liberals.[105] Indeed, the style of passionate charges and impugning opponents' motives may be endemic to American democratic politics. Submerging the issues in passion, using labels as substitutes for thought, questioning motives, these tactics characterized much of the foreign policy debate of the prewar and postwar years as well—a debate in which the liberals frequently triumphed. Developing a more extreme form of this rancorous style, relying upon even wilder charges and more flagrant use of guilt by association, McCarthy and his cohorts flailed the liberals and the Democratic administration.

VII

In looking at the war and postwar years, liberal scholars have emphasized the achievements of democratic reform, the extension of prosperity, the movements to greater economic and social equality. Confident that big business had become socially responsible and that economic security was widespread, they have celebrated the triumph of democratic liberalism. In charting the course of national progress, they frequently neglected or minimized major problems, or they interpreted them as temporary aberrations, or blamed them on conservative forces.[106]

Yet the developments of the sixties—the rediscovery of poverty and racism—suggest that the emphasis has been misplaced in interpreting these earlier years. In the forties and fifties white racism did not greatly yield to the dictates of American democracy, and the failure was not only the South's. The achievements of democratic liberalism were more limited than its advocates believed, and its reforms left many Americans still without adequate assistance. Though many liberal programs were blocked or diluted by conservative opposition, the liberal vision itself was dim. Liberalism in practice was defective, and its defects contributed to the temporary success of McCarthyism. Curiously, though liberalism was scrutinized by some sympathizers[107] who attacked its faith in progress and by others who sought to trace McCarthyism to the reform impulses of earlier generations,[108] most liberals failed to understand their own responsibility for the assault upon civil liberties or to respond to the needs of an "other America" which they but dimly perceived.

Notes

1. See Bernstein, "The Economic Policies of the Truman Administration: A Bibliographic Essay," in Richard Kirkendall, ed., *The Truman Period as a Research Field* (Columbia, Mo., 1967).

2. Also see William Berman, "Civil Rights and Civil Liberties in the Truman Administration," in *ibid.*

3. Also see Richard O. Davies, "Harry S. Truman and the Social Service State," in *ibid.*

4. Gabriel Kolko, "American Business and Germany, 1930-41," *Western Political Quarterly,* XV (December 1962), 713-28; cf. Roland Stromberg, "American Business and the Approach of War, 1935-41," *Journal of Economic History,* XIII (Winter 1953), 58-78.

5. Quoted in Corwin Edwards, *Econimic and Political Aspects of International Cartels,* A Study for the Subcommittee on War Mobilization of the Senate Committee on Military Affairs, 78th Cong., 2nd Sess., pp. 43-44.

6. House Committee on Ways and Means and Senate Committee on Finance, 76th Cong., 3rd Sess., *Joint Hearings on Excess Profits Taxation,* p. 22; *New York Times,* July 26, August 9, 1940; *Wall Street Journal,* July 15, 1940.

7. The next four paragraphs draw upon Bernstein, "The Automobile Industry and the Coming of the Second World War," *Southwestern Social Science Quarterly,* XLVII (June 1966), 24-33.

8. Walter Reuther, *500 Planes a Day* (1940); *CIO News,* December, 1940.

9. Bruce Catton to Robert Horton, Policy Documentation File 631. 0423, War Production Board Records, RG 179, National Archives.

10. Richard Wilcock, "Industrial Management's Policies Towards Unionism," in Milton Derber and Edwin Young, *Labor and the New Deal* (Madison, Wis., 1957), pp. 305-8.

11. Joel Seidman, *American Labor from Defense to Reconversion* (Chicago, 1953), pp. 41-87.

12. *Ibid.,* pp. 131-51. It was in response to the coal strikes led by John Lewis that Congress passed the Smith-Connally Act.

13. 'With few exceptions, throughout the war years labor, not management, made the sacrifices when sacrifices were necessary," concludes Paul A. C. Koistinen, "The Hammer and the Sword: Labor, the Military, and Industrial Mobilization" (unpublished Ph.D. dissertation, University of California at Berkeley, 1965), p. 143.

14. Bernstein, "The Truman Administration and the Politics of Inflation" (unpublished Ph.D. dissertation, Harvard University, 1963), Ch. 2.

15. Senate Special Committee to Study Problems of American Small Business, 79th Cong., 2nd Sess., Senate Document 208, *Economic Concentration and World War II,* pp. 42-64. On concentration, see *ibid., passim;* cf. M. A. Adelman, "The Measurement of Industrial Concentration," *Review of Economics and Statistics,* XXXIII (November 1951), 269-96.

16. *Economic Concentration and World War II,* pp. 22-39.

17. C. Wright Mills, *The Power Elite* (New York, 1956), p. 273.

18. This paragraph is based on Bernstein, "Industrial Reconversion: The Protection of Oligopoly and Military Control of the War Economy," *American Journal of Economics and Sociology,* XXVI (April 1967), 159-72. Cf. Jack Peltason, *The Reconversion Controversy* (Washington, 1950).

19. Gabriel Kolko, *Wealth and Power in America* (New York, 1962), pp. 9-45; quotation from p. 31. Also see U.S. Bureau of the Census, *Income Distribution of the United States* (Washington, 1966), pp. 2-27; and Simon Kuznets, *Shares of Upper Income Groups in Income and Savings* (New York, 1953).

20. Quoted from Francis Biddle, *In Brief Authority* (Garden City, N.Y., 1962), p. 213.

21. Stetson Conn *et al., Guarding the United States and Its Outposts,* in *United States Army in World War II: The Western Hemisphere* (Washington, 1964), pp. 115-49. The Canadian government also moved Japanese away from the coast.

22. Biddle, *In Brief Authority,* p. 219.

23. Quoted from Henry L. Stimson and McGeorge Bundy, *On Active Service* (New York, 1948), p. 406. The prose is presumably Bundy's, but Stimson apparently endorsed the thought (p. xi). Also see War Department, *Final Report: Japanese Evacuation from the West Coast* (Washington, 1943), pp. 9-10.

24. Quoted from Biddle, *In Brief Authority,* p. 219.

25. *Korematsu* v. *U.S.,* 323 US 214, at 219. The Court split and Justice Black wrote the opinion. Justices Roberts, Murphy and Jackson dissented. Also see *Hirabayshi* v. *U.S.,* 320 US 81.

26. *American Epoch* (New York, 1955), p. 528 (italics in original).

27. Apparently Roosevelt refused to condemn the riots. Vito Marcantonio to Roosevelt, June 16, 1943, and reply, July 14, 1943, Vito Marcantonio Papers, New York Public Library. Also see Roosevelt's Proclamation No. 2588, in Samuel Rosenman, ed., *The Public Papers of Franklin D. Roosevelt,* (13 vols.; New York, 1938-50), XII, 258-59.

28. "This was the dark side of an otherwise bright picture," concludes Link, *American Epoch,* p. 529. Also see Frank Freidel, *America in the Twentieth Century* (Cambridge, Mass., 1954), p. 215; Everett C. Hughes, "Race Relations and the Sociological Imagination," *American Sociological Review,* XXVIII (December 1963), 879-90.

29. *Pittsburgh Courier,* July 15, September 2, 9, November 11, 1939; March 2, 9, 1940; April 26, 1941; cited in Richard Dalfiume, "Desegregation of the United States Armed Forces, 1939-1953" (unpublished Ph.D. dissertation, University of Missouri, 1966), pp. ix-x. For other protests, see *Pittsburgh Courier,* September 16, 30, 1939, November 23, and December 7, 1940.

30. *Amsterdam News,* May 10, 1940; Louis Ruchames, *Race, Jobs, and Politics* (New York, 1953), pp. 11-17.

31. Ulysses Lee, *The Employment of Negro Troops,* in *United States Army in World War II: Special Studies* (Washington, 1966), pp. 35-52.

32. Quoted from "For Manhood in National Defense," *Crisis,* XLVII (December 1940), 375. Also see Lee, *Employment of Negro Troops,* pp. 62-65.

33. Lee, *ibid.,* pp. 69-84.

34. Dalfiume, "Desegregation of the Armed Forces," p. 57, is the source of this quotation from the *Baltimore Afro-American,* November 2, 1940. Cf. *Pittsburg Courier,* November 2, 1940.

35. Herbert Garfinkel, *When Negroes March* (Glencoe, Ill., 1959), pp. 37-38.

36. Quoted from the *Pittsburg Courier,* January 25, 1941, and from the *Black Worker,* May 1941.

37. "Proposals of the Negro March-on-Washington Committee" (undated), OF 391, Roosevelt Library. This was called to my attention by Dalfiume, "Desegregation of the Armed Forces," pp. 172-73.

38. Edwin Watson to Roosevelt, June 14, 1941; A. Philip Randolph to Roosevelt, June 16, 1941; both in OF 391, Roosevelt Library; Garfinkel, *When Negroes March,* pp. 60-61.

39. Dalfiume, "Desegregation of the Armed Forces," pp. 173-76, concludes that the Negro leaders may have met defeat. Cf. "The Negroes War," *Fortune,* XXV (April 1942), 76-80ff.; *Amsterdam News,* July 5, 1941; *Chicago Defender,* July 5, 1941; Randolph, "Why and How the March Was Postponed" (mimeo, n.d.), Schomburg Collection, New York Public Library.

40. For the notion that the events of the war years constitute the beginnings of the civil rights revolution, see Dalfiume, "Desegregation of the Armed Forces," pp. 177-89.

41. Ruchames, *Race, Jobs & Politics,* pp. 162-64.

42. *Ibid.,* p. 164.

43. Samuel Lubell, *The Future of American Politics* (New York, 1952), *passim.*

44. Message on the State of the Union, January 11, 1944, in Rosenman, ed., *Public Papers of Roosevelt,* XIII, p. 41. For some evidence that Roosevelt was at least talking about a new alignment of politics, see Samuel Rosenman, *Working with Roosevelt* (London, 1952), pp. 423-29. Probably this was a tactical maneuver.

45. Mary Hinchey, "The Frustration of the New Deal Revival, 1944-1946" (Unpublished Ph.D. dissertation, University of Missouri, 1965), Chs. 1-2.

46. President's statement on signing the GI Bill of Rights, June 22, 1944, in Rosenman, ed., *Public Papers of Roosevelt,* XIII, 180-82, and Rosenman's notes, pp. 183-84. The GI Bill has generally been neglected as an antidepression measure.

47. President's veto of the tax bill, February 22, 1944, in Rosenman, ed., *Public Papers of Roosevelt,* XIII, 80-84.

48. Charles Merriam, "The National Resources Planning Board: A Chapter in American Planning Experience," *American Political Science Review,* XXXVIII (December 1944), 1075-88.

49. Bernstein, "The Truman Administration and the Politics of Inflation," Chs. 3-4.

50. Bernstein, "Charting a Course Between Inflation and Deflation: Secretary Fred Vinson and the Truman Administration's Tax Bill," scheduled for *Register of the Kentucky Historical Society.*

51. Bernstein, "The Truman Administration and Its Reconversion Wage Policy," *Labor History,* VI (Fall 1965), 214-31.

52. Bernstein, "Clash of Interests: The Postwar Battle Between the Office of Price Administration and the Department of Agriculture," *Agricultural History,* XL (January 1967), 45-57; Allen J. Matusow, "Food and Farm Policies During the First Truman Administration, 1945-1948" (unpublished Ph.D. dissertation, Harvard University, 1963), Chs. 1-3.

53. Bernstein, "The Removal of War Production Board Controls on Business, 1944-1946," *Business History Review,* XXXXIX (Summer 1965), 243-60.

54. Bernstein, "The Truman Administration and the Steel Strike of 1946," *Journal of American History*, LII (March 1966), 791-803; "Walter Reuther and the General Motors Strike of 1945-1946," *Michigan History*, IL (September 1965), 260-77; "The Postwar Famine and Price Control, 1946," *Agricultural History*, XXXIX (October 1964), 235-40; and Matusow, "Food and Farm Policies," Chs. 1-3.

55. Bernstein, "The Presidency Under Truman," IV (Fall 1964), 8ff.

56. Truman's message to Congress, September 6, 1945, in *Public Papers of the Presidents of the United States* (8 vols.; Washington, 1961-66), pp. 263-309 (1948).

57. Quoted in Jonathan Daniels, *The Man of Independence* (Philadelphia, 1950), p. 288. For evidence that Truman was trying to head off a bolt by liberals, see *New York Times*, August 12, 1945; Harold Smith Daily Record, August 13, 1945, Bureau of the Budget Library, Washington, D.C.

58. Harold Stein, "Twenty Years of the Employment Act" (unpublished ms., 1965, copy in my possession), p. 2. Also see Stephen K. Bailey, *Congress Makes a Law: The Story Behind the Employment Act of 1946* (New York, 1950).

59. Lubell, *The Future of American Politics*, pp. 8-27, while emphasizing the continuation of the prewar executive-legislative stalemate and the strength of conservative forces in the postwar years, has also been critical of Truman. "All his skills and energies . . . were directed to standing still. . . . When he took vigorous action in one direction it was axiomatic that he would contrive soon afterward to move in the conflicting direction" (p. 10). Cf. Richard Neustadt, "Congress and the Fair Deal: A Legislative Balance Sheet," in Carl Friedrich and John Galbraith, eds., *Public Policy*, V, 351-81.

60. Curtis MacDougall, *Gideon's Army* (3 vols.; New York, 1965-66), I, 102-27. The National Educational Committee for a New Party, which would be explicitly anticommunist, included John Dewey, A. Philip Randolph, Daniel Bell, and Lewis Corey.

61. On the continuity, see Mario Einaudi, *The Roosevelt Revolution* (New York, 1959), pp. 125, 334; Neustadt, "Congress and the Fair Deal"; Eric Goldman, *Rendezvous with Destiny* (New York, 1952), pp. 314-15; and Goldman, *The Crucial Decade and After, America 1945-1960* (New York, 1960).

62. Richard O. Davis, *Housing Reform during the Truman Administration* (Columbia, Mo.) p. 136. The original measure aimed for 1,050,000 units in seven years, at a time when the nation needed more than 12,000,000 units to replace inadequate housing. During the Truman years, the government constructed 60,000 units of public housing (pp. 105-38). Rather than creating programs to keep pace with urban needs, the government in these years fell further behind. In contrast, private industry was more active, and it was assisted by noncontroversial federal aid. Under Truman's government, then, the greatest achievement in housing was that private capital, protected by the government, built houses for the higher-income market.

63. Under the old law, the maximum benefit for families was $85 a month and the minimum was $15, depending on prior earnings. The new minimum was $25 and the maximum $150. *(Social Security Bulletin,* September 1950, p. 3). Unless couples also had other sources of income, even maximum benefits ($1,800 a year) placed them $616 under the BLS "maintenance" standard of living and $109 above the WPA-based "emergency" standard of living—the poverty level. (Calculations based on Kolko, *Wealth and Power*, pp. 96-98.) Since the payments were based on earnings, lower-income groups would receive even fewer benefits. They were the people generally without substantial savings or significant supplementary sources of income, and therefore they needed even more, not less, assistance.

64. *Congressional Quarterly Almanac,*V (1949), 434-35.

65. Bernstein, "Economic Policies of the Truman Administration." Truman had achieved very little: improved unemployment benefits, some public power and conservation projects, agricultural assistance, and a National Science Foundation. He failed to secure the ill-conceived Brannan Plan and two programs suggested by Roosevelt: federal aid to education and health insurance. For his health insurance programs, see his messages of November 19, 1945, in *Public Papers of Truman* (1945), pp. 485-90, and of May 19, 1947, in *ibid.,* (1947), pp. 250-52. In 1951, when the BLS calculated that a family of four needed $4,166 to reach the "maintenance" level, 55.6 percent of the nation's families had incomes beneath that level (Bureau of the Census, *Income Distribution in the United States,* p. 16.).

66. Bernstein, "Economic Policies of the Truman Administration."

67. Truman to William Green, September 13, 1952, PPF 85, Truman Papers, Truman Library.

68. Wilcox, "Industrial Management's Policies Toward Unionism," pp. 305-11; "Public Opinion on the Case Bill," OF 407B, Truman Papers, Truman Library; Robert Brady, *Business as a System of Power* (New York, 1943), Pp. 210-15; Harry Millis and Emily Clark Brown, *From the Wagner Act to Taft-Hartley* (Chicago, 1950), pp. 286-98.

69. R. Alton Lee, *Truman and Taft-Hartley: A Question of Mandate* (Lexington, Ky. 1966), pp. 22-71.

70. Lee, *Truman and Taft-Hartley,* pp. 79-130.

71. Truman's message to Congress, May 25, 1946, in *Public Papers of Truman* (1946), pp. 277-80.

72. Truman's address of July 14, 1940, reprinted in *Congressional Record,* 76th Cong., 3rd Sess., 5367-69.

73. Ruchames, *Race, Jobs & Politics,* pp. 130-36. This section relies upon Bernstein, "The Ambiguous Legacy: The Truman Administration and Civil Rights" (paper given at the AHA, December 1966; copy at the Truman Library).

74. Truman to David Niles, July 22, 1946, and drafts (undated) of an order on nondiscrimination; and Philleo Nash to Niles (undated), Nash Files, Truman Library.

75. Truman to Walter White, June 11, 1946, PPF 393, Truman Papers, Truman Library.

76. Walter White, *A Man Called White* (New York, 1948), pp. 331-32.

77. Robert Carr to Bernstein, August 11, 1966.

78. Interview with Philleo Nash, September 19, 1966.

79. President's Committee on Civil Rights, *To Secure These Rights* (Washington, 1947), pp. 1-95.

80. Clark Clifford, "Memorandum for the President," November 17, 1947, Clifford Papers (his possession), Washington, D.C.

81. Truman's message to Congress, February 2, 1948, in *Public Papers of Truman* (1948), pp. 117-26.

82. Interview with Nash.

83. On the struggle, see Clifton Brock, *Americans for Democratic Action: Its Role in National Politics* (Washington, 1962), pp. 94-99; quotation at p. 98.

84. Grant Reynolds, "A Triumph for Civil Disobedience," *Nation,* CLXVI (August 28, 1948), pp. 228-29.

85. George Houser and Bayard Rustin, "Journey of Reconciliation" (mimeo, n.d., probably 1947), Core Files, Schomburg Collection, New York Public Library.

86. There was no urging of special programs to assist Negroes left unemployed (at roughly double the white rate) in the mild recession of 1949-1950, nor was there open acknowledgement of race hatred.

87. National Council of Negro Women to Truman, November 18, 1950, Nash Files, Truman Library; Senator William Benton to Truman, October 21, 1951, OF 526B, Truman Library.

88. Carl Murphy to Truman, April 10, 1950, OF 93 misc.; Walter White to Truman, November 26, 1948, OF 252K; both in Truman Library.

89. NAACP press release, February 4, 1949, Schomburg Collection, New York Public Library; Hortense Gabel to Raymond Foley, February 26, 1953, Foley Papers, Truman Library; Housing and Home Finance Agency, *Fifth Annual Report* (Washington, 1952), p. 413.

90. President's Committee on Equality of Treatment and Opportunity in the Armed Forces, *Freedom to Serve* (Washington 1950); Dalfiume, "Desegregation of the Armed Forces."

91. Gordon Gray to Truman, March 1, 1950, OF 1285B, Truman Library.

92. Interview with Philip Elman, December 21, 1966.

93. *Shelley* v. *Kraemer,* 334 US 1; *Henderson* v. *United States* 339 US 816; *McLaurin* v. *Board of Regents,* 339 US 641.

94. Interview with Elman; *Brown* v. *Board of Education,* 347 US 483.

95. Karl M. Schmidt, *Henry A. Wallace: Quixotic Crusade, 1948* (Syracuse, N.Y., 1960), pp. 159-60, 252-53, 261-62. On the strategy of letting the liberal intellectuals attack Wallace, see Clifford, "Memorandum for the President," November 17, 1947. On the split in liberal ranks on cooperation with Communists, see Kurtis MacDougall, *Gideon's Army,* I, 122-25.

96. Truman's address of March 17, 1948, in *Public Papers of Truman* (1948), p. 189.

97. Howe and Coser, *The American Communist Party,* 2nd. ed. (New York, 1962), p. 468; see pp. 457-68 for the activity of labor.

98. McGrath's address of April 8, 1949, McGrath Papers, Truman Library, which was called to my attention by Theoharis. Also see Theoharis, "Rhetoric of Politics," n. 37.

99. Quoted from transcript of President's News Conference of June 9, 1949, Truman Library. Also see Sidney Hook, "Academic Integrity and Academic Freedom." *Commentary,* VIII (October 1949), cf., Alexander Meiklejohn, *New York Times Magazine,* March 27, 1949, pp. 10ff. In his veto of the McCarran Act, Truman failed to defend civil liberties effectively and instead emphasized that the act would impair the government's anitcommunist efforts. Veto message of September 22, 1950, *Public Papers of Truman* (1950), pp. 645-53.

100. Theoharis, "Rhetoric of Politics," pp. 32-38.

101. See Truman's addresses of March 27, 1948, in *Public Papers of Truman* (1948), pp. 182-86; and of June 7, 1949, in *ibid.* (1949), pp. 277-80. See Theoharis, "Rhetoric of Politics," pp. 17-27.

102. Quoted from transcript of President's News Conference, March 30, 1950, Truman Library.

103. E.O. 10241, 16 Fed. Reg. 9795.

104. On liberal confusion about this period, see Joseph Rauh, "The Way to Fight Communism," *Future,* January 1962. For the argument that liberal naiveté about Stalinism had led to McCarthyism, see Irving Kristol, "Civil Liberties, 1952–A Study in Confusion," *Commentary,* XIII (March 1952), 228-36.

105. For earlier antitotalitarianism, see Freda Kirchway, "Curb the Fascist Press," *Nation,* (March 28, 1942), 357-58.

106. Although there are no thorough, scholarly histories of these years, there are many texts that embody these characteristics. In addition, much of the monographic literature by other social scientists conforms to the pattern described in this paragraph. For a discussion, see Bernstein, "Economic Policies of the Truman Administration."

107. In particular see the works of Reinhold Niebuhr and the new realism that he has influenced: Niebuhr, *Moral Man and Immoral Society* (New York, 1932); *The Children of Light and the Children of Darkness* (New York, 1944); Arthur Schlesinger, Jr., *The Vital Center* (Cambridge, Mass., 1947). What is needed is a critical study of wartime and postwar liberalism, an explanation for many on "Where We Came Out" (to use the title of Granville Hicks's volume). See Jason Epstein, "The CIA and the Intellectuals," *New York Reveiw of Books,* VII (April 20, 1967), 16-21.

108. See Bell, ed., *The New American Right,* and the tendency to trace McCarthyism back to earlier reform movements and often to Populism. The volume, interestingly, is dedicated to the managing editor of the *New Leader.* For a former radical's attempt to reappraise the liberal past, see Richard Hofstadter, *The Age of Reform* (New York, 1956).

Part Three

POSTWAR POLITICS AND THE DEADLOCK OF DEMOCRACY

Chapter 6 1948:
A STRATEGY OF
GO-FOR-BROKE

*Long-time journalist and Washington
correspondent* CABELL PHILLIPS *paints a
generally favorable portrait of the postwar
chief executive in "The Truman Presidency:
The History of a Triumphant Succession"
(1966), as the book's subtitle indicates. In
the selection printed below, Phillips de-
scribes Truman's zestful campaign of 1948
(and Republican Governor Thomas E.
Dewey's lackluster efforts), which produced
one of the more spectacular upsets in the
history of American elections. Does Phillips
make a clear-cut choice as to which factors,
and voting groups, were the* most *important
in producing that upset? Do you think that
any presidential candidate could duplicate
Truman's feat today, given the innovations
in electioneering techniques introduced since
1948? Is the United States "still a land
which loves a scrapper, in which intestinal
fortitude is still respected"?*

"Nice guys don't win ball games," Leo Durocher, the baseball philosopher, once
observed. The same is often true of the game of politics, and never has it been more
eloquently documented than in the Presidential election campaign of 1948.

Republican Thomas E. Dewey, with deliberate calculation, chose the high road
for his campaign. His effort was as tidy as a new pin, abundantly financed, and
organized with the meticulous efficiency of an electronic computer. Computers of a
sort, in fact, told the Dewey team that they could not lose, so they campaigned not
to win an election but to set up the guideposts and stage props of a new administration. The candidate, with his crisp executive manner and his rich commanding
baritone, exuded so much confidence that he put his followers to sleep.

Democrat Harry S. Truman, no less deliberately, chose the low road. It was a choice of necessity. No one believed he could win, and many had told him so. His party treasury was broke, the party organization was in chaos, and, although he was a sitting President, he was on the defensive as a candidate. So he fought with the heedless, slambang ferocity of the underdog who knows there is only one way out—and set the public imagination on fire. . . .

Truman was not a man to concede that another might know more about the art of politics than he, nor was anyone likely to dispute his assumption. In a real sense, he ran his own show in the 1948 campaign, but he was wide enough to take good counsel when he could get it.

Clustered around the candidate and accompanying him on all his trips was a cadre of the White House "brain trust": Clark Clifford had the role of chief of staff; Jonathan Daniels had been brought back from his newspapers in Raleigh to lend a hand with the speechwriting; Charley Ross, in his gentle, patient way, handled the clamorous demands of the scores of reporters and photographers who accompanied the President wherever he went; and Matt Connelly cast his trained and skeptical eye on the local dignitaries and politicos who pushed and scratched to get a few minutes of the candidate's time or to be photographed in his company whenever his train paused. . . .

Truman's election campaign was to be a life-size version of the experimental whistlestop tour of the previous June. In the view of most of his team, the tour had been a huge success. It created the kind of environment in which the President showed to his best advantage, and it apparently appealed to the public. But a few changes were made. For one thing, prepared speeches would be avoided wherever possible. The President was a poor reader, and his delivery from text was stiff and unconvincing. But in ad-libbing, his natural warmth and sincerity came through splendidly. So his staff avoided scripts for all but the big speeches and provided him with a series of topical cards, each containing only a few highlight sentences to serve as oratorical pump primers. As another precaution, they worked out an elaborate series of "tour books" for each state, containing, for each stop of whatever duration, a brief précis of the local who's who, history, politics, and prevailing taboos and interests. Thus, instead of dedicating an airport to a nonexistent local hero, as he had done in June, he could compliment a trainside audience in Iowa on the fine new sausage factory that had just been opened in their town. These two devices—the natural, homespun speeches and the accurate and intimate hometown lore he was able to put into them—had an important bearing on the outcome of the campaign. . . .

Truman launched his campaign with a Labor Day speech at Detroit, which has become a ritual for Democratic candidates ever since. The event set a pattern that he was to follow almost without deviation for the next eight weeks.

The "Truman Special," with eighty-odd reporters and photographers, details of Secret Service and Signal Corps men, a dozen White House aides and secretaries, and the President and his daughter, Margaret, aboard (Mrs. Truman was attending a christening in Denver), pulled out of Washington's Union Station at 3:40 on the afternoon of Sunday, September 5. It was a sixteen-car train with sleeping and dining cars, a work car for the reporters, a communications car for the Signal Corps and Western Union, and, at the end, the *Ferdinand Magellan,* a Pullman specially adopted for Presidential use in the days of FDR. The *Magellan* contained its own galley and dining area, two spacious bedrooms, and a combination salon and office. An oversized platform at the rear, with a protective striped canopy and a public address system, served as a stage for the endless repetition of a seriocomic folk drama with which hundreds of thousands of Americans were to become familiar in the next two months. A typical day went like this:

The "Truman Special" rolled onto a siding at the station in Grand Rapids, Michigan, shortly before 7 o'clock on a Monday morning. Several hundred people lined the station platform, cheering and shouting a welcome. The local leaders and politicians . . . packed into the President's car for handshakes and coffee, and then into open automobiles for a parade to the town square. Although it was the break-fast hour and Grand Rapids was a heavily Republican city, 25,000 people jammed into the area to hear and see the President and to give him a warm welcome.

Within an hour the train was under way again. At crossings and way stations knots of people were on hand to wave to the President as he whizzed by and get a wave in return. Several times the train stopped briefly at stations where crowds of a few hundred to a few thousand had assembled, and the President stepped out on the back platform to speak for four or five minutes and to shake some of the scores of hands thrust up eagerly toward him. He was genial and good-natured, full of quips and folksiness, and even when he warned them of the perils of sending another Republican Congress to Washington, or electing another Republican governor of Michigan, it was in a joshing, half-serious vein free of venom. Everywhere the people responded warmly, sometimes enthusiastically, occasionally with shouts and whistles of genuine fervor.

Detroit, where the party arrived about noon, wore a carnival aspect, with march-ing bands, flags flying and masses of cheering people along the streets. This was labor's city, labor's holiday, and labor's candidate, and approximately a quarter million working men and their wives and children were packed in Cadillac Square to give the President a noisy workingman's greeting. And he gave them what they had come to hear.

Two years ago, he said, the people had dropped their guard and elected a Republican Congress.

"The Republicans promptly voted themselves a cut in taxes and voted you a cut in freedom. They put a dangerous weapon in the hands of the big corporations, in the shape of the Taft-Hartley law. I vetoed it, but they passed it over my veto."

If the same forces that created Taft-Hartley, he went on, are allowed to stay in power and to elect a Republican President, "labor can expect to be hit by a series of body blows—and if you stay at home as you did in 1946, and keep these reactionaries in power, you deserve every blow you get."

There were roars of assent and shouts of "Pour it on," "Give 'em hell, Harry!" The crowd was with him as he went on to excoriate "that do-nothing Eightieth Republican Congress" for high prices and for blocking minimum wage and Social Security improvements and low-cost housing legislation. He lambasted the "gluttons of privilege" in the Republican Party, and, making it clear he had Dewey in mind, said they were men "with a calculating machine where the heart ought to be."

The yells and applause coming wave upon wave filled Cadillac Square and rattled from radio sets in living rooms, union halls, taverns, and picnic grounds all across the United States. This was not just another Labor Day speech by a President. It was the opening attack in a go-for-broke election campaign. It *had* to be good. It *had* to go over. And it was aimed as much at New York, Pittsburgh, Dallas, and Seattle as it was at Detroit. In the anxiety-ridden Democratic strategy, this was *it.* . . .

The Republicans tipped their hand the next day to the casual, aloof strategy that was to cost them dearly before the campaign ended. Governor Dewey chose to ignore the Truman attack and instead sent Harold Stassen to Detroit to "answer" the President. There was no hope or expectation of matching the huge labor turnout in Cadillac Square of the day before. But the fact that Stassen's indoor audience reached only about 3,000, made up predominantly of Republican business and professional people, and that he concentrated on a defense of the Taft-Hartley Act, created a striking contrast in vitality with the Democratic effort, which every newspaper in the country noted.

This revealed a deliberate Republican strategy, a conscious change of pace. In his 1944 campaign against Roosevelt, Dewey had employed the aggressive cut-and-thrust tactics of the courtroom prosecutor. In his quest for the 1948 nomination, he had slammed and slandered the domestic and foreign policies of the Truman administration with scant reserve. But now, in the election campaign, he chose to give Truman the silent treatment, and to concentrate on elucidating the larger issues of statecraft and creating an air of harmony within Republican ranks.

The rationale for this decision was simply this: Within the Republican Party there was a chronic division of power between the conservative and progressive wings. As a progressive, Dewey's ideas on foreign policy, minimum wages, public housing, and economic controls came a great deal closer to Truman's than they did to such GOP fundamentalists as Styles Bridges and John Taber. But it would do no good to offend their sensibilities by openly espousing his New Dealish views on these issues during the campaign. Moreover, it was reasoned, since Truman was a dead duck anyway, why should Dewey bother trying to trade him punch for punch? It would be a useless and undignified brawl that might inhibit the next President's freedom of action. So it was decided to let Truman make a spectacle of himself shadowboxing against the Eightieth Congress and the outdated ogres of the 1930s, while Dewey declaimed with lofty earnestness on the broad policies of his forthcoming administration. . . .

Governor Warren had little or no part in the strategy. He was counted on mainly to keep California and the Far West safely in line. Senator Taft was counted on to pick up any stray electoral votes that might be floating around in the South. Stassen was an all-purpose troubleshooter and the chief adjutant for the Middle West, although that faithfully Republican farm region was confidently expected to take care of itself.

Thus the main thrust of the Republican campaign was directed toward the intellectual and economic interests of the urbanized Northeast. When its directors sniffed the first scents of danger from the grass roots beyond the Appalachians, it was too late to change direction.

President Truman opened the first of two transcontinental tours he was to make with a memorable appearance at the National Plowing Contest outside Dexter, Iowa, in the broiling midday sun of Saturday, September 18. This occasion was memorable because he uncorked a ploy that had as much to do with winning him the Midwestern farm vote in November as any other factor in the campaign: hanging on the Eightieth Congress responsibility for failing to provide sufficient government storage bins for the year's bumper crop of corn and wheat.

Under the farm price support program, the Commodity Credit Corporation (CCC) lent grain growers 90 percent of parity on their surplus crops. These surpluses, which had run as high as 300,000 bushels a year shortly after the end of World War II, were stored under government control until such time as the market might absorb them. In renewing the CCC authorization in the spring of 1948, Congress failed (apparently without any notable protest from the Democrats) to provide for the acquisition of additional storage bins. (Clusters of these low, silo-like structures, made of corrugated metal, are a familiar feature of the landscape in the corn and wheat country.) The 1948 crop, however, was to be one of historic abundance and therefore one of large surpluses and sliding prices. Between January and September, for example, corn was to drop from $2.46 to $1.78 a bushel, and wheat from $2.81 to $1.97. Without proper storage capacity to hold this enormous yield, many farmers would be unable to get their CCC loans and would have to sell at the depressed market price.

This lapse seems not to have been discovered by the Truman strategists until just before the first major farm speech of the campaign, at Dexter. As the Presidential party was getting ready to leave Washington on September 17, Matt Connelly handed Clifford a brief and disingenuous memo which read: "Charlie Brannan [the new Secretary of Agriculture] suggests that at platform stops in the western area we may be able to develop the following with respect to farmers—failure of Congress to provide storage bins. This action was the responsibility of the Banking and Currency Committee of the House."

Seventy-five thousand farmers (and their wives and children), bankers, mortgage holders, equipment sellers, and produce buyers stood in ankle-deep dust under a 90-degree sun as President Truman mounted the wooden platform on the prairie outside Dexter a few minutes after noon that Saturday. He reminded them that he had been a dirt farmer himself, back in Missouri, and added that he could plow as straight a furrow behind a pair of mules as the next man. He joked them about how well they had prospered under Democratic administrations, as evidenced by the fifty private planes, tied down in an adjacent field, in which many of them had flown to the plowing contest that day. Then he got down to business:

This Republican Congress has already stuck a pitchfork in the farmers' backs. They have already done their best to keep price supports from working.

When the Republican Congress rewrote the charter of the Commodity Credit Corporation this year, there were certain lobbyists in Washington representing the speculative grain trade. These big business lobbyists and speculators persuaded the Congress not to provide storage bins for you farmers. They tied the hands of the administration. They are preventing us from setting up the storage bins that you will need in order to get the support price for your grain.

And when you have to sell your grain below the support price because you have no place to store it, you can thank this same Republican Congress.

There was no sudden cry for revenge from the sweaty multitude at Dexter. This was the very heartland of Republicanism, and many in the crowd sensed that this Democratic President was probably just politicking with his talk about unnamed lobbyists and speculators having subverted the Congress. But they were friendly and responsive, and by God, they conceded, Truman was right about the storage-bin business. This was already hitting a lot of them in the pocketbook, and the shortage was going to get worse as the weeks wore on. Moreover, they remembered, it was only about a week ago that Harold Stassen, speaking presumably for Governor Dewey, had talked disparagingly about farm price supports being responsible for high food prices. Was it a fact, as Truman was now telling them, that the Republicans were out to scuttle the whole farm price support system? It was not too hard to believe.

Truman's well-poisoning operation had worked to perfection. Suspicion over the Republicans' farm policy seeped through the crowd at Dexter that day, and in the days following it raced like a contagion throughout the Farm Belt.

In the press car of the "Truman Special," as it rolled across Iowa that evening, a score of reporters wrote for their papers that the Democratic candidate appeared to have "hit the mark," or that he had "touched a sensitive nerve," in his first big farm speech of the campaign. The country was to hear a lot more about grain storage bins between then and November.

The Truman campaign consisted of two major transcontinental tours of about ten days each, a tour into the Northeast, and a number of lesser forays of one or two days' duration to various parts of the country. In eight weeks he would cover 32,000 miles, make more than 250 speeches, and be seen and heard in the flesh by an estimated 6,000,000 people—a record up to that time for personal campaigning.

For nearly everyone—except, apparently, the candidate himself—it was a bruising, bone-wearying ordeal. The days and the crowds and the scenery and the speeches; the endless succession of high school bands and flag-draped platforms and madly careening motorcades; the ulcerious tensions of successive deadlines, of too little sleep, of cold dinners and warm drinks, and of too many people living too close together for too long—all of these seemed to coagulate into an unintelligible montage for the reporters and the staff men and the flunkies who made up the supporting cast in this extravaganza. But there is a special octane in the bloodstream of a political candidate like Harry Truman that enables him to survive, even to thrive upon, the unconscionable stresses of a campaign. He, after all, has a gambler's stake in each word spoken, each hand shaken, each smile conferred. Every audience is a fresh challenge to his courage or a new boost to his vanity, and the sound of his own voice never palls, even when the setting and the words have been blurred unrecognizably by repetition. . . .

On most days there would be one or two outdoor rallies, or even a major speech, to which the Presidential party would be whirled in a motorcade with screaming police sirens. Afterwards there would be another traffic-stopping dash back to the schedule-bound train. As the train rolled across the countryside, it would pause at station after station where crowds had gathered. Men, women, and children would crowd out onto the tracks at the rear of the train or climb nearby roofs and signal towers for a better view. As the local band struggled through "Hail to the Chief," the "Missouri Waltz," or the state anthem, the President and half a dozen others would step out onto the back platform to be met by cheers and applause—sometimes merely perfunctory, but more often spontaneous and friendly. One of the accompanying guests would introduce the President, not omitting, usually, a plug for his own political interests. Then the President, bareheaded and beaming with a bright smile, would take the microphone and say:

> Every time I come out this way, I feel again the tremendous vitality of the West [or of New England or Oregon of Texas]. This is straight-from-the-shoulder country and it has produced a great breed of fighting men.
>
> I am going to call upon your fighting qualities. For you and I have a fight on our hands, a fight for the future of the country and for the welfare of the people of the United States.

If Truman's words, read today, sound corny, the impression is correct. They *were* corny. But it was a natural, and not a contrived, sort of corn. His words reflected the way he thought and felt, and they sounded right in his flat, unpolished

Missouri accents. And because they sounded right, people were moved to yell approvingly, "Give 'em hell, Harry" to this plain, unpretentious man who was their President.

There might follow a brief allusion to a nearby dam or conservation project or other Federal benefaction from which the locality had gained, and a reminder that this and most other blessings carried Democratic labels. Then, a note of indignation coming into his voice, Truman would say:

> Republicans in Washington have a habit of becoming curiously deaf to the voice of the people. But they have no trouble at all in hearing what Wall Street is saying. They are able to catch the slightest hint from Big Business.
>
> When I talk to you here today about Republicans, I am talking to you about the party that gets most of its campaign funds from Wall Street and Big Business. I am talking to you about the party that gave us the phony Wall Street boom of the nineteen twenties and the Hoover depression that followed. I am talking to you about the party [and here he spaced his words for emphasis] that gave us that no-account do-nothing Republican Eightieth Congress.

Flogging Congress is a safe ploy in almost any political climate. As Mr. Truman did it, it was always good for fresh outbursts of whoops and yells from the crowd. "Give 'em hell, Harry!"

"And now," he would say at the end, "I want you to meet the Boss." Turning proudly, he would reach into the doorway of the car and lead Mrs. Truman out by the hand. Plump and motherly, she would acknowledge the applause with a smile and a wave.

"And here's the one who bosses her," the President would say as Margaret, young, radiant, and usually with an armful of roses, stepped onto the scene. Her appearance always set off the loudest response of all, liberally spiced with wolf whistles from the boys and young men.

As Margaret tossed a rose or two into the crowd, the President would bend down over the railing to grasp a few of the scores of hands thrust toward him and to swap good-natured jibes with whoever could make himself heard over the uproar. The local band would strike up another tune, the engineer would give a warning toot on his whistle, the reporters would scamper down the platform toward the press car, and the "Truman Special" would begin to pull slowly away. The whole event would not have lasted more than fifteen or twenty minutes. But Fence Post, Nebraska, would have a red-letter day to talk about and to mark down in its memory book, and Harry Truman would have done again the one thing he knew best how to do, personal politicking. The same routine would be repeated fifty miles down the line, and again and again until midnight or exhaustion put an end to the day. . . .

And so the Truman cavalcade went rocketing up and down the land, laying down a barrage of political hyperbole, accusation, and ridicule. Much of it was nonsense and some of it was shameful, but there was a seed of truth in most of what he said and an element of low-keyed heroics in the way he said it. This, probably, was what counted most: the impression he created of the game, undaunted underdog. Dewey collaborated unwittingly to enhance this impression.

For the first four or five weeks of the campaign, Dewey and his men behaved almost as if Truman did not exist. They ignored the President's taunts, challenges, and specific allegations, and talked instead in wholesome but bloodless generalities.

"I pledge you," Dewey told a midwestern farm audience, "that your next administration will cooperate with the farmers of the country to protect all people from the tragedy of another dust bowl." Nobody was worried about dust bowls, but farmers were worried about storage bins. And in the Far West Dewey said, "I propose that we develop a national policy that will really save our forests through Federal, state, and local cooperation."

Reporting from the "Dewey Victory Special" as it rolled through California late in September, Leo Egan wrote in the New York *Times:*

Governor Dewey [as candidate] is acting like a man who has already been elected and is merely marking time, waiting to take office. In his speeches and in his manner there is an attitude that the election will be a mere formality to confirm a decision already made.

The basic theme of Mr. Dewey's campaign is that only the election of a Republican President and a Republican Congress can provide the country with the unity it needs to insure peace in a troubled world. Factional divisions within the Democratic party have been referred to but not emphasized. Henry Wallace's third party has been mentioned only once. Governor Thurmond and his States' Rights party have not even been mentioned.

Governor Dewey is deliberately avoiding any sharp controversy with the Democratic incumbent.

The Dewey campaign organization (and this was possibly symptomatic of what was wrong) worked with the awesome efficiency of a computer but it lacked the lively distractions of error, surprise, and human warmth. Schedules were rigorously met. Enough automobiles were always available at trainside to accommodate the traveling party. Speech texts were always ready in advance for the reporters. The candidate was always shielded from rude interlopers by ranks of subordinates. A jerky start of the train from one wayside stop was so unusual as to cause the candidate to expostulate: "What's wrong with that damn fool engineer?" It was *that* kind of mistake that happened on the Dewey train, and this one turned out to be a magnificent blooper. In the skilled hands of Democratic propagandists, it became overnight a jeering anti-Dewey slogan in railroad roundhouses and Union halls all across the country.

In contrast, the Truman entourage lived in a continuing chaos of late arrivals and unexpected departures, overnight shifts in plans, and sudden discoveries that no plan for the next six hours existed. Speech texts, so vital to newspaper coverage in a campaign that rarely could afford radio and television broadcasts, often were unavailable until the hour of delivery. One major speech, on soil conservation, was by some unexplained foul-up delivered to an audience of industrial workers who had come to boo the Taft-Hartley law. The whole campaign came close to folding on the night of September 29 when, according to Jack Redding, the railroad refused to move the "Truman Special" out of the station in Oklahoma City until past charges for transportation were settled. A hasty passing of the hat among oil-rich Democrats in the state averted this humiliating disaster. "For a time," Redding wrote "it seemed possible the whole party might have to alight and get back to Washington the best way they could."

If the Dewey party lived in a cloudland of euphoria, the Truman camp was pitched in the slough of despond. As their train rattled back and forth across the country, the men around the President came increasingly to feel—up to the last couple of weeks, at least—that they were just going through the motions of campaigning. What kept them going was their loyalty to Truman, whose spirits, as far as the eye could detect, never flagged. Clark Clifford has recalled what he believes was the low point of the group's morale:

> One day around the middle of October, somebody hopped off the train at some town out in the Middle West—I've forgotten where it was—and bought a current copy of *Newsweek* magazine. We knew they were going to publish this high-powered poll by fifty leading political writers around the country on the election outlook. We were pretty apprehensive, but we had to see it.
>
> Well, there it was, in great big black type—"Fifty political experts unanimously"—get that, "unanimously"—"predict a Dewey victory." Not a one of them gave the Old Man a chance; the score was Dewey, 50, Truman zero. Boy. . . .!
>
> We took it back and showed it to Mr. Truman. He blinked a little, but he didn't let it faze him. He gave us that big grin and said, "Oh, well, those damn fellows; they're always wrong anyway. Forget it, boys, and let's get on with the job."
>
> So everybody takes a deep breath, squares his shoulders, and gets on with what really appeared to be a hopeless task.
>
> I don't think Mrs. Truman and Margaret really thought he could win, and in his very deepest heart I suspect the President didn't think so, either. But he had too much experience and courage to ever let on, if he felt that way.

However, as the weeks wore on and November approached, spirits aboard the "Truman Special" began to lift. It was a subtle but exhilarating change. No one was quite sure what it was, but the motion and hubbub on the Truman train began to acquire a sense of purpose. The visible factor was that the crowds were getting larger, friendlier, and noisier. On a swing through hard-rock Republican Indiana, 25,000 people turned out at Kokomo to Greet the President, 20,000 at Hammond, and more than 12,000 at Logansport. Dewey had been over the same route a week earlier and had not done as well. Five thousand people waited beside the tracks in a downpour of rain in Albany, New York, to greet the President's train when it rolled in at 8 o'clock one late October morning. Six thousand filled every available seat in the armory at Springfield, Illinois, and other hundreds gathered outside in this citadel of Republicanism to hear the Democratic candidate lambaste Dewey for not having a farm program. In St. Paul, he filled the 15,000-seat civic auditorium and three adjacent halls and drew applause forty-two times with his excoriation of the "do-nothing Eightieth Congress." Dewey drew only 7,000 in the same auditorium. At the traditional "Friday night before election rally" in the Brooklyn Academy of Music (some of its organizers had been prominent in the "dump Truman" drive at the convention) the crowd gave him a twelve-minute ovation when he rose to speak.

Something was in the air, all right: the biggest political upset in history. "We felt it, but we just couldn't believe it," Clark Clifford remembers. So did many of the reporters and political experts who had followed the campaign. Robert C. Albright, a veteran of the political staff of the Washington *Post,* wrote: "Now and then a particularly large crowd or a noisy ovation starts a mighty surge of hope in the rear staff car. Some of it filters forward to the press car, and hardbitten reporters ask themselves, 'Could we be wrong?" Some began cautiously to hedge their predictions, but they could not trust their eyes above their judgment—or at least above the collective judgment of the journalists' tribe. They were trapped by professional timidity into going along with the consensus that Dewey was bound to win, and win big.* That was what the pros in the various states had told them; that was what they told one another in endless bull sessions in the press car; that was what all the polls told them.

The Gallup poll four days before election had it cold: Dewey, 49.5 percent of the popular vote, Truman 44.5 percent, the rest to Wallace, Thurmond, *et al.* The New York *Times* had it even colder. At great cost and earnest effort it had deployed a small battalion of reporters across the country for an entire month to take the national pulse. Its findings: Dewey, 29 states with 345 electoral votes (266 needed to win); Truman, 11 states with 105 electoral votes; Thurmond, 4 states with 38 votes; the rest "in doubt." Willard Kiplinger, one of Washington's most profound pundits, also had it cold. Publisher of a new weekly magazine, *Changing Times* with an immovable Saturday deadline, he hit the newsstands Monday, November 1, election eve, with a front cover proclaiming in inch-high type, WHAT DEWEY WILL DO.

Everybody had it cold, apparently, except Truman himself and Howard

---

* This reporter was no exception!—C. P.

McGrath, his campaign chairman. On the Sunday before election, McGrath and Redding, sitting alone amidst the debris and overflowing ashtrays in their New York headquarters, telephoned a score of top Democratic state leaders across the country to get their last-minute estimates of the outlook. One after another they gave almost identical replies: "Things have been looking up in the last couple of weeks. We'll certainly carry the state for the Senator [or Governor or Congressman], but the President probably won't make it."

When the roundup was completed, McGrath looked at Redding and said: "You can't win all the things they say they're going to win and not elect a President too. After all, he's at the top of the ticket."

"We're either going to lose everything—every senatorial race, every congressional race, every courthouse—or we'll elect a President. I think we elect Truman. . . ."

All across the country men and women made a dutiful bedtime check of their radios and televisions, just to see how things were going—and then stayed glued to them past midnight, into the dawn, and even through the breakfast hour. Suddenly they were spectators at a contest as thrilling as that between David and Goliath, and containing the same dramatic ingredients.

Truman picked up an early lead in popular votes, and, though it expanded and narrowed harrowingly through the night, he never lost it. The commentators said at first this was to be expected. This was the city vote, they said, but wait until the rural precincts are heard from. But about midnight, Iowa—Iowa, the heartland of midwestern Republicanism—dropped irretrievably into the Democratic column. The commentators were not so sure any more, and they noted that the crowds had drifted away from the Dewey victory celebration at the Roosevelt Hotel, leaving a pall of apprehension and untouched cases of champagne behind them.

The electoral vote seesawed back and forth agonizingly as the hours ticked on. At 4:30 Wednesday morning, Jim Hagerty, Dewey's press man, broke a long and ominous silence to tell reporters, "We're still in there fighting." Then came the shocking news that Illinois had conceded—Democratic. At 6 o'clock, Truman had a commanding lead in both popular and electoral votes but not enough to win. His electoral score was 227 to 176 for Dewey. But a few states, including Ohio and California, were still out, and the experts had all said Ohio was a shoo-in for Dewey and that Governor Warren could hardly be expected to lose his home state.

Then, at 9:30, came the climax, a tension-snapping end to one of the most exhausting cliffhangers of all time. As idling teletypes in a hundred newsrooms across the nation suddenly began to chatter, bleary-eyed radio announcers grabbed their microphones to proclaim almost hysterically: "Ohio has gone Democratic! This puts Truman over the top with 270 electoral votes. Ladies and gentlemen, President Truman has won the election!"

What happened? How did this greatest of political miracles come to pass?
The Presidential vote statistics are as follows:

Candidate	Popular Vote	Electoral Vote	States
Truman	24,045,052	304	28
Dewey	21,896,927	189	16
Wallace	1,137,957	—	—
Thurmond	1,168,687	38	4
Others	240,594	—	—
Total	48,489,217	531	48

The vote for Congress was as follows, with figures in parentheses showing the previous membership:

	Democratic	Republican
Senate	54 (45)	42 (51)
House	263 (188)	171 (246)

It was the closest Presidential election since 1916. Truman's margin over Dewey was 2,148,125. He won by a plurality, not by a majority. His percentage of the popular vote was 49.5; Dewey's, 45.1. In a general way, each man lost where he assumed he was strongest, and won where his prospects seemed thinnest. Dewey swept all of the industrial Northeast, from Maryland through Maine, except for Massachusetts and Rhode Island. This was traditional Democratic territory. Truman captured many of the important farm states, most notably Wisconsin, Iowa, and Colorado, which were traditionally Republican. In addition, he swept the whole tier of eleven western states (excluding Oregon), in which, though they are traditionally Democratic, the Republicans had confidently expected to make important gains. Thurmond deprived Truman of four states in the once-solid South—South Carolina, Alabama, Mississippi, and Louisiana. And Wallace certainly robbed him of New York (the Progressive Party total there was approximately twice Dewey's winning margin), and probably of New Jersey.

What were the factors in this upset?

There were many, but in this writer's view the controlling one was this: Truman had, in the November 1947 memorandum by Clifford and the political strategy board, a basic campaign strategy that was unique to his needs and to his capacities, and he stuck with it. It was a strategy of go-for-broke; of recognizing that he was the underdog and that he had little to lose and much to gain; of seizing the initiative and pressing it with every weapon and against all risks. His banner was the New Deal; his targets were familiar and well defined; and the obstacles were starkly and realistically portrayed. The strategy called for courage and persistence, which Truman supplied in absolute measure. He did not deviate essentially from his master plan throughout the campaign. The result was that he knew what he was doing every step of the way.

Three voting blocs supplied the margin for Truman's victory: labor, Negro (plus other minorities), and farm. Throughout the campaign Truman had emphasized day after day his fights with the Eightieth Congress over civil rights for the Negroes, housing, minimum wages, and his veto of the Taft-Hartley Act. When the votes were counted, he had carried the thirteen largest industrial cities, where labor and Negro votes are decisive, some by pluralities greater than Roosevelt's in 1944. This swelled his popular vote score. It was not enough to outbalance the Republican "upstate" vote in places like New York, Pennsylvania, and Michigan, which gave their electoral votes to Dewey, but it was sufficient in Ohio and Illinois, and possibly in California.

The tradition of the eleven Great Lakes and Plain states—the nation's biggest grocery basket—is Republican. Seven went for Dewey in 1944, and six for Wilkie in 1940. Dewey, presuming on a revulsion against New Deal and postwar regimentation of the farmer, expected to sweep them all with the possible exception of Illinois and Minnesota. Instead, he took only five—Indiana, North and South Dakota, Nebraska, and Kansas. Iowa's swing behind Truman was, psychologically, the most crushing blow of all to the GOP. This was the very citadel of Republicanism, which had remained faithful since 1936. When Iowa defected to the Democrats in 1948, she took every other important farm and cattle state, except the aforementioned five, with her. It was a tribute to the efficacy of the grain-storage-bin issue and to a drastic mid-October break in farm prices. The farmers were riding a high crest of prosperity that year, but Truman frightened them into thinking that a Republican administration might take it away from them.

Another major factor was the contrast in campaign techniques and in the motivational appeals to the voters. The Truman campaign was positive, hard-hitting, and directed to the gut interests of the voters. He named names and places and gave chapter and verse (with whatever injury the cause of accuracy) when he criticized something. And for every wrong and every fear, he had a palpable villain—the Eightieth Congress and, by extrapolation, Republican candidates and Republican officeholders in general. He gave the voters something to be "agin," which is the most powerful motivator of voter behavior.

By contrast, both Dewey's campaign and his personality were arid. He avoided direct controversy with his opponent. He was seldom specific or convincing when he elucidated the larger issues. Intellectually, his campaign was on a higher level than Truman's, just as it was in the matter of taste and decorum. By the same token it was overlaid with a palpable superciliousness. It was, said Clarence Buddington Kelland, national Republican committeeman from Arizona, "smug, arrogant, stupid. . . . It was a contemptuous campaign, contemptuous alike to our enemies and to our friends."

In fact, the demerits of the Dewey campaign technique may have bulked as large in the outcome as did the merits of the Truman technique. Jules Abels, in *Out of the Jaws of Victory,* pointed to what may have been a decisive and fatal factor in the Dewey operation in these words:

The election was not thrown away by indifference or lack of effort. Preparation and more preparation had always been the distinguishing characteristic of Dewey and his team throughout his career. . . . The truth is that the type of campaign was the result not of careless, but of too careful and painstaking calculation. The Dewey campaign line was frozen into inertia not because it had been underthought, but because it had been overthought.

The consequence of this, as Abels and others have pointed out, was that when the first turbulence of a Truman tide began to appear late in October, the Dewey crew, geared for smooth water only, were unable to trim sails in order to meet the rising seas.

Still another factor of importance was Truman's handling of the Russian blockade of Berlin. This had occurred in midsummer, and it had created an air of anxiety over the whole tenuous peace of Europe. The airlift that Truman had ordered seemed at first an act of desperation—which it probably was. But as the weeks wore on and tons of supplies continued to pour daily into Berlin, it became an act of defiance and of calling the Russian bluff. The country experienced a surge of pride, of which President Truman was the inevitable beneficiary. While foreign policy, per se, never became a flammable issue in the campaign, largely because of Dewey's forbearance, the dramatic success of the Berlin airlift greatly enhanced Truman's image as a leader.

Finally, in assessing the factors of the 1948 upset, there was the widespread miscalculation that the old New Deal dynamic had been buried in the grave with FDR. Dewey and his men believed that the concepts of the managerial revolution, so captivating to the Eastern elite in the postwar years, had captivated the rest of the country as well. In this new dogma the old political clichés, slogans, and alliances were written off as decadent, including particularly belief in the New Deal-forged coalition of labor, Negroes, city bosses, and Southern Bourbons. In its place was an aggressive, up-to-date, all-purpose conservatism of Republican hue with a base as wide as the continent.

They were wrong. Truman campaigned on an orthodox New Deal-Democratic platform. He held Dewey to a smaller proportion of the total vote (45.1 percent) than Dewey got running against Roosevelt in 1944 (45.8 percent). If the figures are recast to lump the essentially Democratic Wallace and Thurmond votes along with Truman's, the Democratic 1948 total becomes 54.9 percent, which is 1.6 percent above what FDR drew in 1944. In other words, it is clear that, instead of diminishing, the Democratic potential under Truman had grown.

Republican theorists in their postmortems attempted to explain Dewey's poor showing as attributable to Republican stay-at-homes who didn't bother to vote. Sam Lubell, in an expert analysis of the campaign for the *Saturday Evening Post* two months after the election, came to a quite different conclusion:

GOP victories in the industrial east were won less through new Republican adherents than by the apathy which kept much of the old FDR vote from the polls. Far from costing Dewey the election, the [Democratic] stay-at-homes may have saved him almost as crushing a defeat as Landon suffered in 1936.

At all events, Harry Truman was now President in his own right, his record was vindicated, and his leadership was open to no man's challenge. "You just have to take off your hat," the New York *Sun*, which rarely had said anything kind about him before, editorialized the day after election, "to a beaten man who refuses to stay licked!.... The next few days will produce many long and labored explanations of what has happened. To us of the *Sun* there is no great mystery about it. Mr. Truman won because this is still a land which loves a scrapper, in which intestinal fortitude is still respected."

Chapter 7 COMPROMISE MADE TRUMAN PRESIDENT

*In 1951 SAMUEL LUBELL, political
pollster, analyst, and columnist, published
one of the more important and provocative
books dealing with American politics to
appear during the present century. In the
excerpt that follows from "The Future of
American Politics," Lubell depicts President
Truman as a figure quite different from the
"go-for-broke" crusader and leader described
by Cabell Phillips. Instead, Lubell believes
that Truman's personality, background, and
experience fitted him perfectly to preside as
a compromiser or "broker" over an inherited
political deadlock between the presidency
and Congress, between liberals and conservatives. Truman's claim to greatness, if there is
one, resides in this fact, Lubell asserts. Do
you agree with Lubell's tentative evaluation,
as stated in a footnote to the 1965 edition
of his book, that "the verdict of history
[seems] to favor Truman on domestic issues
and in Europe but [remains] a question
mark in Asia"?*

The Truman Riddle

When the Seventy-fifth Congress reconvened in January, 1938, most of the
Senators were dismayed to find that the first order of business before them was the
antilynching bill. Particularly among those Senators whose constituencies straddled
Northern and Southern prejudices the prospect of having to vote on the proposal
stirred much anguish. As one of these Senators explained to a leader of the
Southern opposition, "You know I'm against this bill, but if it comes to a vote I'll
have to be for it."

This Senator went on to recall how a favorite uncle had served in the Confed-
erate Army and how his mother still associated all Republicans with the "redleg"

Abridgement of "The Man Who Bought Time" from *The Future of American Politics* 3rd
Edition Revised (Colophon) by Samuel Lubell. Copyright © 1951, 1952, 1956, 1965 by
Samuel Lubell. Reprinted by permission of Harper & Row, Publishers, Inc.

abolitionists who had helped make the Kansas-Missouri border a guerrilla battlefield during the Civil War period. "All my sympathies are with you," the Senator fervently declared, "but the Negro vote in Kansas City and St. Louis is too important."

Turning to go, Senator Harry S. Truman added almost wistfully. "Maybe the thing for me to be doing is to be playing poker this afternoon. Perhaps you fellows can call a no quorum."

This episode is related here for the first time in print, not to raise doubts about President Truman's sincerity in the matter of civil rights—of that more later—but because it brings into focus so clearly the essential political qualities which made Truman President and which remained the key to his whole administration. Few Presidents seemed more erratic and puzzling to their contemporaries; yet few occupants of the White House ran more consistently true to form.

Truman was commonly pictured as "a little man" hopelessly miscast for the "biggest job in the world." Yet how many of our Presidents gave the historians more to write about? Almost any one of a number of his actions would have made his Presidency memorable—the dropping of the first atomic bomb, the Truman Doctrine of resistance to communism, the Marshall Plan, the Berlin Airlift, his spectacular election triumph in 1948, his abandonment of the tradition of "no entangling alliances" with the signing of the North Atlantic Defense Treaty, our armed intervention in Korea, the firing of General Douglas MacArthur.

The strange thing about these precedent-shattering actions is how basically unchanged things were left. After seven years of Truman's hectic, even furious, activity the nation seemed to be about on the same general spot as when he first came to office.

Consider the three principal conflicts which dominated the Truman years and whose interweavings formed the fabric of our times:

Domestically, our economy trembled with the alternating fevers and chills of threatened inflation and threatened depression, even as it did when World War Two ended. The cold war with Russia continued to pursue its malarial course, now and then sinking into endemic concealment, only to flare up in blood-letting recurrence. Although both the Wallaceites and Dixiecrats were discredited in 1948, the civil war inside the Democratic party raged on relentlessly through Truman's entire administration.

Nowhere in the whole Truman record can one point to a single, decisive breakthrough. All his more important policies reduced themselves to one thing—to buying time for the future. Far from seeking decision, he sought to put off any possible showdown, to perpetuate rather than break the prevailing stalemate.

The mystery of where Truman was heading can be answered simply. All his skills and energies—and he was among our hardest-working Presidents—were directed to standing still.

This persistent irresolution can hardly be blamed on a lack of personal courage.

A less courageous—or less stubborn—man, in fact, would not have been so resolutely indecisive. It took courage to order American troops into Korea. It also took courage to dismiss General MacArthur at a time when the Republicans were howling so furiously for Secretary of State Dean Acheson's English mustache. Characteristically, both these moves, each so bold in itself, neatly neutralized themselves into a policy of limited action.

This faculty for turning two bold steps into a halfway measure—no mean trick— was Truman's political hallmark. If it applied solely to our relations with the Soviets one might conclude that it was the only shrewd course left between an inability to make peace and an unwillingness to go to war. But the same middle touch could be seen in Truman's handling of domestic political and economic problems. When he took vigorous action in one direction it was axiomatic that he would contrive soon afterward to move in the conflicting direction. In the end he managed to work himself back close to the center spot of indecision from which he started.

In the fight against inflation, for example, Truman warned again and again of the calamitous consequences of uncontrolled price rises and, just as repeatedly, he followed these warnings with actions which aggravated the dangers of inflation. When World War Two ended, he eloquently called for holding the line against inflation to avoid another boom and collapse such as followed World War One. Still, despite the enormous backlog of spending power left over from wartime savings and profits, Truman supported repeal of the excess profits tax, wage increases and liberal credit policies, all of which pumped still more money into the economy.

Again, when Truman called a special session to enact the Marshall Plan, he demanded legislation to control prices. When the Korean War broke out, however, he pointedly refrained from requesting price control powers, even while asking for the broadest authority to mobilize the economy. Why did he seek price control in 1948 but not in 1950? Could it have been that in 1948 he requested legislation which he knew would not be enacted so he could blame the Republican-controlled Congress for whatever happened, while in 1950 he feared that price powers *would* be given him, leaving him no alibi for failing to check the rise in living costs?

Even after Congress forced price control powers on him, Truman delayed acting for several months, while wholesale prices leaped 14 per cent and the real value of every defense dollar was cut by one fifth. By the spring of 1951, with the renewal of price control at issue, Truman had once again donned the armor of the champion of the voting consumer.

There is a good deal more behind this curious jerkiness which characterized Truman's administration than the politician's common desire to face both ways at the same time. Partly it can be attributed to Truman's personality. Where Franklin Roosevelt radiated serene self-confidence, Truman seemed afflicted by an inner sense of inferiority. It might have been because of nearsightedness, or of the financial failures of his father who lost the family farm speculating on the grain market and was reduced to the job of night watchman, or of Truman's own business reverses and his lateness in getting into politics. Thirty-eight years old when he ran for his first political office, he was fifty when he won his seat in the U. S. Senate. On reaching Washington he felt his inadequacy so keenly that he announced he intended to go to law school at night.

Whatever the psychological reason, Truman's personality seemed to demand that he alternate between crafty caution and asserting himself boldly, even brashly, as if proving something to himself. His usual instinct appeared to be to play things close to his vest, but periodically he had to unbutton his vest and thump his chest.[1]

Many of his explosive flare-ups probably were forced by his irresolution in allowing situations to build up until drastic action became unavoidable. With the RFC and Internal Revenue Bureau frauds for example, he let matters drift for months until it became clear that a major scandal was in the offing and only then instituted his own "shake-up."

The real key to Truman's determined indecision, however, is the fact that he was the product of political deadlock. It was because stalemate fitted his nature so snugly that he became President. Truman can be considered a "political accident" in the sense that Roosevelt's death brought him to the White House. But there was nothing accidental about his being in the line of succession. Only a man exactly like Truman politically, with both his limitations and strong points, could have been the Democratic choice for Roosevelt's successor.

How Presidents Are Made

The ruthless, Darwinian process of natural selection which Truman had to undergo to reach the White House was provided by the fierce struggle between the President and Congress which burst into the open early in 1937 with Roosevelt's proposal to pack the Supreme Court and which has continued to the present.

Roosevelt's winning a third and fourth term has obscured the fact that the last major measure of a New Deal nature which he was able to get through Congress was the Wages and Hours Law in mid-1938. With the failure of the attempted purge of the more conservative Democratic Senators and the Republican gains in the 1938 Congressional election, the anti-New Deal coalition came into undisputed control on Capitol Hill. After that Roosevelt never could work his will with Congress. Through the power of veto, he usually could hold the rebellious Congress in check. Congress, for its part, was able to block any Roosevelt proposal it disliked.

That this President-Congress deadlock did not paralyze the effective functioning of the government can be credited largely to the development of a new profession in Washington—that of the so-called "border-state" politician, who undertook to act as political brokers between the White House and Capitol Hill.

Although many members of this bloc actually came from the border states, the label really represented a state of mind. In favor of Roosevelt's foreign policy, the border Democrats were middle of the roaders on domestic issues. They leaned more toward the farmer than toward labor, but still were not antilabor. In fact, they consciously made a point of remaining acceptable to both the liberals and conservatives, to both the isolationists and interventionists.

Theirs was the balance of compromise, which they employed to mediate between the Democratic extremes, being careful never to throw their influence finally on one side or the other. Probably the most effective single member of the group, until his elevation to the Supreme Court, was South Carolina's Jimmy Byrnes, whose talents were admirably suited to cloakroom negotiation.

In many ways this border-state bloc, which included Senators like Dick Russell of Georgia and Carl Hatch of New Mexico, constituted the real locus of political power in Washington. Roosevelt soon learned what Truman discovered, that to get any proposal through Congress required the approval of these middle-of-the-road Democrats. Throughout Truman's administration whenever the border-state Democrats swung their influence against the Administration it got beaten.

By political geography and personal temperament, Truman was a typical border-state Senator. Campaign biographies usually describe him as having been one of Roosevelt's most faithful supporters and in his first year in the Senate Truman did go down the line for every New Deal measure. But in the struggle within the Democratic party, which developed during Roosevelt's second term, Truman had a way of straying in and out of both camps.

He backed the resolution introduced early in 1937 by Byrnes condemning sit-down strikes. Although supporting Roosevelt on packing the Supreme Court, Truman voted for Pat Harrison of Mississippi for Senate majority leader against Alben Barkley, the White House choice. A regular member of John Garner's convivial "Board of Education," Truman supported the Vice-President's efforts to block a third term. . . .

Nor was Roosevelt especially friendly toward Truman. Several times Truman complained to James A. Farley, then Democratic National Chairman, of being treated unfairly on patronage matters. Roosevelt preferred to consult with Missouri's Governor Lloyd Stark, who was planning to oppose Truman for the Senate. Late in 1939 Roosevelt tried to get Truman to withdraw in Stark's favor by offering him a $10,000-a-year appointment to the Interstate Commerce Commission.

Truman has described the 1940 Democratic primary as the crucial battle of his entire political career. With Boss Pendergast in jail, the Kansas City organization could not be counted upon for its usual ingenious vote. Truman had no funds of his own for campaign purposes—he couldn't even prevent the family farm from being foreclosed.

One noon at lunch in the office of Edward Halsey, then secretary of the Senate, Truman complained of his difficulties in raising funds for radio talks and political advertising. Byrnes was at the same table. In 1938 Byrnes had taken the lead in opposing Roosevelt's efforts to purge some of the more conservative Senators like Walter George, Bennett Clark, Millard Tydings, Pat McCarran and Guy Gillette. Although Truman was not being openly purged by Roosevelt, Byrnes still felt that no President should interfere in Democratic primary contests. Byrnes sought out Bernard M. Baruch, who had helped finance the fight against the purge, and interested him in Truman's behalf. . . .

It was Baruch, moreover, who sparked the idea which inspired Truman's successful 1948 campaign strategy. Shortly after the Republican Convention, Baruch suggested to Truman that he call the Republican-controlled Congress back into special session, thus providing an arena in which the Republican performance could be matched against the newly drafted Republican platform. Truman was so enthusiastic over this suggestion that he sent Clark Clifford to New York City to discuss the idea more fully with Baruch on the eve of the latter's departure for Europe.

That Baruch should have been interested in Truman by Byrnes, who became a leader of the anti-Truman opposition within the Democratic party, must surely rate as one of the more ironic footnotes in American political history. The irony deepens in view of how the famous Truman Defense Investigating Committee came to be set up.

Early in 1941 Representative Eugene Cox of Georgia, an uncompromising Roosevelt foe, began demanding an investigation of defense spending. The prospect of an inquiry headed by Cox, a zealot by nature, sent shivers through the heads of the defense agencies. One day Roosevelt explained the concern of the Army and Navy to Byrnes, without referring to Cox by name. "I can fix that by putting the investigation into friendly hands," Byrnes assured the President. Under its rules, Byrnes explained, the House could not authorize an investigation for a week but the Senate could act in a few hours.

Some weeks earlier Truman had introduced a resolution for an investigation, which had been referred to the Committee on Audit and Control which Byrnes headed. Calling Truman to his office, Byrnes asked him why had he introduced the resolution? Truman explained that some Missouri contractors were complaining that the big companies were getting all the defense construction contracts. A little pressure on the War Department, he felt, would be a good thing.

"What would you do if the resolution were reported out?" Byrnes asked.

"I know there isn't a chance in the world of your reporting it out," Truman replied. "But if you did I wouldn't conduct the investigation in a way that would hurt defense. You could count on me for that."

Shortly afterward the resolution was reported out and, although no one dreamed it, a new President was in the making.

Truman's able management of the Defense Investigating Committee transformed him into a figure of national importance, earning him a reputation for honesty and fearlessness. What was not widely appreciated was how adroitly Truman appealed to both Democratic factions. Since his Committee's reports were sharply critical of the defense agencies the conservative Democrats were pleased, as were the Republicans. Since the "military" was a favorite committee target the New Dealers also were gratified. An informal understanding existed between the Truman Committee staff and Donald Nelson, the chairman of the War Production Board. Whenever Nelson ran into particular difficulty with the War or Navy departments, he would "leak" his troubles to the Truman Committee, which would then bring pressure on the military.

While the Truman Committee was conducting its able investigations, the attrition of the wartime "Battle of Washington" was steadily shifting the political balance against Roosevelt in favor of Congress. A variety of factors entered into this—the off-year Republican gains in 1942; the vengeful fury of the isolationists who, although supporting the war, drummed constantly with criticism of home front bungling; the failure to bring prices and wages under control; the feuding and squabbling among the government administrators; also the rising resistance in various quarters to wartime restrictions.

In one case of the rubber crisis, the rumbling resentment on Capitol Hill broke through with the passage of a bill which would have disrupted the whole mobilization machinery by Donald Nelson. Roosevelt vetoed the measure. But, confronted with the likelihood that his veto would be overridden, he called upon Baruch, Harvard president James B. Conant, and Karl Compton, then president of the Massachusetts Institute of Technology, to investigate the situation. Their report, unsparing in criticizing the administrative irresponsibility, save Roosevelt's veto.

The following month Roosevelt pulled Byrnes off the Supreme Court and made him "assistant president" with an office in the White House. The political significance of this action was largely overlooked. It meant that Congress had gained the ascendancy in Washington. After that, the overhanging political question facing the administration became how to come to terms with the dominant coalition in Congress. . . .

By the time the 1944 Democratic convention opened in Chicago, the balance of Washington power had shifted so strongly that Roosevelt's running mate had to be acceptable to the conservative Democrats in the Senate. Henry Wallace, on whom Roosevelt had soured before the end of the 1940 campaign, was never really in the running. He served as a stalking-horse behind whom labor and the big city delegates could hold their votes and bargaining power. The logistics of the Battle of Washington required that the Vice-Presidency go to one of the border-state Democrats who had made a veritable profession of reconciling the warring Democratic wings. The real choice lay between Byrnes and Truman, who had gone to Chicago to nominate Byrnes.

Three principal objections were raised to Byrnes. Negro leaders opposed him as a Southerner. Ed Flynn, the Democratic boss closest to Roosevelt, argued that

Byrnes would "hurt the ticket" since he had been converted from Catholicism. Then, as "assistant president," Byrnes had been too forceful for the liking of some labor leaders.

Truman's record, by contrast, could hardly have been more shrewdly tailored to the needs of a compromise candidate. Usually a safe administration vote, he enjoyed the asset of having been opposed for re-election by Roosevelt, which reassured the more conservative. Democrats. He had supported Roosevelt in the World Court and Neutrality battles, yet two of the Senate's leading isolationists, Burton Wheeler and Bennett Clark, were the men Truman usually looked to for political guidance. Although acceptable to labor, Truman had opposed the sit-down strikes and had voted for the Smith-Connally antistrike act, but not to override Roosevelt's veto of it.

Truman had voted for price control but against the wartime limitation of $25,000 a year on salaries. He had favored all relief appropriations but had helped kill the WPA theater project.

In nominating Truman the embattled Democrats actually were voting to keep the line of succession to the Presidency from passing to either the Northern or Southern Democrats. The 1948 convention found the deadlocked Democrats in the same plight—with the same result. When the Philadelphia convention opened, the clamor to ditch Truman was joined in by such factional rivals as Dixiecrat Southerners and the Americans for Democratic Action, by James Roosevelt and by city bosses like Jacob Arvey of Chicago and Frank Hague of Jersey City. Their unanimity in desiring to get rid of Truman was surpassed only by their inability to agree on anyone to take his place.

This same necessity to preserve the precarious balance within the party dictated the nomination of Barkley, another border-state Senator, as Vice-President.

The Red Queen

Compromise made Truman President and—despite the controversies he stirred, the officials he fired and the terrible-tempered letters he wrote—compromise remained the unswerving objective of his Presidency. If this has been obscured it is because of a failure to appreciate that the only form of compromise possible in Truman's administration was stalemate.

Broadly speaking, any middle-of-the-road politician faces one of two prospects. He can allow himself to be torn in two by the forces he is attempting to conciliate. Or he can draw strength from both irreconcilable extremes by playing one off against the other. In view of Truman's Senate record it is not surprising that he followed the latter course.

His role was to raise all issues but to settle none. He repeatedly pressed vigorous recommendations on Congress knowing they would be rejected—not only on inflation control but on civil rights and repeal of the Taft-Hartley Law. During the 1948 campaign he could think of sending Justice Vinson to Moscow on a "peace mission," not long after he had publicly denounced the Soviet leaders as men whose word could not be trusted. One doesn't have to question Truman's sincerity to observe that he appeared happiest when able to make a dramatic show of activity, secure in the knowledge that nothing much was going to happen.

Harsh as that estimate may sound it was Truman's claim to greatness. There is much to be said, after all, for the mariner who, knowing that he cannot quiet the storm, contrives somehow to stay afloat until the storm has died down of itself. The major problems Truman grappled with were mainly inherited. All were fearfully difficult, perhaps impossible of harmonious solution. As the President of the last center of hope in the world, Truman could hardly confess helplessness. Unable either to reconcile or to ignore the forces in conflict, he tried to stall them off hoping that time would make decision unnecessary.

The contradictions in Truman's actions vanish when one appreciates that actually he dreaded moving too far in any direction, of doing too much or too little. Even his acrobatic economics find their consistency in the fact that he was afraid of both rising and falling prices. When prices went up, Truman wanted them to come down. When they started down, as in 1949, he would become frightened of a possible recession and start up the government's inflationary credit engines. Truman's apologists may contend that this is what is known as a "managed economy"—but the motivating force was to put off politically painful economic adjustments.

Similarly, in foreign affairs Truman would lash out boldly when his hand was forced, as in Korea. When it came to seeing things through, however, he would drag action, as if hoping for something to turn up to make it unnecessary to go too far. Not for two years after the North Atlantic Defense Pact was signed was anything much done to implement it, although in the interval the Soviets exploded their first atomic bomb. So leisurely was the timetable for mobilization laid down in 1950, that it really represented a gamble that the Soviet Union did not intend to go to war. Our slow rate of rearming could be justified only on the basis of faith in Stalin's desire for peace.

If over the course of his Presidency Truman's personal standing rocketed up and down like a roller coaster, it was not because he, himself, was so erratic, but because of changes in the stresses and strains of the forces in conflict.

As the costs and frustrations of continued stalemate grew more burdensome the middle ground on which Truman pitched his political tent tended to crack and crumble. The tensions of office told on him personally as, like Alice's Red Queen, he had to run ever faster in order to stand still. In the glaring light of threatened showdown, all his weaknesses became mercilessly exposed—the wavering evasions, the lack of any policy for achieving decision.

But if that was the source of his weakness, it also explains his astonishing recoveries from the abysmally low levels of public esteem to which he fell at times.

The choices of action which Truman tried to evade were all extremely difficult ones, such as splitting the Democratic party or letting the economy run loose to find its natural level, or precipitating a showdown with the Soviets which might cause them to back down but could also bring on war. Truman's constant gamble was that the American public, when confronted with the unpleasant implications of decisive action, would prefer to continue with his policy of calculated drift.

The secret of Truman's political vitality was that he shrewdly planted himself on the furiously dead center of stalemate to which irreconcilables must repair if they are to make a bargain. Whenever the balance of the raging conflict shifted in favor of conciliation, Truman inherited the situation. But could the stalemated forces be held at arm's length indefinitely? Eventually wouldn't they wrench apart whoever stood in the middle?

There we have the essential drama of Truman's Presidency. It was the drama of a man fighting stubbornly and, yes, courageously, to avoid decision. Whether, in standing against these pressures, Truman was a pitiful or heroic figure cannot be answered finally today. Although his place in history is set, as the man who bought time, one all-crucial question remains unanswered:

In whose favor has time been working?

Has time been operating to strengthen the cause of peace? Or has it been giving the Soviet Union a breathing spell to overcome its weaknesses and amass the strength to make an eventual war bloodier and more difficult to win?

Has time been working to invigorate and stabilize our economy or has it been merely piling the inflationary bricks ever higher for a bigger crash?

Has time, in its not always obvious workings, been managing to bring into existence the conditions which will consolidate the Democrats as the nation's majority party? Or have its clashing elements been driven ever more hopelessly apart until they must split?

In short, have the processes of time in these atomic-riven days been of a self-healing or a cancerous nature?

If the verdict of history vindicates Truman,[2] he will rate as one of our greatest presidents, as much for what he did not do as for what he did. If the verdict proves hostile, Truman is likely to appear as another James Buchanan, who also considered himself a crafty, dexterous politician, but who wasted the last remaining years of conciliation and left the White House with his own party ready to break up and a disunited country drifting into bloody war.

Whatever the judgment of the future, it should be clear that Truman was incapable of breaking the stalemate which gripped us and was probably even unwilling to try. Deadlock was the essence of the man. Stalemate was his Midas touch. . . .

Notes

1. After he left the White House, Truman spoke out bluntly and sharply on every possible occasion, but this was not how he operated as President.

2. By 1965 the verdict of history seemed to favor Truman on domestic issues and in Europe but remained a question in Asia.

Part Four

KOREA AND THE PROBLEM OF LIMITED WAR

Chapter 8 TIME WAS ON THE AMERICAN SIDE

*The Korean War occasioned the gravest
confrontation between a president and a
military figure in American history. The
specific questions at issue involved immediate strategic decisions arising out of the
armed conflict in Korea. But beyond that
the Truman-MacArthur encounter also
involved larger matters: the nature of the
Cold War, the feasibility of "limited" war,
the nature of war itself, and ultimately the
supremacy of the civil over the military
powers in American government. In the
selection that follows, JOHN W. SPANIER
outlines the Truman administration's
position on these matters as presented to a
congressional hearing in 1951 following
President Truman's "firing" of General
MacArthur. Among Spanier's other published works are "American Foreign Policy
Since World War II" (1962) and "World
Politics in an Age of Revolution" (1967)**

MacArthur had condemned the Administration's Korean and Chinese policy in
forthright and unequivocal terms. "I was operating in what I call a vacuum. I could
hardly have been said to be in opposition to policies which I was not aware of even.
I don't know what the policy is now." No doubt MacArthur overstated his case
somewhat for dramatic effect, but his words illustrate the intensity of his frustration after Communist China's intervention. Washington was fighting an accordion
war—up and down—at a "staggering" cost. "It isn't just dust that is settling in
Korea . . . it is American blood." His own plan, he maintained, would be decisive,
and it would quickly achieve the desired results—victory in the field, a united

Reprinted by permission of the publishers from John W. Spanier, *The Truman-MacArthur
Controversy and the Korean War* (Cambridge, Mass.: The Belknap Press of Harvard University
Press, Copyright, 1959, by the President and Fellows of Harvard College), pp. 239-256. Foot-
notes omitted.

Korea, and an end to hostilities. His only requirement was that the restrictions, imposed upon him by the politicians in Washington should be lifted. It is to these two themes—the Administration's indetermination and his own resolution—to which MacArthur constantly returned. His course was positive; Truman's negative. He stood for victory; the President for stalemate. The choice was clear, the alternatives simple.

The Truman Administration, not unnaturally, saw MacArthur's strategy in a different light. It would, as Secretary of State Acheson emphasized, accept the "large risk of war with China, risk of war with the Soviet Union, and a demonstrable weakening of our collective-security system—all this in return for what? In return for measures whose effectiveness in bringing the conflict to an early conclusion are judged doubtful by our responsible military authorities." The United States could not, therefore, allow its field commander's desire to achieve military victory in a local area to govern its entire global foreign policy, particularly since his strategic recommendations were militarily unfeasible and politically undesirable.

To clarify these points, to emphasize them, and then once more to re-emphasize them, the Administration brought an impressive array of witnesses before the Senate committee: Secreatry of Defense Marshall, the Joint Chiefs of Staff, the Secretary of State, and ex-Secretary of Defense Louis Johnson. Altogether, they testified for almost a month, from May 7 to June 7 (1951). MacArthur had testified for three days.

During his days on the witness stand, MacArthur had argued that his military program to defeat Communist China had received the endorsement of the Joint Chiefs of Staff, and that the limitations imposed upon him were political. The Joint Chiefs quickly denied both of these notions. They made it quite clear that they had opposed an extension of the war on strictly military grounds; in other words, their professional opinion was that MacArthur's program was militarily impracticable. Perhaps the most important military testimony in this respect came from the Air Force Chief of Staff. . . .

In declaring his opposition to the bombing of Manchuria, General Vandenberg prefaced his remarks with the comment that the role of air power was not well understood in the United States. Strategic air power, he said, should be employed only for the destruction of the enemy's industrial centers. He did not doubt that the air force could lay waste the cities of Communist China and Manchuria, but the result might not be conclusive. In war, there could first of all be no guarantee, no certainty. More important, Communist China's arsenals lay in the Soviet Union; despite large-scale bombing of Manchuria and continental China, therefore, the Russians would still be in a position to supply the weapons of war from across the Manchuria border.

Destruction of Red Chinese and Manchurian cities would, in addition, require "full" application of the Strategic Air Command's power. Anything less would be unable to achieve the task, since the rate of attrition would be too high. The air force would lose planes and crews more quickly than they could be replaced. The resulting loss would deprive the air arm of its capacity for "massive retaliation" against the Soviet Union. ". . . The United States Air Force, if used as a whole, can lay waste Manchuria and (the) principal cities of China, but . . . the attrition that would inevitably be brought about upon us would leave us, in my opinion, as a Nation, naked for several years to come . . ." The bombing of Manchuria would require twice the number of bombers then available to the Strategic Air Command. Under present circumstances, therefore, the air force could not afford to "peck at the periphery." SAC must be kept ready for its principal role—to deter the Soviet Union from attack and to preserve the global balance of power; or, if it did not succeed in this task, to destroy the heart of international Communism's power, the Soviet Union's industrial complex. . . .

It was, therefore, better to concentrate on the 200 miles of supply line in North Korea—"we can exercise very concentrated attacks on that supply line. If you extend the length another hundred miles back into Manchuria, you can get certain other bases, but with the same air power you would thin out your present attacks against the 200 miles of supply line that is Korea."

Not only could the country not afford to attack Manchuria because the rate of attrition which the air force would suffer would undermine its deterrent capacity, but "going it alone" would seriously affect its over-all strength in another way. If we "went it alone" in Asia, we probably would have to "go it alone" in Europe. This would deprive the United States of its bases in both Europe and North Africa. The advantages of keeping these bases were obvious. . . . Vandenberg estimated that minus its overseas bases, the United States would require an air force five to six times the size it at present possessed. European bases, while not therefore "absolutely essential," were "highly desirable."

An economic blockade too would be limited in its effectiveness in bringing enough pressure to bear upon Communist China to quickly end the war. The limitation was, according to Admiral Sherman, dictated by two factors. The first consideration was the nature and stage of Communist China's economic development. This was still sufficiently lacking in industrialization and specialization that a blockade would not have the same immediate impact as it would on a more highly industrialized country. A blockade could only be an effective long-run weapon.

The second consideration limiting the effectiveness of a blockade of Communist China was the thoroughness with which China could be cut off from the essential supplies she had to import. The long Sino-Russian border would make any blockade incomplete. Admiral Sherman stressed that the loss of imports enforced by a naval blockade would force Communist China to rely more upon the Soviet Union, and thereby place an increasing drain on both the Soviet economy and the Trans-Siberian railroad. This long railway, which was subject to easy disruption by bombing, sabotage, or naval raiding parties, was already overtaxed and could not therefore adequately replace the supplies stopped on the sea; moreover, it could attempt to do so only at the expense of supplying the Soviet Union's own forces in the Far East. The other members of the Joint Chiefs were less optimistic than Admiral Sherman. General Bradley, the chairman of the Joint Chiefs, qualified Sherman's analysis: the Trans-Siberian railroad could handle 17,000 tons a day in addition to its own tonnage-maintenance requirements. Russia had also built up supply depots and certain war industries to relieve the railway of some of its load during wartime. The implication was clear: Russian forces in the Far East had a "considerable military capacity": they could for a time get along with fewer supplies. This available tonnage could be switched to supply Communist China.

A blockade by itself could not, therefore, speedily terminate hostilities. A blockade could necessarily yield only slow results since it relied for effects principally on starvation and attrition. Only if combined with other military measures, such as air bombardment, could a naval blockade yield immediate results; short of such supplementary means, a blockade could not seriously hamper China's capacity to continue its conduct of the war. The Admiral also emphasized that the key to an effective United Nations naval blockade would be the wholehearted cooperation of our allies. Any effective blockade must include Port Arthur and Dairen, over which the Soviet Union exercised certain military rights and privileges under the Sino-Soviet treaty. The Russians would "very probably" demand unimpeded access to both ports; stopping her ships might provoke her entry into the war. "If the United Nations should declare a naval blockade, the Russians would probably respect it, as they did the United Nations blockade of Korea. If the United States should declare a blockade unilaterally, the Russians might not respect it, and it is conceivable that they might oppose it by force."

The implication of Admiral Sherman's words is clear: a unilateral blockade by the United States would signify the isolation of this country from its allies. Since this would for all practical purposes neutralize the United States Air Force, Moscow might be tempted to break the blockade of Aairen and Port Arthur. With NATO's massive retaliation nonexistent, the Strategic Air Command could, in the event of war, operate at only 15 to 20 per cent of its effectiveness. If, on the other hand, the United States imposed the blockade in cooperation with its Atlantic allies, any Soviet counteraction would risk the possibility of an immediate reaction by NATO, or more specifically, American strategic air power based on Western European and North African soil. "The fact is that our allies have been unwilling to join in a naval blockade of China, and have been slow to establish a tight economic blockade."

Another reason for the need of a United Nations blockade was equally obvious; most of the strategic imports and ships carrying goods to Communist China bore the flags of non-Communist United Nations members. Sherman recommended that greater effort be concentrated on increasing the effectiveness of the economic blockade. In recent weeks, he said, United States efforts along these lines had been successful. The British government had prohibited any further sales of rubber for the rest of the year, and the General Assembly had on May 18 by a vote of forty-five to four approved a resolution calling for an embargo on arms, ammunition, petroleum, and other materials of war, although as Secretary Acheson stressed, "Many countries were already doing this . . . ; others were not."

In expanding this point, Acheson emphasized that . . . the "facts show there already exists on the part of the major industrial countries of the free world an economic embargo with respect to materials of primary strategic significance." The economic blockade made the naval blockade much less important. "I think it is clear that we cannot get nations to go further in regard to a naval blockade than they are willing to go on an economic blockade, since it is a more drastic sanction."

Thus the Administration, particularly its military advisers, doubted the efficacy of winning the Korean War through the application of air power and the imposition of a naval blockade. MacArthur had always denied that his prescription would need few (many?) extra ground troops. General Collins, Army Chief of Staff, did not agree. The successful implementation of MacArthur's strategy would require the United States to send "considerably" more troops to Korea. General Bradley, indeed, thought that a decision could be effected only if American troops were actually sent into China proper. . . . The Communist army in Korea could be decimated; but it could not be defeated without hitting its center of power. The air force and navy could hamper China's capacity to fight; but they could not destroy it. If there were no alternative to military victory, there could also be no substitute to military invasion and occupation. MacArthur had himself recognized at the time of the North Korean aggression that air and naval forces alone would not suffice to halt the Communist attack; ground troops would be needed. If this was true for a Soviet satellite, it was certainly true for Communist China.

In any case, even if it were not necessary to employ American troops inside continental China, large reinforcements would be needed. An all-out war with Communist China would require "substantially" more naval, air, and ground power, as well as an increase in supply and service troops to support the forces at the front. These could not, however, be furnished without a more intensive program of mobilization and greater effort to produce the ammunition and other implements of war.

Could these troops not be supplied by Nationalist China? The Joint Chiefs thought not. Chiang would need his troops to safeguard Formosa; and his soldiers were anything but first-class. General MacArthur's mission to Formosa had "indicated a state of readiness which didn't seem to be conducive of successful action by those troops. . . ." The Nationalist troops "had very limited capabilities, particularly for offensive action. As General MacArthur himself pointed out, they would have to have almost complete logistical support from ourselves, transportation furnished . . . their leadership, equipment, and training were all of such a state that they would be of limited use in offensive operations." Any diversionary action against continental China would, in addition, require excessive United States naval and air support—excessive, that is, to the returns that could be expected from such an investment. Nor was the reason purely the military's unfavorable estimate of

Chiang's troops. Of greater importance, although not explicitly stated during the hearings, was the Administration's evaluation of Chiang Kai-shek's political prospects on the continent. The only circumstances under which Nationalist troops might reconquer vast portions of China, if not the whole mainland, would be if upon their landing, the Chinese Communist army rallied to Chaing Kai-shek as the French people and the Bourbon army had rallied to Napoleon upon his return to French soil from Corsica. In the Administration's opinion, it was precisely this confidence of the masses which Chiang lacked; its loss had accounted for his defeat in the first place, for his fall in four short years from "the undisputed leader" of the Chinese people to a "refugee" on a small island off the coast of China. It was extremely doubtful that a year's absence had restored the Chinese people's affection for their old leader.

There was, in short, no substitute for American troops. But concentrating American armed power in Korea meant stripping other areas of their forces, lowering the deterrent to Soviet intervention in these parts of the world, and increasing their vulnerability to attack. In fact, the attrition of American military strength, particularly air and ground strength, might well deprive the United States of its ability to counter emergencies elsewhere, and perhaps even weaken the United States sufficiently to attract a Soviet attack. This country could not therefore afford to engage "too much of our power in an area that is not the critical strategic prize." Yet, this is precisely what MacArthur's strategy would entail; nothing would probably delight the Kremlin more. It would, in General Bradley's famous phrase, "involve us in the wrong war, at the wrong place, at the wrong time, and with the wrong enemy."

Indeed, it might also involve us with the right enemy, since bombing Communist China and inflicting a severe defeat upon the Soviet Union's closest and strongest ally would probably leave the Kremlin no alternative but to intervene. As Secretary Acheson said:

We know of soviet influence in North Korea, of Soviet assistance to the North Koreans and to Communist China, and we know that understandings must have accompanied this assistance. We also know that there is a treaty between the Soviets and the Chinese Communists. But even if this treaty did not exist, China is the Soviet Union's largest and most important satellite. Russian self-interest in the Far East and the necessity of maintaining prestige in the Communist sphere make it difficult to see how the Soviet Union could ignore a direct attack upon the Chinese mainland.

To be sure, General MacArthur had argued that the Soviet Union would not intervene if the United States and its allies acted with determination and without hesitation; the Administration, however, remembered that he had said the same thing just before Communist China had entered the battle. (It might have added that MacArthur's foresight had proven itself equally fallible on other occasions. In 1939, he had declared Japan would not attack the Philippines; proponents of such a view, he had said, failed to understand "the logic of the Japanese mind." If Japan did covet the islands, however, his Filipino forces would prove themselves more than a match for the invading army. In early 1941, he had doubted that the Japanese would commit suicide by attacking as mighty a naval power as the United States, but if Japan should launch such an attack, American, British, and Dutch forces could handle her with half the forces they then had in the Far East!) Admittedly, the Administration had shared MacArthur's mistaken estimate of Peking's intentions before November 24; but it was unwilling to take a second chance. "I cannot accept the assumption," said Secretary Acheson, "that the Soviet Union will go its way regardless of what we do. I do not think that Russian policy is formed that way any more than our own policy is formed that way. This view is certainly not well enough grounded to justify a gamble with the essential security of our Nation."

There were a number of courses the Russians could follow. Acheson believed that "They could turn over to the Chinese large numbers of planes with 'volunteer' crews for retaliatory action in Korea and outside. They might participate with the Soviet Air Force and the submarine fleet." or, the "Kremlin could elect to parallel the action, taken by Peiping and intervene with a half million or more ground-force 'volunteers'; or it could go the whole way and launch an all-out war. Singly, or in combination, these reactions contain explosive possibilities, not only for the Far East, but for the rest of the world as well."

Hostilities with the Soviet union at the present time had, however, to be avoided. Not only was a war unnecessary because Soviet imperialism had been contained and denied the fruits of its aggression; it was also undesirable because the United States might have to fight such a war alone. Our allies, as Secretary Acheson said,

> are understandably reluctant to be drawn into a general war in the Far East—one which holds the possibilities of becoming a world war—particularly if it developed out of an American impatience with the progress of the effort to repel aggression, an effort which in their belief offers an honorable and far less catastrophic solution. . . .

Allied fears of a large-scale war in the Far East and a corresponding shift of American power from Eurpoe to the opposite side of the world—or World War III, which would probably see the Russians occupying their countries—were not the only reason for Washington's reluctance to test MacArthur's opinions about Soviet intentions. Even if the United States were willing to "go it alone" and alienate its allies, it had to resist this temptation for one simple reason—the United States was unready to fight a global war. . . . General Bradley was . . . emphatic: "I would not be a proponent of a policy which would ignore the military facts and rush us headlong into a showdown before we are ready."

Even in Asia, the Russians possessed the capacity to intervene and put up a good fight; contrary to General MacArthur's opinion, Administration witnesses considered Soviet power in the Far East "a very serious matter." They had "many thousands of planes in the other areas of Vladivostok, Dairen-Port Arthur, in Harbin, Manchuria, and troop concentrations as Sakhalin near to Japan." The Russians had over the past few years also been building up their Far Eastern industries, and they had "undoubtedly" been accumulating sufficient supplies to sustain their divisions "for a considerable length of time."

Refusal to accept MacArthur's military program did not, therefore, in the opinion of the chairman of the Joint Chiefs, constitute "appeasement."

There are those who deplore the present military situation in Korea and urge us to engage Red China in a larger war to solve this problem. Taking on Red China is not a decisive move, does not guarantee the end of the war in Korea, and may not bring China to her knees. We have only to look back to the five long years when the Japanese, one of the greatest military powers of that time, moved into China and had almost full control of a large part of China, and yet were never able to conclude that war successfully. I would say from past history one would only jump from a smaller conflict to a larger deadlock at greater expense. My own feeling is to avoid such an engagement if possible because victory in Korea would not be assured and victory over Red China would be many years away . . .

Some critics of our strategy say if we do not immediately bomb troop concentration points and airfields in Manchuria, it is "appeasement." If we do not immediately set up a blockade of Chinese ports—which to be successful would have to include British and Russian ports—it is appeasement. These same critics would say that if we do not provide the logistical support and air and naval assistance to launch Chinese Nationalist troops into China it is "appeasement."

These critics ignore the vital questions:

Will these actions if taken, actually assure victory in Korea?

Do these actions mean prolongation of the war by bringing Russia into the fight?

Will these actions strip us of our allies in Korea and in other parts of the world?

From a military viewpoint, appeasement occurs when you give up something, which is rightfully free, to an aggressor without putting up a struggle, or making him pay a price. Forsaking Korea—withdrawing from the fight unless we are forced out—would be an appeasement to aggression. Refusing to enlarge the quarrel to the point where our global capabilities are diminished, is certainly not appeasement but is a militarily sound course of action under the present circumstances.

Did the rejection of MacArthur's program mean that the Administration would continue to "go on as before"? Would it continue to sacrifice American lives, as MacArthur had charged, "without justified purpose..? The answer to the first question was "yes," to the second "no." American lives in Korea had not been sacrificed in vain.

The operation in Korea has been a success. Both the North Koreans and the Chinese Communists declared it to be their purpose to drive the United Nations forces out of Korea and impose Communist rule throughout the entire peninsula. They have been prevented from accomplishing their objective.

It has been charged that the American and allied forces in Korea are engaged in a pointless and inconclusive struggle.

Nothing could be further from the fact. They have been magnificent. Their gallant, determined, and successful fight has checked the Communist advance and turned it into a retreat. They have administered terrible defeats to the Communist forces. In so doing, they have scored a powerful victory.

Their victory has dealt Communist imperialist aims in Asia a severe setback.

The alluring prospect for the Communist conspiracy in June 1950—the prospect of a quick and easy success which would not only win Korea for the Kremlin but shake the free notions of Asia and paralyze the defense of Europe—all this has evaporated.

But the achievements gained by the United States and her friends were not simply negative:

Instead of weakening the rest of the world, they have solidified it. They have given a more powerful impetus to the military preparations of this country and its associates in and out of the North Atlantic Treaty Organization.

We have doubled the number of our men under arms, and the production of material has been boosted to a point where it can begin to have a profound effect on the maintenance of the peace.

The idea of a collective security has been put to the test, and has been sustained. The nations who believe in collective security have shown that they can stick together and fight together.

New urgency has been given the negotiation of a peace with Japan, and of initial security arrangements to build strength in the Pacific area.

These are some of the results of the attack on Korea, unexpected by—and I am sure most unwelcome to—the Kremlin.

Korea had thus been a success. But how could fighting now be ended? Could this really be achieved without carrying the war into China as General MacArthur had recommended? Could the hostilities actually be concluded without risking the dire consequences pointed out by the government's witnesses? Their testimony seemed to suggest that the United States would continue to fight indefinitely, that is until Communist China finally tired of the war; this impression, needless to say, was not welcome to the American public, and must be attributed largely to the Administration's inability to clarify the nature of previous cold-war clashes and their relationship to the present war in Korea.

A comprehensive presentation of Administration policy would have clarified that in each of the East-West conflicts which had preceded Korea, both sides had aimed only at limited objectives and pursued these aims by limited means. The Soviet rulers had in no case aimed at a knock-out blow of the Western powers, since this purpose could have been achieved only by means of total war. Each Communist challenge had been met by the Western powers, particularly the United States, with an equally limited response; the West, too, had been reluctant to resort to global hostilities.

Each side had been unwilling to precipitate atomic warfare. The almost equal distribution of power between them and the very destructiveness of modern weapons had limited the objectives which they could safely seek. Both blocs had therefore surrendered the notion that they could impose their respective wills upon one another; neither pursued total military victory nor unconditional surrender.

The means, in short, had limited the end, and necessity had become the mother of moderation. Consequently, the Administration believed: first, that the United States must restrain its efforts to counter expansionist Soviet moves to the restoration of the *status quo;* and second, that the Soviet government acted upon the assumption that if the Western nations resisted its thrusts successfully, it was safest to break off the engagement and accept the pre-crisis situation. In this context, the American government viewed the intermittent American-Soviet trials of strength as a series of conflicts whose aim it was to determine the precise location of the boundary which divided the Communist states from the free world; American containment would allow no further Russian encroachment beyond this line, and Soviet imperialism could satisfy its ambitions only as the risk of all-out war. . . .

Korea fell into the same category as Berlin. It was "only the latest challenge in this long, hard, continuing world-wide struggle. We are applying there the same policy that has been successfully applied in the attempted aggressions that preceded it elsewhere in the world." This war, too, was being fought under certain ground rules. The Chinese Communists possessed a "privileged sanctuary" in Manchuria, but the United States possess a similar sanctuary in Japan, Okinawa, and South Korea, particularly around the main port of Pusan. "They are not bombing our ports and supply installations," said General Bradley, "and they are not bombing our troops."

The objective too was limited. The purpose of the fighting was to restore the situation that had existed before the North Korean attack on June 25, 1950. When Senator Alexander Smith said that he was "a little bit confused" by the idea of "stopping where we began," Acheson replied:

> Senator, if you accomplish what you started out to do, I don't think that is synonymous with saying you stopped where you began.
>
> We started out to do two things. One is repel the armed attack and the other is to restore peace and security in the area.
>
> Now, if we do these two things, we have done what we started out to do, and I should think that is success

Thus, without admitting outrightly that the Administration had abandoned the goal of a militarily unified Korea, the Secretary of State informed the Communists that it was willing to call a cease-fire on the 38th Parallel. The price of a united Korea was too high; the *status quo* was therefore acceptable.

To be sure, Acheson had always insisted that the United States had never harbored any other aim, but this explanation will not withstand critical examination. That the attempt to unify Korea by force had been made, but that circumstances had necessitated acceptance of the present solution, is evident from General Bradley's testimony:

> General Bradley . . . as we went farther north and the United Nations again came out with a resolution to establish a unified Korea, united and free Korea; that was the mission they gave to General MacArthur in late September. (Actually the United Nations resolution was approved on October 7, though Bradley is correct when he says that the mission was originally assigned to MacArthur by Washington in late September.)
>
> Senator Cain. And yet to carry out that mission from a military point of view or that objective from a political point of view, it will, before we are through, if we do not change that mission, be required to defeat the enemy and to repel him, not from South Korea but we must repel the enemy from Korea, or otherwise, sir, how can we make Korea a free, independent, and democratic nation?
>
> General Bradley. Well, I think we could have an intermediate military objective . . .

In late September and early October, the Administration had argued that the parallel had to be crossed to safeguard South Korea's security; for if North Korea were not defeated, South Korea might be subjected to a further attack at some future date when the enemy had recovered his strength and reorganized his army. Administration witnesses did not repeat this argument after Communist China's

intervention, even though the threat to South Korea's future existence remained—
only, of course, on a more potent scale. This time they explained that although a
cease-fire on the 38th Parallel would only reaffirm the position that had existed at
the time of the initial challenge, it could be made to contain safeguards to deter
another invasion. Why such an arrangement had not been considered in October of
1950 was not said; but the implication was that it had not then been a question of
accepting such a cease-fire or nothing. The opportunity for a militarily united
Korea had been rendered possible by the destruction of the North Korean army.
Circumstances had not changed. The *status quo* had been restored at the 38th
Parallel and the Administration was willing to call an end to the fighting on this
line.

There remained only one question: would the Chinese Communists, as the
Russians before them, settle on the basis of the 38th Parallel, the line from which
the North Korean advance had originally started? Secretary Acheson believed they
would, although he could not predict the time when this would happen. But Berlin
had taken fifteen months to settle; Greece eighteen months; Korea was then in its
tenth month. Hope for an early finish of the fighting, however, was good for several
reasons. First, "the offensives of the enemy have been broken and thrown back
with enormous enemy casualties. These defeats . . . present grave problems for the
Communist authorities in China. While the manpower resources of China are vast,
its supply of trained men is limited. They cannot cover up their casualties. They
cannot gloss over the draft of more and more men for military service." Second, the
"Chinese Red leaders have betrayed their long-standing pledge of demobilization
and the military demand for man power has, instead, been increased." And third,
"Peiping has also broken its promises of social and economic improvement. In the
great cities, dependent on imported materials, unemployment increases. The regime
has not lightened the burdens of the people. It has made them heavier." The
dissatisfaction caused by this increasing toll of dead and injured, as well as by the
broken pledges, were already "reflected in a sharp increase in repressive measures,
and in propaganda to whip up the flagging zeal of their own people. In the light of
all these factors," Acheson concluded, "I believe that the aggression can best be
brought to an end with a minimum risk and a minimum loss, by continuing the
punishing defeat of the Chinese in Korea." The infliction of heavy casualties on the
Chinese army, the destruction of its morale and "trained fabric" would, in other
words, bring the Chinese Communists to negotiate an end to hostilities without the
risk of World War III.

Shortly after Acheson made this statement, the Communists made their first
move to end the war. On June 23, 1951, the Russian delegate to the United
Nations, Jacob Malik, intimated that the Soviet Union was ready for a cease-fire in
Korea. The Communists, therefore, having also tried unsuccessfully to conquer the
entire Korean peninsula, had finally decided to incorporate the stalemate on the

38th Parallel into the almost global stalemate along the line determined in previous engagements.

The meek had inherited; they had restored the Republic of Korea to its prewar boundaries; they had managed to avoid an enlarged war and its attendant dangers in the Far East; they had preserved the unity of the Atlantic community and through the rearmament program increased their power several times; and they had husbanded their strength to balance Russian power and to create "unassailable barriers" in the path of Soviet expansion. They had refused to dissipate their military power on the periphery of the Communist empire, but had conserved it for its primary function, the continued denial of Communist ambitions and the encouragement of trends within the Soviet political and social system which would so increase its strains and stresses that they would moderate the ambitions of its leaders.

It was this article of faith upon which the Administration's case, in the final analysis, rested: Soviet imperialism could be contained without the horror of another global conflict, that the indefinite frustration of the Kremlin's appetite could cause the regime to become more accommodating and negotiate outstanding issues, and to accept a live-and-let-live attitude based upon the realities of military strength and the necessity of compromising with power. "For no mystical, Messianic movement—and particularly not that of the Kremlin," George Kennan had predicted, "can face frustration indefinitely without eventually adjusting itself in one way or another to the logic of that state of affairs." United States containment policy, therefore, "has it in its power to increase enormously the strains under which Soviet policy must operate, to force upon the Kremlin a far greater degree of circumspection than it has had to observe in recent years, and in this way to promote tendencies which must eventually find their outlet in either the break-up or the gradual mellowing of Soviet power." Or, as Secretary Acheson expressed it during the hearings: ". . . what we must do is to create situations of strength, then I think that the whole situation in the world begins to change so far as the potentialities of the Soviet Union being able to achieve its present purposes is concerned; and with that change there comes a difference in the negotiating positions of the various parties, and out of that I should hope that there would be a willingness on the side of the Kremlin to recognize the facts which have been created by this effort of ours and to begin to solve at least some of the difficulties between east and west." Time, in short, *was* on the side of the United States and her allies—if the Western powers could remain united, contain further Communist expansion, and preserve the balance of power on the basis of the *status quo*.

Chapter 9 THE AMERICAN PEOPLE WERE INCREASINGLY DISSATISFIED

*In the article that follows, two specialists in
international politics and military strategy,
ALVIN J. COTTRELL and JAMES E.
DOUGHERTY, take issue with the Truman
administration's conduct of the Korean War,
even while they do not give unequivocal
support to General MacArthur's proposals.
In what sense, in the authors' opinion, was
the so-called "atomic question" a false issue
in the context of the Korean War? How do
the authors differ with Spanier in their
assessment of the meaning and result of the
Communists' decision to seek a truce in the
summer of 1951? Would you say that events
in Indochina after 1951 tended to confirm
Cottrell and Dougherty's evaluation of the
long-term effects of the Korean war? To
confirm Mao Tse-tung's writings, "On the
Protracted War"?*

The Korean War represented a crucial turning point in the struggle between the communists and the Free World. The manner of the American response to the North Korean attack demonstrated to the communists the West's ability to react swiftly and decisively to an act of outright aggression. But more important still, the Korean War revealed the inadequacy of Western democratic governments to deal with a conflict situation which is protracted and kept indecisive. It was the experience of this war, more than any other single factor, which has given rise ... to the debate over the readiness of the United States to wage so-called "limited wars." This debate, insofar as it has centered upon the size and the mobility of American

From Alvin J. Cottrell and James E. Dougherty, "The Lessons of Korea: War and the Power of Man," *Orbis*, II (Spring 1958), pp. 39-65. Footnotes omitted. Reprinted by permission of *Orbis*, a quarterly journal of world affairs by the Foreign Policy Research Institute, Philadelphia, Pa.

tactical forces on the periphery of the Sino-Soviet bloc, completely misses the crucial point: namely that the problem of waging "limited war" is essentially not one of military power but of political will.

Through the years 1950-1953, the United States was, in terms of sheer military power, the superior contestant. Narrow limits were indeed imposed upon the Korean conflict, but "it was obviously the stronger Power which imposed them and made them stick." It is fair to ask whether the United States, if it had in being all of the elaborate force levels called for by contemporary proponents of the "limited war" doctrine, would even now be able to avoid a repetition of Korea. Since the memory of the Korean War, with all its bitter frustrations, continues to permeate American thinking in the present discussion on weapons policy, a review of United States strategy in that war may serve to remind us that mere possession of the requisite military power does not provide, by itself, an answer to our problem: namely how to meet the intermediate—"limited"—challenges of the communists.

Imposed Limitations on the War

The Korean War has been the only military conflict directly involving the United States and members of the communist bloc. The conflict was limited in several ways: The hostilities were confined to a precise geographical area. The nearby territory of Formosa was "neutralized" and the territory north of the Yalu River was delcared off limits. The war was limited with regard to the nationality of the forces eligible to participate, for the armed forces of the Nationalist Chinese Government, a member of the Security Council, which urged U.N. members to resist the aggression, were not allowed to take part in the action. Furthermore, the war was limited as to weapons employed, types of targets selected and kinds of supplementary operations undertaken. Thus, weapons of mass destruction were not used; the rail and supply line of the Chinese communists were not hit; and long range American aerial reconnaissance was ruled out.

It is significant that none of these limitations were or could have been forced upon the United States by the enemy. They all were voluntarily assumed by the United States. The reasons given for accepting these limitations were various, but practically all of them were reducible to fears of one sort or another: fear that the United States would alienate its European allies by prosecuting too vigorously a war in Asia; fear of antagonizing the Asian neutrals if Chiang's forces were utilized; and, above all, fear that the war, if it was not rigidly localized, would become general and global.

The difficulties encountered by the United States during the Korean War sprang in the first instance from a failure to view the struggle against the total strategic background. Probably the communists themselves did not foresee the full strategic implication of the border crossing on June 24, 1950, and they may not have anticipated the prompt response of the United States and the U.N. Security Council. The United States entered the war for definite enough a purpose: the defense of a free nation against flagrant communist aggression. At the outset, the United States and its friends in the United Nations were under no misapprehension as to the fundamental issues, political and moral, raised by the attack on South Korea.

. . . By October of 1950, when U.N. forces began their offensive to the Yalu, the General Assembly went beyond the original objective of merely defending South Korea and defined the U.N.'s goal as the establishment of a "unified, independent and democratic government in the sovereign state of Korea." This policy statement was intended and interpreted as an authorization for General MacArthur to move northward to the Yalu River.[1] In the same month, the situation changed ominously when the Chinese communists began to pour into Korea. Then the Korean War began to assume a different meaning: MacArthur called it an "entirely new war." The West was slow to evaluate the strategic consequences of the conflict with Communist China. Since the war had started over the Korean question, Western diplomats and commentators persisted in regarding it as a war over Korea, in which the additional features of Chinese communist intervention now had to be taken into account. A mental block obscured the full significance of the fact that the war was now between Communist China and the United States. It took the communists four months—from June to October 1950— to develop a novel strategy for turning Korea to their own strategic advantage.

Once the Chinese were in the fight, the unity of purpose of the United States and its allies in the U.N. began to flag. While India began to view Korea as an arena of the Cold War in which she vowed to be neutral, Great Britain "became anxious to minimize her responsibility for sponsoring the decisive resolution" concerning MacArthur's authority to cross the 38th Parallel.

Once it was known that China was the antagonist, what were the decisions to be made by the United States? Some of these decisions, by their very nature, could not even be faced unless the United States formulated for itself a reasonably clear picture of the over-all Sino-Soviet strategy in Asia. Policy-making flows from analysis, and analysis hinges on framing the right questions. Several questions had to be asked, and at least hypothetical answers had to be given to them. There is some cause for wondering whether American policy-makers did pose the right questions in October 1950. Why did Communist China enter the Korean War? Did she come in enthusiastically to defend herself against an American-U.N.-dominated Korea on her border, or did she come in somewhat reluctantly and fearfully as a result of Soviet cajolery, pressure and promises? Was Mao Tse-tung confident of his estimate of the Korean situation before committing himself? Or did he use the gradual build-up of "volunteer" forces during October to probe his enemy and thus to gauge the Western reaction to his move? Was Stalin prepared to divert sizable and much-needed resources from the Soviet Union to support the Chinese in the event of large-scale fighting? Were the communists prepared to face atomic conflict? What were the strategic implications of China's move for American interests in Japan,

Formosa, Indochina, and elsewhere? What did the communist bloc really stand to gain in Korea? How great and how genuine was the danger that the Korean tinder-box would spark a world conflagration? What was the relation of American objectives in the Far East to American objectives in the NATO community? These and similar questions impinged upon the decisions which had to be made in the fall of 1950, particularly those concerning the role of Chiang's army, the application of an economic and naval blockade to China, going beyond the Yalu and using atomic weapons.

The gravest American error in Korea was the failure to respond decisively during the first few days of the Chinese communist intervention. Since the United States temporized in the face of Mao Tse-tung's probingly cautious, "unoffical" entry into the war, Mao was able gradually to build up his ground forces in North Korea. The initiative passed out of American hands, and the war became prolonged. The longer the war dragged on, the more often the debate within the United States over the Korean War raised the specter of general war. Whenever it was suggested that the United States take steps to regain the military initiative, the proposals were invariably rejected on the grounds that they involved the danger either of provoking general war or of offending the friends of the United States. The major proposals put forth for regaining the initiative concerned the use of Chiang Kai-shek's Nationalist forces on Formosa, the application of a blockade against China, operations beyond the Yalu River and the introduction of atomic weapons.

The Use of Chiang's Forces

There may have been justification for the neutralization of Chiang's forces on Formosa by executive order of June 27, 1950, under which the Seventh Fleet was to protect Formosa and thus restrain Chiang from carrying out air or sea attacks against the mainland. Secretary of State Dean Acheson had argued that if Chinese troops from Taiwan were to join the U.N. forces in Korea, the Red Chinese might decide to enter the conflict precisely to weaken Chiang's army and thus diminish his capability of defending the island against a potential communist assault. Another and perhaps the most important reason for the U.S. refusal to permit Chiang's participation was, in a sense, a political one, imposed upon the United States by foreign sentiment and by its own reluctance to offend that sentiment. It was summed up succinctly by W. Averell Harriman in the report which he gave to President Truman on his meeting with General MacArthur in early August 1950:

> He [General MacArthur] did not seem to consider the liability that our support of Chiang on such a move would be to us in the Far East. I explained in great detail why Chiang was a liability and the great danger of a split in the unity of the United Nations on the Chinese-Communist-Formosa policies; the attitude

of the British, Nehru and such countries as Norway, who, although stalwart in their determination to resist Russian aggression, did not want to stir up trouble elsewhere.

This decision to hold Chiang "under wraps" should have come in for review and modification as soon as Chinese intervention loomed seriously on the horizon. The argument about non-interference in the Chinese Civil War, if it ever had any validity, lost all its effectiveness in October 1950. When intelligence reports were received through Indian and British diplomatic channels concerning an impending Chinese military move into Korea, "intelligence reports" should have immediately been filtered through the same channels to the communists concerning an impending "deneutralization" of Formosa. Had this been done, Mao may well have reconsidered his policy of introducing "volunteers," who could conceivably have been recalled and publicly "chastised" for unauthorized activities. The pretext of "volunteers" reflected Mao's extreme caution. October and November 1950 were doubtless the critical months in the Korean War, when Mao scanned carefully American responses to his moves and took the measure of the U.N.'s firmness of purpose. The U.S. might at this point have blocked China from entering the war, and Mao could have recalled the "volunteers" with a minimum loss of face. General MacArthur, at the time of his dismissal, proposed that restrictions be removed from the deployment of Chiang's forces and that these forces be given substantial American logistical support against China. Regardless of how helpful Chiang's army may have been on the Korean peninsula, it is not mere hindsight to conclude that, had the Chinese Nationalists been poised for action across the Formosa Straits, the communists would not have felt free to remove sizable forces from the Fukien area for use in Korea. . . .

Among the arguments often advanced against accepting Chiang's offer of troops was that the United States might unwittingly commit itself to deploying American ground forces to achieve Chiang's major objective: re-establishing the Nationalist Government on the mainland. This reasoning would have us believe that America could not have controlled the scope of its operations on the Chinese mainland, even though it had demonstrated its ability to impose precise limits on its Korean actions. The U.S. certainly could have supplied Chiang with enough material to allow him to carry out diversionary attacks against the Chinese communists without running the risk of being drawn into the morass of China. The United States could have reduced or cut off the aid to Chiang if and when his operations conflicted with American strategic objectives. . . .[2]

Economic Sanctions

The question of invoking economic warfare measures against China raised problems of coalition diplomacy for the United States. There can be little doubt that an intensified application of economic sanctions against Communist China, reinforced by a naval blockade against communist shipping along the coast of China, would have greatly reduced the strength of the Chinese armies in Korea. Admiral Forrest Sherman, Chief of Naval Operations, made this statement during the Senate hearings:

> A naval blockade by the United Nations would substantially reduce the war potential of Communist China. . . . China is not capable of taking countermeasures that could appreciably reduce the effectiveness of such a blockade.
>
> A naval blockade by the United Nations would be advantageous from a psychological standpoint. It would demonstrate to the Chinese Communists, and to the neighboring Asian peoples, the power of the forces against communism—it would demonstrate the effectiveness of sea power, a power that the Chinese communists can do little to thwart.

The general arguments against economic weapons were reducible to one, namely that they could have little effect because of the agricultural character of the Chinese economy and because China would still be able to receive goods from the Soviet bloc. . . .

American allies were firmly opposed to boycott and blockade, because such policies would have hurt their Far East trade, which totals several hundred shiploads per year. Britain, moreover, was concerned over the precarious position of Hongkong. Consequently, the United States was unable to expect its allies to favor General MacArthur's proposal for applying economic sanctions. Nevertheless, the failure to apply sanctions enabled China to protract the conflict without suffering any unusual economic strains. The fact that China was an underdeveloped agrarian nation made her almost totally dependent upon imports for the success of her first five-year plan. Every shipload of goods received in the eastern ports helped to lessen China's need for making demands upon her Soviet ally or the East European satellites. The supply lines from the Soviet Union to Korea, some 4,000 miles in length, were already operating under a heavy strain.

Had the United States been able to persuade all the U.N. members who had branded China as an aggressor to cut off trade with her, the impact of an embargo upon Communist China's economy and war effort would have proved considerable. Mao was, no doubt, agreeably surprised to see that he was free to make strategic moves in Korea without being forced entirely to rely upon his own meager resources and those of his Soviet ally, who was ill-prepared to increase aid shipments. Central to the Chinese communist leader's concept of protracted war is the notion of altering the relative power distribution between oneself and the enemy, strengthening the former and weakening the latter by every available means.

Operations beyond the Yalu

There were two principal suggestions for extending operations beyond the Yalu River. The first was to reconnoiter Manchuria and the Chinese coastal areas. As early as July 1950, the Air Force had contemplated flying high—level photo missions over Dairen, Port Arthur, Vladivostok and the Kuriles. When President Truman heard about these proposed flights over Soviet-controlled territory, he instructed Secretary of the Air Force Finletter not to allow his Far East commanders "to engage in activities that might give the Soviet Union a pretext to come into open conflict with us." This decision to refrain from sweeping reconnaissance over Soviet areas on the Pacific coast may have been justified at the time, although such restraint precluded our gaining the very intelligence needed to corroborate the Central Intelligence Agency estimate that the U.S.S.R. did not intend to intervene on a large scale in the Far East. Certainly, official policy on reconnaissance should have undergone review when it became apparent that General MacArthur's post-Inchon offensive would take U.N. forces into North Korea or, at the very latest, when the State Department learned through Indian and British diplomatic channels that the Chinese communists had made a definite threat to intervene. Had reconnaissance been conducted, the request for authority to bomb the Yalu bridges could have been made in time to hinder the Communist Chinese build-up of massive ground armies in the Korean peninsula. The continued failure to reconnoiter the area above the Yalu even after MacArthur reiterated the need for such operations in the spring of 1951 was indefensible.

The second suggestion for going beyond the Yalu related to actual offensive operations in Manchuria, including "hot pursuit" of communist fighter planes and the bombing of enemy supply routes and industrial centers. It should be made clear that at no time were ground force operations by American forces north of the Yalu contemplated. Air components alone could have executed whatever additional measures the Chinese intervention made imperative.

The limitations which the United States placed upon itself with respect to the use of air power along the Yalu not only prevented the carrying of the war into Manchuria but, furthermore, prevented the U.N. forces from holding their line of farthest advance because it deprived them of maximum effective air support. . . .

The communists held a unique advantage in being able to use Manchuria as a privileged sanctuary into which their MIG's could retreat after attacking American forces in Korea. On November 13, 1950, the State Department wired instructions to its embassies in six nations to inform the allied governments

that it may become necessary at an early date to permit U.N. aircraft to defend themselves in the air space over the Yalu River to the extent of permitting hot pursuit of attacking enemy aircraft up to 2 or 3 minutes' flying time into Manchuria air space.

It is contemplated that U.N. aircraft would limit themselves to repelling enemy aircraft engaged in offensive missions to Korea.

We believe this would be a minimum reaction to extreme provocation, would not in itself affect adversely the attitude of the enemy toward Korean operations, would serve as a warning, and would add greatly to the morale of U.N. Pilots. . . .

The instructions made it clear that the United States was not seeking the concurrence of the governments concerned. Nonetheless, in the face of the "strongly negative responses" received from those governments, the State and Defense Departments decided that the plans for "hot pursuit" ought to be abandoned. On this issue, too, coalition diplomacy came into conflict with tactical operations which were considered necessary or desirable from a military point of view.

After the United States' allies reacted unfavorably to the "hot pursuit" proposals, it was practically a foregone conclusion that General MacArthur's recommendations for more ambitious operations beyond the Yalu, i.e., bombing Manchuria, would be received with even less enthusiasm in the NATO capitals. General MacArthur frequently stressed the fact that his objective was not to extend the scope of ground operations into China itself, but rather to force China to remove herself from the Korean War by the continued application of added pressure on the Chinese supply lines in Manchuria. Nevertheless, Canada's Lester Pearson publicly expressed doubts that his government could participate in any program in Asia involving commitments on the mainland of China, and the British House of Commons carried on a long discussion about war on the Chinese mainland if MacArthur's policies were adopted. Secretary of State Acheson testified to the Senate that he deemed it "highly probable" that the Sino-Soviet agreement of 1950 included a Soviet promise to assist China if the Manchurian Railway were subjected to a bombing attack by a foreign power. Secretary Acheson did admit, however, hat his views on the risk of direct Russian intervention were based on an analysis of Russian self-interest and treaty obligations, not on specific information from intelligence and diplomatic sources concerning Soviet intentions.

The Use of Atomic Weapons

There is no question that of all the proposals advanced for regaining the initiative the suggestion to introduce atomic weapons in Korea was the one fraught with the most serious implications. Despite the fact that by the end of November 1950 approximately 400,000 Chinese had poured into Korea, there were some credible reasons why atomic weapons should not have been used at that time. The American atomic stockpile was then earmarked primarily for use by the Strategic Air Command. The diversion of atomic weapons to Korea might have retarded the build-up of the West's far-flung system of atomic air bases, on which Western deterrent power hinged. Moreover, the technology of tactical atomic weapons and delivery systems had not been developed beyond its earliest stages when the fighting in Korea was at its peak; experiments with low-yield atomic weapons for use against troop concentrations in the immediate battle-zone had scarcely begun. Consequently, Americans and their allies, with the disturbing image of atomic bombs dropped by strategic aircraft on Hiroshima and Nagasaki still vivid in their minds, were unable or unwilling to distinguish between the tactical use of nuclear weapons against enemy armies in the field and their strategic use against urban populations deep in enemy territory.

The West, therefore, cavilled at any suggestion that atomic weapons should or could be used in Korea. In particular the European allies of the United States, more vulnerable to atomic attack than the American Continent, took a less sanguine view of the atomic risks than some American policy-makers. On November 30, 1950, President Truman, perhaps in an effort to bring United States nuclear capability into close support of American diplomacy, hinted at a press conference that the introduction of atomic weapons into the Korean conflict was being discussed. "Naturally, there has been consideration of this subject since the outbreak of the hostilities in Korea, just as there is consideration of the use of all weapons whenever our forces are in combat. Consideration of the use of any weapon is always implicit in the very possession of that weapon." If this guarded reference was intended to frighten the Chinese communists, the effort backfired. Before the news could have any impact on the strategic thinking of the Chinese communist leadership, the British Labour Government reacted to this veiled threat with open concern, and Prime Minister Clement Attlee hurried to Washington in order to obtain Mr. Truman's assurance that the Korean War would remain "conventional." Domestic critics voiced misgivings to the effect that, since the atom bomb had become a popular symbol of cataclysmic destruction, its use under any circumstances would set off an uncontrollable chain of events which would propel the world into an unwanted total war. Others argued that, even if global war would not be touched off by atomic warfare in Korea, the peoples of Asia would be even more deeply offended by a new exhibition of "American contempt for Asian lives" than they had been five years earlier at the time of Hiroshima and Nagasaki.

In retrospect, the American decision to forego the actual use of atomic weapons in Korea was the most defensible of all the negative decisions made in Washington. The "atomic question," in a sense, was a false one, for probably it would never have been raised had other conventional alternatives, which were available for dealing with Communist China's aggression, been adopted with vigor and determination. It was one thing, however, to decide that the United States would not bring to bear its most powerful military weapon upon a given conflict situation; it was quite another thing to forfeit the psychological and political value inherent in the possession of the atomic bomb by communicating such a decision baldly to the enemy. The disclosure of our intentions may well have served to reassure our allies or to placate an ill-informed public incited by irresponsible party politicians and segments of the press. But however much the Western public may have wished to ignore the fact, the Korean War was fought in the atomic age, and one of the contestants in this war was an atomic power. Hence atomic weapons had a role to play in the strategy of the war, even if they were never actually employed.

Today, when nuclear weapons constitute such an important component of the Western defense establishment, it is essential that we read correctly the lessons of the Korean War with regard to the American decision not to use the atomic bomb. For some Americans, who for the first time had occasion to pass prior judgment upon the potential use of atomic weapons, the problem was a moral one. For others the problem was political, since they conceived of it in terms of Asian sentiments or NATO solidarity. These objections were, at least in the context of the Korean War, more logical than those which sprang from a fear that the use of atomic weapons was certain to touch off World War III. There are weighty reasons for concluding that the Soviet Union was willing to be drawn, in 1950-51, into a general war with the West neither in Korea nor, as some people feared, in Europe. In either case, the question confronting the Russians was identical: Were they ready for general war? It is clear now that the time was not at all appropriate for the Kremlin to risk large-scale conflict with the West had the latter applied additional pressure upon Communist China. Stalin was in no position to enter the Korean War openly. His Far East air force was not strong enough to stand a contest of attrition and replacement production with the United States. The Soviet Union, moreover, would have encountered serious logistic difficulties in attempting to establish and supply operational bases in North Korea, some 4,000 miles from the locus of Russian industrial power. Had the United States increased military pressure in Korea, one wonders how long the communist bloc would have attempted to match the West in a war in which technical equipment and material resources (rather than manpower, which was far more expendable for the communists) were being devoured at a steadily increasing rate. The Soviets, had they attempted to intervene massively against the United States in the Far East or launched an attack aginst Western Europe, could not have avoided the type of war which has long been the nightmare both of the Tsarist and bolshevik strategists: a two-front all-out war against a powerful enemy. During World War II, the Kremlin had been at pains to avoid a showdown with the Japanese while holding off the Germans in the West. By contrast, the United States, between 1942 and 1945, was strong enough to take on two powerful enemies on opposite sides of the globe.

Most important of all, Russian atomic stockpiles and strategic delivery capabilities were distinctly inferior to those at the disposal of the U.S. Communist conflict doctrine prescribes the postponement of the all-out, decisive engagement until overwhelming victory is assured. It is, therefore, unlikely that the Soviet Union would have allowed itself to be drawn into a war beyond its borders under circumstances as unfavorable as those surrounding the Korean War. When asked whether the bombing of Manchurian air bases would bring the Soviets into the conflict and thereby touch off World War III, General Mark Clark replied to the Senate Subcommittee investigating the War: "I do not think you can drag the Soviets into a world war except at a time and place of their own choosing. They have been doing too well in the Cold War."

War by Truce: Panmunjom

Despite the limitations which the United States imposed upon itself, it was the consensus of Western observers at the scene that the U.N. forces were on the verge of breaking through the communists' lines in June 1951. At this point, the communists feared that the United States was about to mount a tactical offensive in Korea, supported by the extension of air operations into Manchuria. They switched to a strategy of protracted truce negotiations to prevent being driven out of Korea and to demoralize the West by weakening its will to take up the fight again later. This was the second crucial juncture of the war. Just as the circumspect use of "volunteers" had enabled Mao's forces to enter the war with a minimum risk of provoking a commensurate action by the United States against China, the change-over to truce talks in June 1951 eliminated, for all practical purposes, any further danger that Mao's forces might suffer a serious military reversal. Thus the negotiations provided a perfect alibi for a Chinese withdrawal from the shooting war—with their major units intact and well-trained and with the prestige of having fought the United States to a stalemate. The first American strategic mistake had been the failure to act swiftly in November 1950 to counter the stealthy Chinese entrance into the war; the second major blunder by the United States was the virtual decision to accept the communist demand for a cessation of hostilities prior to the opening of truce negotiations.

Had the U.S. followed the World War I example of continuing the offensive until the armistice was actually signed, the Korean War might well have ended by midsummer of 1951 on much more favorable terms for the Free World and for Korea. Instead, the United States gave the communists an invaluable breathing spell.

Korean Balance Sheet

In the light of the contemporary debate over U.S. military strategy, it is important to review the after-effects of the Korean War. The Chinese communists used the war as a training school in which the most up-to-date technical weapons were available. Thus Korea helped them transform their ill-equipped revolutionary forces into a modern army. Meanwhile, the "Resist America, Aid Korea" campaign conducted by Peking helped considerably to consolidate the new regime at home and to stiffen the political loyalty of the Chinese people. China won and the United States lost considerable prestige in Asia, for this was the first time in history that an

Oriental nation held the technically superior West at bay. The Korean War, more-over, gave tremendous impetus to the international communist campaigns for propagating pacifism, especially through such devices as the Stockholm Peace Appeal, and strengthening neutralism throughout the Arab-Asian world. Neutralist India, originally a supporter of the U.N. decision to counter North Korean aggres-sion, began to sound a strident note of hostility against the United States as soon as Communist China became a contestant; the defense of a small republic then be-came, in Indian eyes, a case of American intervention in Asian affairs. When, in mid-1951, the Soviet Union espoused the role of peacemaker, the Asians seemed to forget entirely that the war had been instigated by a puppet government armed by the Soviets. By manifesting a willingness to settle for a draw in Korea, the West virtually admitted that Communist China's right to intervene in the peninsula was equal to that of the United Nations.

The United States, by waging the kind of war it did in Korea from November 1950 on, allowed the strategic initiative to pass into the hands of an enemy leader who had frequently stressed in his military writings that any army, once it can be forced into a passive position or deprived of its freedom of action, is on the road to defeat. Mao Tse-tung fully realized that the side which enjoys superiority at the outset of the conflict need not retain the initiative throughout the campaign:

> In the course of a struggle, a correct or incorrect command may transform inferiority into superiority or passivity into initiative, and vice versa. . . . The inferior and passive side can wrestle the initiative and victory from the side possessing superiority and the initiative by securing the necessary conditions through active endeavour in accordance with actual circumstances.

One of the most suitable means of achieving superiority and seizing the initiative from the enemy, Mao wrote, is to create illusions in the mind of the enemy, including the illusion that he is up against overwhelming strength. Mao applied his superior understanding of strategic principles in Korea to compensate for the over-whelming superiority of American technological power. Throughout 575 truce meetings, the communist leaders stalled for time. The Chinese communists built up their military power and international support, while the United States suffered all the "internal and external contradictions" which Mao had forecast for all his ene-mies: mounting casualty lists, consumption of war material, decline of troop morale, discontented public opinion at home and the gradual alienation of world opinion.

The United States imposed upon itself a number of severe limitations in con-ducting the Korean War. The motivation for these restraints was largely a political one. American policy-makers hoped that, with a war policy of forbearance unprece-dented in modern history, the United States would earn the respect both of its new

Atlantic allies and the uncommitted peoples. This hope, unfortunately, proved to be an illusory one. The United States built up very little credit either in Europe or in Asia: Americans, in fact, found themselves in the incredible position of having to defend themselves against charges of waging "germ warfare," forestalling the "natural integration" of Formosa with the Chinese Mainland, and preventing the restoration of peace in the Far East by keeping Red China out of the United Nations. While Europeans placed little credence in communist propaganda, most were inclined to blame the United States for placing too much emphasis on the conflict in Korea. Finally, few people in Europe and Asia believed that the United States deserved any praise for limiting the war—for American political leaders, in their efforts to justify the Korean policy, argued frequently that any extension of the war would lead to general war and risk of communist retaliation against the United States. American motives, consequently, were taken to be more selfish than altruistic.

The decision to meet communist aggression in Korea in June 1950 was both courageous and wise. But the United States failed to foresee the future implications of the outcome of the Korean War—that popular political support for all subsequent responses to communist peripheral attacks would to a large extent hinge upon the success of the first direct encounter between American and communist forces.

There can be little question but that Secretary of State Acheson was confronted by serious political problems during the course of the Korean War. The United States had scarcely begun to construct a defense of Europe through the North Atlantic Treaty Organization when the Korean War broke out. The Europeans, especially the British, were inclined to dissociate the crisis in the Far East from their security interests and feared that an American emphasis of Asia might slow down the development of the Atlantic Alliance. The United States, on the other hand, had historically been oriented more towards Asia than Europe, and emerged from World War II as the dominant power in the Pacific. Whereas Great Britain was in the process of reducing her political commitments in Asia, the United States, which had borne the greatest burden among the Western powers in fighting the Axis on both fronts, realized its growing strategic responsibilities in both theaters. This divergence of basic interests in the Western Alliance was aggravated by Mao's entry into the war.

There is no doubt, however, that the success of Communist China was in large measure due to Mao's strategy of delay and attrition. Had the United Nations been able to conclude the war with MacArthur's Inchon offensive, America would have been spared many a diplomatic dilemma. Mao, by entering the Korean War, shored up the faltering regime of North Korea and denied the U.N. a decision with finality. Then, by switching in June 1951 to "attritional" truce talks which lasted for two years, the communists were able to camouflage their flagging capabilities and resources and, at the same time, to wear down the American will to resume the kind of energetic initiative needed to bring the war to a successful conclusion.

The American people were increasingly dissatisfied with the conduct of the Korean War, which they found both frustrating and pointless. After the experience, in the twentieth century, of two world wars, both of which had ended in climactic, overwhelming victories, it was difficult for Americans to readjust their thinking to the notion of a war which, for two years, had to be fought out along the "line of scrimmage." What Americans objected to was not the fact that the war was kept limited, or waged at a level lower than that of a general war, but rather the fact that its limitations whittled down the real superiority of the United States. Since American policymakers had posed a false dilemma—either a protracted stalemate or all-out war—popular opinion within the United States tended to conclude that American conventional forces had been misused in Korea. Perhaps the most serious effect of this was to inhibit the freedom of action of the U.S. policymakers when confronted by subsequent crises in so-called peripheral areas.

The communists, doubtless realizing to what an extent the Korean War had served as a conditioner of the American mind, were able to parlay their psychological gains in Korea into a swift victory in Indochina. A successful prosecution of the war in Korea by the United States might have either convinced the Chinese communists that a new adventure in Indochina should not be risked or, failing this, prepared the American people for intervention in Indochina.

In recent years, far too much criticism has been hurled at the Dulles policy of "massive retaliation" on the grounds that it did not prevent the loss of North Vietnam. Such criticism, unfortunately, does not go to the root of the problem. Most of the critics of the declaratory policy of "massive retaliation" imply that statements of this sort are relatively worthless in meeting the intermediate range of communist military threats and that, first and foremost, the United States needs to increase its tactical force levels to fight limited wars in any part of the globe. Yet the experience of Korea shows clearly that the possession of forces "in being" does not of itself assure an effective defense against communist aggression. . . .

In the current quest for a sound military policy, the need for many different types of weapons is recognized as a matter of course. But, as Korea amply attested, hardware without courage and firmness of purpose is of little value. Mao Tse-tung, who now must be ranked with the great classical strategists, long ago warned against the fallacy of the mechanistic assumption that "weapons mean everything." He wrote that the view of the communists differs from that of the capitalist: "We see not only weapons, but also the power of man. Weapons are an important factor in war but not the decisive one; it is man and not material that counts."

Notes

1. The vote in the General Assembly was 47-5. India fearing that action in North Korea would bring in Communist China, abstains.

2. General MacArthur told the Senate "I have said that I can conceive of no condition in which I would attempt to land United States ground forces in continental China."

Part Five

THE STATE OF THE AMERICAN SYSTEM

Chapter 10 NOT TOWARD SOCIALISM, BUT PAST SOCIALISM

Editor, essayist, and popular historian FREDERICK LEWIS ALLEN *and his graceful literary style commanded large audiences for his studies in American social history, such as the widely-read "Only Yesterday: An Informal History of the 1920s" (1931). In "The Big Change: America Transforms Itself, 1900-1950" (1952), Allen rhapsodized those developments which, in his estimation, had converted the United States from a dog-eat-dog capitalist society to a democratic welfare state during the course of the twentieth century. The "dynamic logic of mass production," a more enlightened business outlook, the organization of workers and other groups into a system of counterbalancing powers, and government intervention had produced a pluralistic society characterized by a broad area of consensus on basic values. This "mixed" system best met the needs of the mass of Americans, and might also serve as a beacon to peoples throughout the world. A prime example of the "celebrationist" history that helped produce what seemed like another "era of good feelings" in the mid-1950s, "The Big Change" also served indirectly to enhance President Truman's stature as the man who had presided over the further perfection and extension of "the Great American Discovery" in the post-World War II era.*

As we enter upon the second half of the twentieth century and pause to take stock of our situation, let us look to see, first, what has happened to the gap that once yawned so widely between rich and poor.

In money terms—income terms—the change has not been overwhelming. There are still islands of deep poverty in the United States, and there are families and individuals by the millions who through illness, age, adversity, or marginal ability, live on the ragged edge of want. And the average represents nothing like affluence. Yet even so, what has happened over half a century, but most impressively since 1940, has been striking enough to be described by the definitely unhysterical

Abridged from pp. 183, 186-188, 193-194, 201-204, 227, 234, 240-244, 249-257 in *The Big Change 1900-1950* (Perennial Edition) by Frederick Lewis Allen. Copyright, 1952, by Frederick Lewis Allen. Reprinted by permission of Harper & Row, Publishers, Inc.

director of research of the National Bureau of Economic Research as "one of the great social revolutions of history. . . ."

What do these figures mean in human terms? That millions of families in our industrial cities and towns, and on the farms, have been lifted from poverty or near-poverty to a status where they can enjoy what has been traditionally considered a middle-class way of life: decent clothes for all, an opportunity to buy a better automobile, install an electric refrigerator, provide the housewife with a decently attractive kitchen, go to the dentist, pay insurance premiums, and so on indefinitely. . . .

At the top of the scale there has likewise been a striking change. The enormous lead of the well-to-do in the economic race has been considerably reduced.

Let us see what has happened to the top five per cent of the population, income-wise—roughly speaking, the people who have been living on incomes of $8,000 or over.

According to the elaborate calculations of Simon Kuznets of the National Bureau of Economic Research, during the period between the two wars the people in this comparatively well-off group were taking a very big slice of the total national income—no less than 30 percent of it, before taxes; a little over 28 per cent after taxes. But by 1945 their slice had been narrowed from 30 to 19½ per cent before taxes, and from 28 to 17 per cent after taxes. Since 1945 this upper group has been doing a little better, relatively, but not much.

As for the top one per cent, the really well-to-do and the rich, whom we might classify very roughly indeed as the $16,000-and-over group, their share of the total national income, after taxes, had come down by 1945 from 13 per cent to 7 per cent.

A question at once arises. Have we, in reducing the slice received by these upper groups, and increasing the slice received by lower groups, simply been robbing Peter to pay Paul? (It often looks that way to Peter, especially around March 15.) [Formerly, income tax filing deadline.]

The answer is that Peter has been getting a smaller relative slice of a much larger pie. Even after one has made allowance for rising prices, one finds that the total disposable income of *all* Americans went up 74 per cent between 1929 and 1950. That is a very considerable enlargement. So that although the well-to-do and the rich have suffered *relatively,* it is much less certain that they have suffered *absolutely.*

And one might add at this point an interesting footnote. The big hike in wages that we were speaking of a moment ago has not, by and large, reduced profits. In fact when we compare the 1929 totals with the 1950 ones, we discover that total profits rose in the interval a little more sharply than total wages and salaries! To quote the apt slogan of the New England Council: "The rising tide lifts all the boats." (And why did the rich not gain heavily thereby? Because the profits were in part retained for business expansion; because dividends were more widely distributed; and also, of course, because taxes were much higher). . . .

Much more impressive, however, than the narrowing of the gap in *income* between rich and poor has been the narrowing of the gap between them in their *ways of living.* . . .

Let us proceed from clothes to the equipment of daily living. As Professor H. Gordon Hayes pointed out in *Harper's* in 1947, the rich man smokes the same sort of cigarettes as the poor man, shaves with the same sort of razor, uses the same sort of telephone, vacuum cleaner, radio, and TV set, has the same sort of lighting and heating equipment in his house, and so on indefinitely. The differences between his automobile and the poor man's are minor. Essentially they have similar engines, similar fittings. In the early years of the century there was a hierarchy of automobiles. At the top were such imported cars as the Rolls-Royce, Mercedes-Benz, and Isotta Fraschini; to possess one of these was a mark of lively wealth. There was also an American aristocracy of the Pierce Arrow, Peerless, and Packard. Then came group after group, in descending scale, till you reached the homely Model-T Ford. Today, except for a few survivals such as the obstinately rectangular Rolls-Royces of the old school, and a few oddities such as the new British sports cars, which to the American eye would seem to have been constructed for exceptionally dashing midgets, there is a comparative absence of class groupings. And, although the owner of a big, brand-new car probably has a large income, he may merely be someone who adjusts a slender income to cover the costs of the machines that entrance him.

In the matter of running water and plumbing, the breakdown of distinctions has proceeded much more slowly but nevertheless steadily. There have been, it is true, some injuries to Southern mountaineers who at first glimpse of a water closet decided that one was supposed to stand in it to wash one's feet; but today only the older and poorer tenements and dwellings in American cities and towns lack running water, bathtubs or showers, and water closets, and these conveniences are fast being installed in farmhouses the country over.

Meanwhile the servant class has almost vanished, especially in the North and West, although servants' wages have a purchasing power today from five to ten times or more greater than in 1900 (and, if the servants live in, offer an exceptional opportunity for saving). Their virtual disappearance, which has imposed upon all but a tiny fraction of American families the chores of cooking and cleaning and washing, not only marks the absorption of the immigrant proletariat of yore into general American society, in which domestic service has been regarded as humiliating, but also removes another contrast between the ways of living of the prosperous and the poor. Today the daughter of comfortably circumstanced parents had better know how to cook well—and their son, too, may find the knowledge pretty nearly essential. . . .

Today the cult of informality is pervasive. Its advance has been so long-continued that one would momentarily expect a reaction toward elegance; but for every step taken in the direction of formality, two steps are presently taken in the direction of an easier code of manners.

Look at the male American of today. The cutaway coat is obsolescent, except for borrowed or rented wear at weddings. . . .

Sports attire is gradually on the way in, ranging from the separate tweed jacket and flannel or khaki slacks to the fancy-patterned shirt and slacks favored in California and Florida. Work clothes of various sorts tend likewise to be popular for easy-going wear. Young men shun neckties except as occasional concessions to formality, and the standard costume of an undergraduate out for a day with a girl at a girls' college is likely to be a shirt or T-shirt and slacks, with wool socks and unpolished shoes. If he wishes to follow the very strictest code of aristocratic propriety, he may insist upon wearing a plain white or plain blue shirt with buttoned-down collar (left open, of course) rather than anything of Hawaiian aspect and dingy white shoes rather than dingy brown ones; but he won't get into a regular two-piece suit, with necktie, until dinner. And on many a campus the two-piece suit plays today almost, though not quite, the part that the dinner coat played in the early years of the century: it is what one wears on a formal occasion. Otherwise one is happy in khaki slacks and a T-shirt, sport shirt, sweater, lumberman's shirt, or windbreaker, the combination chosen depending on the weather. So steady is the campaign of attrition against the formerly orthodox male costume, in fact, that one suspects that its one-hundred-and-twenty-five-year reign may be approaching its end.

Among women the trend toward informality of attire is not so clearly defined. Yet it is amusing to note with what enthusiasm the supposedly omnipotent moguls of the dress trade and the advertising trade decree from time to time the return of elegance, and how widely spaced and brief are their triumphs; while the majority of the younger women, and many older ones too, go hatless all year round, go stockingless in summer, and wear flat-heeled loafers or ballet shoes and peasant kerchiefs. . . .

Whatever one's view of the cult of informality, it is distinctly a manifestation of the all-American standard of living and behavior. . . .

There are a great many people today, there have been a great many people throughout American history, who have in effect called the United States a Carthage. There are those who argue that during the past half century, despite the spread of good living among its people, it has been headed in the Carthaginian direction; that it has been producing a mass culture in which religion and philosophy languish, the arts are smothered by the barbarian demands of mass opinion, and the life of the spirit wanes. There are millions in Europe, for instance, to whom contemporary American culture, as they understand it, is no culture at all; to whom the typical American is a man of money, a crude, loud fellow who knows no values but mechanical and commercial ones. And there are Americans aplenty, old and young, who say that achievement in the realm of the mind and spirit has become ominously more difficult in recent years, and that our technological and economic triumphs are barren because they have brought us no inner peace. . . .

Does the all-American standard . . . threaten quality? Are we achieving a mass of second-rate education, second-rate culture, second-rate thinking, and squeezing out the first-rate?. . . .

Let us look at the market for art. The painter of today faces two great difficulties. The first is that his work is offered to the public at high prices (if he can get any price at all) because he can sell only his original work, to one collector or institution, and cannot dispose of thousands at a time; and collectors with ample money are scarce. The second is that the abler young painters of the day have mostly swung all the way to the abstract, which to most potential buyers is about as comprehensible as contemporary poetry. Yet the signs of interest among the public are striking. Forbes Watson is authority for the statement that there were more sales of paintings in the nineteen-forties than in all the previous history of the United States; that in the year 1948 there were a hundred exhibitions of American art in American museums; and that the total attendance at art exhibitions that year was over 50 million. One should also take note of the greatly enlarged number of local museums; of the lively promotion of an interest in art by many universities and colleges; the rising sale of reproductions, in book form and otherwise; and also the recent sharp increase in the number of Sunday amateur dabblers with a paint-brush. Lyman Bryson reports tht the lowest estimate he has been able to find of the number of people who paint in the United States today is 300,000. And the Department of Commerce says that the sales of art supplies went up from four million dollars in 1939 to forty million in 1949—a tremendous leap. The suspicion comes over one that there is something stirring here, too, and that the plight of the contemporary artist, like the plight of the contemporary writer, may be partly due to the fact that the market for his output may not yet be geared to the potential demand.

We turn to music—and confront an astonishing spectacle.

In 1900 there was only a handful of symphony orchestras in the country; by May 1951 there were 659 "symphonic groups"—including 32 professional, 343 community, 231 college, and a scattering of miscellaneous amateur groups. Fifteen hundred American cities and towns now support annual series of concerts. Summer music festivals attract audiences which would have been unimaginable even thirty years ago. To quote Cecil Smith,

> The dollar-hungry countries of Europe are setting up music festivals by the dozen, not to give American tourists the music they would not hear at home, but to make sure they do not stay at home because of the lack of music in

Europe. The programs at Edinburgh, Strasbourg, Amsterdam, Florence, and Aix-en-Provence are designed as competition for Tanglewood, Bethlehem, Ravinia, the Cincinnati Zoo, and the Hollywood Bowl.

Mr. Smith cites further facts of interest: that the Austin, Texas, symphony recently took over a drive-in movie for out door summer concerts; that Kentucky hill people come in their bare feet when the Louisville orchestra plays in Berea; and that "an all-Stravinsky program, conducted by the composer, strikes Urbana, Illinois, as a perfectly normal attraction."

A good deal of the credit for this extraordinary state of affairs goes to the radio. The first network broadcast of a symphony orchestra was held in 1926, the first sponsored one came in 1929, the Metropolitan Opera was put on the air in 1931, and Toscanini was engaged as conductor of the NBC orchestra in 1937; by 1938 it was estimated that the Music Appreciation Hour, conducted by Walter Damrosch, was being heard each week by seven million children in some 70,000 schools, and that the Ford Sunday Evening Hour, featuring the Detroit Symphony, was fifth among all radio programs in popularity. Millions upon millions of people were getting music of all sorts—popular, jazz, and classical— in such quantity, year after year, that businessmen and housewives and school children who had never until a few years earlier heard a symphony orchestra or a string quartet were getting an ample opportunity to find out for themselves whether "Roll Out the Barrel" or "One O'Clock Jump" or Beethoven's Seventh sounded best on a fifth or tenth hearing. In the late nineteen-forties the radio network production of classical music began to weaken as television made spectacular inroads upon the radio business; but long before this another way of communicating music had jumped into prominence.

During the nineteen-twenties the phonograph record business had been threatened with virtual extinction by the rise of radio. But presently, it began to expand: people who had developed a lively interest in music began to want it on their own terms. The expansion was accelerated by the wild vogue of jazz, whose more serious votaries soon learned that if you were to become a really serious student of what Benny Goodman and Duke Ellington were producing, you must collect old recordings and become a connoisseur of Handy, Beiderbecke, and Armstrong. By the nineteen-forties, young people who in earlier years would have gone off dancing of an evening were finding that it was very agreeable to sit on the floor and listen to a record-player, with a few bottles of beer to wash the music down. Many whose taste in books and in art was very limited were not only becoming able to identify the most famous symphonies by their first few notes, but were developing a pride in their acquaintance with the works of Bach's obscure contemporaries, and in their connoisseurship of the comparative merits of recordings by various orchestras. A very rough estimate of the sales of records during the year 1951, made by *Billboard* magazine, put the grand total at some 190 million—more than one for every man, woman, and child in the United States—and the total sale of records in the "classical" category at perhaps ten to fifteen per cent of that 190 million: let us say something like twenty to thirty million classical records. To give a single example: as many as 20,000 sets of Wanda Landowska's harpsichord recordings of the Goldberg Variations were sold during the first three months after they were issued. And a shrewd student of American culture tells me that as he goes about the United States he keeps being told, in place after place, "our town is sort of unusual. I suppose the most exciting thing, to us, that's going on here isn't anything in business but the way we've put over our symphony orchestra (or our string quartet, or our community chorus)."

Verily, as one looks about the field of the arts, the picture is confused. Here is an incredible boom in public interest in music, along with expanding audiences for the ballet, old-style and new-style. Here is the Broadway theater almost ready for the pulmotor—and local civic theaters and college theaters in what look like a promising adolescence. Here are the movies, beloved by millions (and berated by highbrow critics) for decades, losing audiences little by little to television, which has not yet outgrown a preposterous crudity. Here is architecture, which has outgrown its earlier imitation of old European styles and is producing superb industrial buildings along with highly experimental and sometimes absurd modern residences—while the peripheries of our great cities, whether New York or Chicago or St. Louis or Los Angeles, display to the bus traveler from airport to town almost no trace of the handiwork of any architects at all. Here are lovely (if monotonous) motor parkways—and along the other main highways a succession of roadtown eyesores (garages, tourist courts, filling stations, billboards, secondhand auto salesrooms, junk dealers, and more billboards) which make the motor parkways seem, by contrast, like avenues for escapists.

Is not the truth of the situation perhaps something like this: Here is a great nation which is conducting an unprecedented experiment. It has made an incredible number of people, previously quite unsophisticated and alien to art or contemptuous of it, prosperous by any previous standard known to man. These multitudes offer a huge market for him who would sell them equipment or entertainment that they can understand and enjoy. To compare them with the people who in other lands have been lovers and students of literature and the arts is grossly unfair. They are not an elite, but something else again. Let us say it in italics: *This is something new; there has never been anything like it before. . . .*

If this is what auspicious economic conditions can bring . . . the all-American culture may prove to have been, not the enemy of excellence, but its seed-bed.

Walt Whitman saw the possibilities when he wrote, fancifully depicting the arrival of the muse, a migrant from ancient Greece to the New World:

By thud of machinery and shrill steam-whistle undismay'd
Bluff'd not a bit by drain-pipe, gasometers, artificial fertilizers;
Smiling and pleas'd with palpable intent to stay,
She's here, install'd amid the kitchen-ware!. . . .

For the March 4, 1951, issue of *This Week,* a magazine that goes as a supplement to over ten million readers of Sunday newspapers, the editor, William I. Nichols, wrote an article (later reprinted in the *Reader's Digest*) called "Wanted: A New Name for 'Capitalism.' " Arguing that the word is no longer the right one to fit our present American system, because in too many people's minds, especially in other parts of the world, "it stands for the primitive economic system of the nineteenth century," Mr. Nichols asked: "How shall we describe this system—imperfect, but always improving, and always capable of further improvement—where men move forward together, working together, building together, producing always more and more, and sharing together the rewards of their increased production?" He said he had heard various suggestions, such as "the new capitalism," "democratic capitalism," "economic democracy," "industrial democracy," "distributism," "mutualism," and "productivism," but wondered if there might not be a better term. And he invited readers to write in their own suggestions in a coupon printed in the magazine.

Fifteen thousand coupons came back with suggestions. "Never in my whole editorial experience," said Mr. Nichols afterward, "have I touched so live a nerve."

Perhaps one reason for this extraordinary response was that the idea of asking readers to do something simple and easy about an idea thrown at them—"as if it were a box-top contest," as Mr. Nichols said—was an apt journalistic stroke. But surely it also suggested the existence in the United States of a very wide-spread feeling that we've got something here—something working reasonably well and at any rate going full tilt—that defies all the old labels.

And I suspect that one reason why so many people feel this way is that here in the United States we have not been constructing a system as such, but tinkering with and repairing and rebuilding, piece by piece, an old system to make it run better; . . . and that accordingly we have arrived at a transformed product which might be likened to an automobile continually repaired, while running, by means of new parts taken from any old car which seemed to suit the immediate purpose of the repairers, with the result that in the end it is hard to say whether what we have is a Buick or a Cadillac or a Ford. . . .

I have tried to show how this patchwork process has taken place. In the nineteenth century we had in the United States a combination of federal and state and local government—the federal component being small and very limited in its duties—which left business to operate pretty much as it pleased. But these governments permitted businessmen to organize corporations which were given special rights and privileges, and while these rights and privileges worked wonderfully in providing incentives for men to build up lively and inventive businesses, they had other unforeseen effects. They made the lone workman, whose income was determined by the Iron Law of Wages, pretty nearly helpless before his employer; they gave an enormous share of the fruits of the enterprise to this employer; and they also gave huge power to the men who controlled the supplies of money without which the employers found it difficult to operate. At the turn of the century America seemed in danger of becoming a land in which the millionaires had more and more and the rest had less and less, and where a few financiers had a strangle hold, not only on the country's economic apparatus, but on its political apparatus too.

This outraged the democratic spirit of the country, the national sense of fair play. So we went to work to change things—not by revolution but by a series of experimental revisions of the system. When it broke down badly in the Great Depression the repair work and reconstruction were pretty drastic, and some was foolish, but the same basic principle of unrevolutionary and experimental change prevailed. After some years of this there was considerable uncertainty whether the engine would ever run again without wheezing and knocking. But when World War II came along, we discovered that if Washington jammed the accelerator right down to the floor boards the engine began to run smoothly and fast. And when the war was over, and Washington released the accelerator, it still hummed. What had happened to bring about this astonishing result?

The answer, in brief, is that through a combination of patchwork revisions of the system—tax laws, minimum wage laws, subsidies and guarantees and regulations of various sorts, plus labor union pressures and new management attitudes—we had repealed the Iron Law of Wages. We had brought about a virtually automatic redistribution of income from the well-to-do to the less well-to-do. And this did not stall the machine but actually stepped up its power. Just as an individual business seemed to run best when it plowed part of its profits into improvements, so the business system as a whole seemed to run better if you plowed some of the national income into improvements in the income and status of the lower income groups, enabling them to buy more goods and thus to expand the market for everybody. We had discovered a new frontier to open up: the purchasing power of the poor.

That, it seems to me, is the essence of the Great American Discovery. And it has its corollary: that if you thus bring advantages to a great lot of previously under-privileged people, they will rise to their opportunities and, by and large, will become responsible citizens.

At present we have a very large and powerful central government. It continues to expand as if in response to some irresistible law of growth—not only because of the obligations which war and Cold War have imposed upon it, but because of our increasing interdependence as a more and more urbanized people with more and more complex institutions. The government regulates business in innumerable ways. . . . It constantly interferes with the operations of the once almighty economic law of supply and demand, the law of the market place. It provides all sorts of subsidies and guarantees to groups who have convinced it, rightly or wrongly, that they need such help. And furthermore it acknowledges two great responsibilities, the recognition of which was forced upon it during the miserable years of the Great Depression. One of these is a responsibility for seeing that people in an economic jam are helped to their feet—if not by their relatives and friends, or by local relief, or by state relief, then by federal relief if necessary. And the other is a responsibility for seeing that the economic system as a whole does not break down.

The government therefore maintains certain control powers over the national economy *as a whole;* and in a time of emergency like that which has followed the onset of the Korean War, these powers are extended. But it does not try to run our individual businesses (with certain exceptions such as the atomic power industry, which for security purposes is an island of socialism in a sea of private management). For we recognize that our businesses are better run if they remain in private hands. The past dozen years or so have offered a triumphant demonstration of the validity of this belief. For they have seen privately managed American business not only do a brilliant job of huge-scale war production, but also foster a startling variety of advances in technology.

Nor, for that matter, does the federal government take over the power of our state and local governments, though it subsidizes them to do many things which they cannot adequately do unaided. So there is a wide distribution of governmental powers. Our road system, for instance, is part local, part state, and only in minor degree federal. Our university and college system is partly state run, partly independent. And our school system is mostly locally run (by local public authority), partly church run, partly independent.

Furthermore we have an extraordinarily wide and proliferating assortment of voluntary institutions, associations, and societies which in their manifold ways contribute to the public good. Not only universities, schools, churches, hospitals, museums, libraries, and social agencies in great variety, but also societies for the protection or promotion of practically everything: if you want to feed European children, or protect our wild ducks, or promote zoning systems, or agitate for more freedom for corporations, or extend church work, or make boys into Boy Scouts, or save the redwoods, you will find a private organization dedicated to this purpose, and sometimes there will be several of them. There are also the foundations, offspring of idealism and the estate tax. And an endless range of trade associations, professional associations, alumni and alumnae associations, service clubs, and lodges. As a people we are great joiners, campaigners, and voluntary group helpers and savers and reformers and improvers and promoters. Get together half a dozen like-minded Americans and pretty soon you'll have an association, an executive secretary, a national program, and a fund-raising campaign.

Nor is it easy to draw a sharp line between the voluntary organizations on the one hand and either business or the government on the other. When a good part of the money contributed in a Community Chest campaign comes from local corporations, and a mighty foundation draws its resources from an automobile company, and the private air lines fly over airways maintained by the federal government, and a university may be partly state-supported and partly privately supported (and in addition may be subsidized for certain research work by the federal government), the lines are blurred indeed. . . . There is constant consultation and collaboration between people who are working on the same problem in private business, in private public-service organizations, in the government, and in state and private institutions of learning.

Under such circumstances it is fair to say that the moral and intellectual strength of the United States is based in considerable degree upon private organizations which are as consecrated to the idea of public duty as governmental ones could be, and in part perform services almost indistinguishable from governmental ones, but provide at the same time vastly more diversity and flexibility of approach, and vastly more opportunity for the free play of individual talent and interest, than could be harnessed in any other way. And that the American system as a whole is such a mixture of different things, arrived at in such diverse, unsystematic, and even haphazard ways, that possibly its strength lies in the very fact that you can't put a label to it.

Over every proposal for a further change in the complicated design of the national economic machine there is hot argument. Will this measure undermine the incentive to work and save and invest and invent? Will it give tyrannical power to Washington? Does this group of people, or this industry, really need aid? Can the government afford it? Does it set a good or a bad precedent? People can get apoplectic over such issues—and no wonder, for the development of this new American system is highly experimental, and we don't know whether we can continue to make it work.

Take a look at a few of the uncertainties.

During the postwar years inflation, though never acute, has been almost uninterrupted, and in sum has been a serious menace to our economic health. We don't know whether we can maintain our fast pace without continuing inflation.

Even before the Korean war we had pretty nearly reached the limit of taxation—the limit beyond which the burden would become so intolerable that the incentive to produce would be weakened and tax evasion would become a monumental rather than a minor problem. We don't know whether we can reduce this load or increase our productivity fast enough to take care of it.

If the Soviets should change their policy so convincingly that we could ease up on military expenditures, we don't know whether we could step up domestic production fast enough to prevent a depression.

If total war should come, we don't know whether the federal debt would become so astronomical that the credit of the federal government would be shaken.

In any case, we don't know whether the government has taken on so many financial responsibilities, since it added to its own previous authority much of the authority once exercised by Wall Street, that there is not a danger of a new kind of panic and financial collapse at some time in the future—a panic resulting from the inability, not of private financiers, but of public financiers, to maintain the values they have undertaken to guarantee. We think we know a great deal more about economics than we did a generation ago, but we cannot be surer that we are living in a New Era than were the moguls of Wall Street who cherished that innocent faith in 1929.

And in addition, we don't know at exactly what point a policy of aid to disadvantaged men and women degenerates into a demoralizing policy of handouts to people who would rather accept federal bounties than extend themselves. Some are sure we have already crossed this line; others are sure we haven't.

So it is just as well that every time we tinker with this experimental system there should be energetic and protracted debate.

But the fury of our political campaigns, and the angry disputes over this or that congressional bill, detract our attention from a remarkable fact: that despite the purple language which is tossed about, very few Americans seriously propose any *really wholesale* change in our evolving American system. (And at that, our stormiest debates in recent years have not been over domestic policy but over foreign policy, or over the supposed influence of American Communists and their friends and alleged friends over foreign policy.) There is a large amount of antipathy to the administration in power in Washington. There are numerous people who would like to curb federal power, repeal various laws now on the books, pare down the bureaucracy, minimize relief. There are others who want the government to take on new labors and new powers, like that of running a great medical insurance program. Yet the vast majority of Americans agree that the government should continue to accept an overall responsibility for relief when necessary; that it should supervise and regulate business to *some* extent; that it should subsidize and guarantee various groups to *some* extent—but that it should keep its intervention limited, and should let the great bulk of business remain under private management. The seething debate is over how much of this and how much of that we need, but the area of virtual agreement is very wide; and this includes letting private business remain in private hands.

For we believe we have domonstrated that business can be far more resourcefully and ingeniously run by private managers; and furthermore that these private managers can run most if not all of it with such consideration for the general public welfare that they can achieve for us all that government ownership would bring, plus the efficiency, flexibility, and adventurousness which government ownership would jeopardize—and without the danger of tyranny that government ownership might invite.

In short, there is subconscious agreement among the vast majority of Americans that the United States is not evolving *toward* socialism, but *past* socialism. . . .

Yet the delusion persists that the trend of the times is toward socialism—and perhaps even toward communism. Though our production, our wealth, our standard of living are the wonder of the worlds; though Britain under Socialist leadership had to come to us for financial aid; though, as Isabel Lundberg wrote in 1947, we are in a position to offer tangible goods and expert technological services to nations to whom the Russians, for all their loud talk of material benefits, could not offer so much as a shoelace; though our evolved system is potentially the most revolutionary force on earth, nevertheless so fixed in our minds is this delusion that when we face foreign problems we instinctively consider ourselves the natural allies of conservatism, and we tend to behave as if we wanted to stifle the natural hopes of mankind for a decenter way of life. Instinctively we set our faces against change. And preposterously we think of Soviet Russia—which has submerged the historic Communist aim of a better life for the masses of people in an aim of national aggrandizement through barbaric means—as if it and its allied zealots and dupes represented radicalism, represented a disposition of things toward which we ourselves might drift if we did not hold fast against change; as if Soviet Russia were something other than a despotic medievalism which was developed out of a revolutionary attempt to meet the problems of the nineteenth century—problems which we ourselves have long since surmounted.

It is time we rid ourselves of this notion about Russia. It is time we realize that when we battle against communism, we are battling against the past, not against the future. It is time, too, we rid ourselves of the notion that the direction of change at home is toward socialism or communism, and that therefore loyal Americans must stand pat. This notion is a stultifying force in our life. It causes well-meaning people to imagine that anyone with unorthodox ideas must be suspect of subversive intent. It tends to cramp men's imaginations into a timid conformity. It tends to constrict our generous impulses as a people. Combined with the fear of large-scale war, and especially of atomic war, it eats away at our bold confidence in ourselves and our destiny.

We would do better to put it out of our minds, and to realize that our sobering position of leadership in the world is founded upon the fact that we have not stood still. The story of the changes in the contours of American life that we have hammered out in the first half of this twentieth century, is a triumphant story, however harsh may have been some of our experiences in the interim and however obscure may be the shape of the future. We would do well to think of our accomplishment thus far as but the preface to what we may accomplish in the second half of the century if we can continue to invent, improve, and change—and can keep a good heart. The courageous nation, like the courageous man, is not unhappy at the thought of dangers beside the road ahead, but welcomes them as challenges to be faced and overwhelmed along an adventurous course.

Chapter 11 THE POWER ELITE

*Although sociologist C. WRIGHT MILLS,
who died in 1962, purported to have little
use for history as a scholarly discipline,
historians along with other social scientists
owe much to his insightful studies of
American society in such works as "The
New Men of Power: America's Labor
Leaders" (1948) and "White Collar: The
American Middle Classes" (1951). In "The
Power Elite" (1956), Mills brought into
prominent display the thesis that an
industrial-military complex had emerged as
the dominant feature of the American power
structure in its fifth, and latest, epoch of
chronological development, and the ensuing
debate over the concept's validity has
continued to this day. How convincing are
the arguments that Mills employs to differ-
entiate his thesis from orthodox Marxism?
To what extent does Frederick Lewis Allen's
portrait of American society substantiate
Mills' analysis, even though their conclusions
may differ widely? Have circumstances since
the mid-1950s tended to weaken or
strengthen Mills' thesis?*

Official commentators like to contrast the ascendancy in totalitarian countries of a tightly organized clique with the American system of power. Such comments, however, are easier to sustain if one compares mid-twentieth-century Russia with mid-nineteenth-century America, which is what is often done by Tocqueville-quoting Americans making the contrast. But that was an America of a century ago, and in the century that has passed, the American elite have not remained as patri-oteer essayists have described them to us. The 'loose cliques' now head institutions of a scale and power not then existing and, especially since World War I, the loose cliques have tightened up. We are well beyond the era of romantic pluralism.

The supremacy of corporate economic power began, in a formal way, with the Congressional elections of 1866, and was consolidated by the Supreme Court decision of 1886 which declared that the Fourteenth Amendment protected the corporation. That period witnessed the transfer of the center of initiative from government to corporation. Until the First World War (which gave us an advanced showing of certain features of our own period) this was an age of raids on the government by the economic elite, an age of simple corruption, when Senators and judges were simply bought up. Here, once upon a time, in the era of McKinley and Morgan, far removed from the undocumented complexities of our own time, many now believe, was the golden era of the American ruling class.[1]

The military order of this period, as in the second, was subordinate to the political, which in turn was subordinate to the economic. The military was thus off to the side of the main driving forces of United States history. Political institutions in the United States have never formed a centralized and autonomous domain of power; they have been enlarged and centralized only reluctantly in slow response to the public consequence of the corporate economy.

In the post-Civil-War era, that economy was the dynamic; the 'trusts'—as policies and events make amply clear—could readily use the relatively weak governmental apparatus for their own ends. That both state and federal governments were decisively limited in their power to regulate, in fact meant that they were themselves regulatable by the larger moneyed interests. Their powers were scattered and unorganized; the powers of the industrial and financial corporations concentrated and interlocked. The Morgan interests alone held 341 directorships in 112 corporations with an aggregate capitalization of over $22 billion—over three times the assessed value of all real and personal property in New England.[2] With revenues greater and employees more numerous than those of many states, corporations controlled parties, bought laws, and kept Congressmen of the 'neutral' state. And as private economic power overshadowed public political power, so the economic elite overshadowed the political.

Yet even between 1896 and 1919, events of importance tended to assume a political form, foreshadowing the shape of power which after the partial boom of the 'twenties was to prevail in the New Deal. Perhaps there has never been any period in American history so politically transparent as the Progressive era of President-makers and Muckrakers.

The New Deal did *not* reverse the political and economic relations of the third era, but it did create within the political arena, as well as in the corporate world itself, competing centers of power that challenged those of the corporate directors. As the New Deal directorate gained political power, the economic elite, which in the third period had fought against the growth of 'government' while raiding it for crafty privileges, belatedly attempted to join it on the higher levels. When they did so they found themselves confronting other interests and men, for the places of decision were crowded. In due course, they did come to control and to use for their own purposes the New Deal institutions whose creation they had so bitterly denounced.

But during the 'thirties, the political order was still an instrument of small propertied farmers and businessmen, although they were weakened, having lost their last chance for real ascendancy in the Progressive era. The struggle between big and small property flared up again, however, in the political realm of the New Deal era, and to this struggle there was added, as we have seen, the new struggle of organized labor and the unorganized unemployed. This new force flourished under political tutelage, but nevertheless, for the first time in United States history, social legislation and lower-class issues became important features of the reform movement.

In the decade of the 'thirties, a set of shifting balances involving newly instituted farm measures and newly organized labor unions—along with big business—made up the political and administrative drama of power. These farm, labor, and business groups, moreover, were more or less contained within the framework of an enlarging governmental structure, whose political directorship made decisions in a definitely political manner. These groups pressured, and in pressuring against one another and against the governmental and party system, they helped to shape it. But it could not be said that any of them for any considerable length of time used that government unilaterally as their instrument. That is why the 'thirties was a *political* decade: the power of business was not replaced, but it was contested and supplemented: it became one major power within a structure of power that was chiefly run by political men, and not by economic or military men turned political.

The earlier and middle Roosevelt administrations can best be understood as a desperate search for ways and means, within the existing capitalist system, of reducing the staggering and ominous army of the unemployed. In these years, the New Deal as a system of power was essentially a balance of pressure groups and interest blocs. The political top adjusted many conflicts, gave way to this demand, sidetracked that one, was the unilateral servant of none, and so evened it all out into such going policy line as prevailed from one minor crisis to another. Policies were the result of a political act of balance at the top. Of course, the balancing act that Roosevelt performed did not affect the fundamental institutions of capitalism as a type of economy. By his policies, he subsidized the defaults of the capitalist economy, which had simply broken down; and by his rhetoric, he balanced its political disgrace, putting 'economic royalists' in the political doghouse.

The 'welfare state' created to sustain the balance and to carry out the subsidy, differed from the 'laissez-faire' state: 'If the state was believed neutral in the days of T.R. because its leaders claimed to sanction favors for no one,' Richard Hofstadter has remarked, 'the state under F.D.R. could be called neutral only in the sense that it offered favors to everyone.'[3] The new state of the corporate commissars differs from the old welfare state. In fact, the later Roosevelt years—beginning with the entrance of the United States into overt acts of war and preparations for World War II—cannot be understood entirely in terms of an adroit equipoise of political power.

We study history, it has been said, to rid ourselves of it, and the history of the power elite is a clear case for which this maxim is correct. Like the tempo of American life in general, the long-term trends of the power structure have been greatly speeded up since World War II, and certain newer trends within and between the dominant institutions have also set the shape of the power elite and given historically specific meaning to its fifth epoch:

I. In so far as the structural clue to the power elite today lies in the political order, that clue is the decline of politics as genuine and public debate of alternative decisions—with nationally responsible and policy-coherent parties and with autonomous organizations connecting the lower and middle levels of power with the top levels of decision. America is now in considerable part more a formal political democracy than a democratic social structure, and even the formal political mechanics are weak.

The long-time tendency of business and government to become more intricately and deeply involved with each other has, in the fifth epoch, reached a new point of explicitness. The two cannot now be seen clearly as two distinct worlds. It is in terms of the executive agencies of the state that the rapprochement has proceeded most decisively. The growth of the executive branch of the government, with its agencies that patrol the complex economy, does not mean merely the 'enlargement of government' as some sort of autonomous bureaucracy: it has meant the ascendancy of the corporations's man as a political eminence.

During the New Deal the corporate chieftains joined the political directorate; as of World War II they have come to dominate it. Long interlocked with government, now they have moved into quite full direction of the economy of the war effort and of the postwar era. This shift of the corporation executives into the political directorate has accelerated the long-term relegation of the professional politicians in the Congress to the middle levels of power.

II. In so far as the structural clue to the power elite today lies in the enlarged and military state, that clue becomes evident in the military ascendancy. The warlords have gained decisive political relevance, and the military structure of America is now in considerable part a political structure. The seemingly permanent military threat places a premium on the military and upon their control of men, material, money, and power; virtually all political and economic actions are now judged in terms of military definitions of reality: the higher warlords have ascended to a firm position within the power elite of the fifth epoch.

In part at least this has resulted from one simple historical fact, pivotal for the years since 1939: the focus of elite attention has been shifted from domestic problems, centered in the 'thirties around slump, to international problems, centered in the 'forties and 'fifties around war. Since the governing apparatus of the United States has by long historic usage been adapted to and shaped by domestic clash and balance, it has not, from any angle, had suitable agencies and traditions for the handling of international problems. Such formal democratic mechanics as had arisen in the century and a half of national development prior to 1941, had not been extended to the American handling of international affairs. It is, in considerable part, in this vacuum that the power elite has grown.

III. In so far as the structural clue to the power elite today lies in the economic order, that clue is the fact that the economy is at once a permanent-war economy and a private-corporation economy. American capitalism is now in considerable part a military capitalism, and the most important relation of the big corporation to the state rests on the coincidence of interests between military and corporate needs, as defined by warlords and corporate rich. Within the elite as a whole, this coincidence of interest between the high military and the corporate chieftains strengthens both of them and further subordinates the role of the merely political men. Not politicians, but corporate executives, sit with the military and plan the organization of war effort.

The shape and meaning of the power elite today can be understood only when these three sets of structural trends are seen at their point of coincidence: the military capitalism of private corporations exists in a weakened and formal democratic system containing a military order already quite political in outlook and demeanor. Accordingly, at the top of this structure, the power elite has been shaped by the coincidence of interest between those who control the major means of production and those who control the newly enlarged means of violence; from the decline of the professional politician and the rise to explicit political command of the corporate chieftains and the professional warlords; from the absence of any genuine civil service of skill and integrity, independent of vested interests.

The power elite is composed of political, economic, and military men, but this instituted elite is frequently in some tension: it comes together only on certain coinciding points and only on certain occasions of 'crisis.' In the long peace of the nineteenth century, the military were not in the high councils of state, not of the political directorate, and neither were the economic men—they made raids upon the state but they did not join its directorate. During the 'thirties, the political man was ascendant. Now the military and the corporate men are in top positions.

Of the three types of circle that compose the power elite today, it is the military that has benefited the most in its enhanced power, although the corporate circles have also become more explicitly intrenched in the more public decision-making circles. It is the professional politician that has lost the most, so much that in examining the events and decisions, one is tempted to speak of a political vacuum in which the corporate rich and the high warlord, in their coinciding interests, rule.

It should not be said that the three 'take turns' in carrying the initiative, for the mechanics of the power elite are not often as deliberate as that would imply. At times, of course, it is—as when political men, thinking they can borrow the prestige of generals, find that they must pay for it, or, as when during big slumps, economic men feel the need of a politician at once safe and possessing vote appeal. Today all three are involved in virtually all widely ramifying decisions. Which of the three types seems to lead depends upon 'the tasks of the period' as they, the elite, define them. Just now, these tasks center upon 'defense' and international affairs. Accordingly, as we have seen, the military are ascendant in two senses: as personnel and as justifying ideology. That is why, just now, we can most easily specify the unity and the shape of the power elite in terms of the military ascendancy.

But we must always be historically specific and open to complexities. The simple Marxian view makes the big economic man the *real* holder of power; the simple liberal view makes the big political man the chief of the power system; and there are some who would view the warlords as virtual dictators. Each of these is an oversimplified view. It is to avoid them that we use the term 'power elite' rather than, for example, 'ruling class.'[4]

In so far as the power elite has come to wide public attention, it has done so in terms of the 'military clique.' The power elite does, in fact, take its current shape from the decisive entrance into it of the military. Their presence and their ideology are its major legitimations, whenever the power elite feels the need to provide any. But what is called the 'Washington military clique' is not composed merely of military men, and it does not prevail merely in Washington. Its members exist all over the country, and it is a coalition of generals in the roles of corporation executives, of politicians masquerading as admirals, of corporation executives acting like politicians, of civil servants who become majors, of vice-admirals who are also the assistants to a cabinet officer, who is himself, by the way, really a member of the managerial elite.

Neither the idea of a 'ruling class' nor of a simple monolithic rise of 'bureaucratic politicians' nor of a 'military clique' is adequate. The power elite today involves the often uneasy coincidence of economic, military, and political power.

Even if our understanding were limited to these structural trends, we should have grounds for believing the power elite a useful, indeed indispensable, concept for the interpretation of what is going on at the topside of modern American society. But we are not, of course, so limited: our conception of the power elite does not need to rest only upon the correspondence of the institutional hierarchies involved, or upon the many points at which their shifting interests coincide. The power elite, as we conceive it, also rests upon the similarity of its personnel, and their personal and official relations with one another, upon their social and psychological affinities. In order to grasp the personal and social basis of the power elite's unity, we have first to remind ourselves of the facts of origin, career, and style of life of each of the types of circle whose members compose the power elite.

The power elite is *not* an aristocracy, which is to say that it is not a political ruling group based upon a nobility of hereditary origin. It has no compact basis in a small circle of great families whose members can and do consistently occupy the top positions in the several higher circles which overlap as the power elite. But such nobility is only one possible basis of common origin. That it does not exist for the American elite does not mean that members of this elite derive socially from the full range of strata composing American society. They derive in substantial proportions from the upper classes, both new and old, of local society and the metropolitan 400. The bulk of the very rich, the corporate executives, the political outsiders, the high military, derive from, at most, the upper third of the income and occupational pyramids. Their fathers were at least of the professional and business strata, and very frequently higher than that. They are native-born Americans of native parents, primarily from urban areas, and, with the exceptions of the politicians among them, overwhelmingly from the East. They are mainly Protestants, especially Episcopalian or Presbyterian. In general, the higher the position, the greater the proportion of men within it who have derived from and who maintain connections with the upper classes. The generally similar origins of the members of the power elite are underlined and carried further by the fact of their increasingly common educational routine. Overwhelmingly college graduates, substantial proportions have attended Ivy League college, although the education of the higher military, of course, differs from that of other members of the power elite.

But what do these apparently simple facts about the social composition of the higher circles really mean? In particular, what do they mean for any attempt to understand the degree of unity, and the direction of policy and interest that may prevail among these several circles? Perhaps it is best to put this question in a deceptively simple way: in terms of origin and career, who or what do these men at the top represent?

Of course, if they are elected politicians, they are supposed to represent those who elected them; and, if they are appointed, they are supposed to represent, indirectly, those who elected their appointers. But this is recognized as something of an abstraction, as a rhetorical formula by which all men of power in almost all systems of government nowadays justify their power of decision. At times it may be true, both in the sense of their motives and in the sense of who benefits from their decisions. Yet it would not be wise in any power system merely to assume it.

The fact that members of the power elite come from near the top of the nation's class and status levels does not mean that they are necessarily 'representative' of the top levels only. And if they were, as social types, representative of a cross-section of the population, that would not mean that a balanced democracy of interest and power would automatically be the going political fact.

We cannot infer the direction of policy merely from the social origins and careers of the policy-makers. The social and economic backgrounds of the men of power do not tell us all that we need to know in order to understand the distribution of social power. For: (1) Men from high places may be ideological representatives of the poor and humble. (2) Men of humble origin, brightly self-made, may energetically serve the most vested and inherited interests. Moreover (3), not all men who effectively represent the interests of a stratum need in any way belong to it or personally benefit by policies that further its interests. Among the politicians, in short, there are sympathetic *agents* of given groups, conscious and unconscious, paid and unpaid. Finally (4), among the top decision-makers we find men who have been chosen for their positions because of their 'expert knowledge.' These are some of the obvious reasons why the social origins and careers of the power elite do not enable us to infer the class interests and policy directions of a modern system of power.

Do the high social origin and careers of the top men mean nothing, then, about the distribution of power? By no means. They simply remind us that we must be careful of any simple and direct inference from origin and career to political character and policy, not that we must ignore them in our attempt at political understanding. They simply mean that we must analyze the political psychology and the actual decisions of the political directorate as well as its social composition. And they mean, above all, that we should control, as we have done here, any inference we make from the origin and careers of the political actors by close understanding of the institutional landscape in which they act out their drama. Otherwise we should be guilty of a rather simple-minded biographical theory of society and history.

Just as we cannot rest the notion of the power elite solely upon the institutional mechanics that lead to its formation, so we cannot rest the notion solely upon the facts of the origin and career of its personnel. We need both, and we have both—as well as other bases, among them that of the status intermingling.

But it is not only the similarities of social origin, religious affiliation, nativity, and education that are important to the psychological and social affinities of the members of the power elite. Even if their recruitment and formal training were more heterogeneous than they are, these men would still be of quite homogeneous social type. For the most important set of facts about a circle of men is the criteria of admission, of praise, of honor, of promotion that prevails among them; if these are similar within a circle, then they will tend as personalities to become similar. The circles that compose the power elite do tend to have such codes and criteria in common. The co-optation of the social types to which these common values lead is often more important than any statistics of common origin and career that we might have at hand.

There is a kind of reciprocal attraction among the fraternity of the successful— not between each and every member of the circles of the high and mighty, but between enough of them to insure a certain unity. On the slight side, it is a sort of tacit, mutual admiration; in the strongest tie-ins, it proceeds by intermarriage. And there are all grades and types of connection between these extremes. Some overlaps certainly occur by means of cliques and clubs, churches and schools.

If social origin and formal education in common tend to make the members of the power elite more readily understood and trusted by one another, their continued association further cements what they feel they have in common. Members of the several higher circles know one another as personal friends and even as neighbors; they mingle with one another on the golf course, in the gentleman's clubs, at resorts, on transcontinental airplanes, and on ocean liners. They meet at the estates of mutual friends, face each other in front of the TV camera, or serve on the same philanthropic committee; and many are sure to cross one another's path in the columns of newspapers, if not in the exact cafes from which many of these columns originate. As we have seen, of 'The New 400' of cafe society, one chronicler has named forty-one members of the very rich, ninety-three political leaders, and seventy-nine chief executives of corporations.

'I did not know, I could not have dreamed,' Whittaker Chambers has written, 'of the immense scope and power of Hiss' political alliances and his social connections, which cut across all party lines and ran from the Supreme Court to the Religious Society of Friends, from governors of states and instructors in college faculties to the staff members of liberal magazines. In the decade since I had last seen him, he had used his career, and, in particular, his identification with the cause of peace through his part in organizing the United Nations, to put down roots that made him one with the matted forest floor of American upper class, enlightened middle class, liberal and official life. His roots could not be disturbed without disturbing all the roots on all sides of him.'[5]

The sphere of status has reflected the epochs of the power elite. In the third epoch, for example, who could compete with big money? And in the fourth, with big politicians, or even the bright young men of the New Deal? And in the fifth, who can compete with the generals and the admirals and the corporate officials now so sympathetically portrayed on the stage, in the novel, and on the screen? Can one imagine *Executive Suite* as a successful motion picture of 1935? Or *The Caine Mutiny?*

The multiplicity of high-prestige organizations to which the elite ususally belong is revealed by even casual examination of the obituaries of the big businessman, the high-prestige lawyer, the top general and admiral, the key senator: usually, high-prestige church, business associations, plus high-prestige clubs, and often plus military rank. In the course of their lifetimes, the university president, the New York Stock Exchange chairman, the head of the bank; the old West Pointer—mingle in the status sphere, within which they easily renew old friendships and draw upon them in an effort to understand through the experience of trusted others those contexts of power and decision in which they have not personally moved.

In these diverse contexts, prestige accumulates in each of the higher circles, and the members of each borrow status from one another. Their self-images are fed by these accumulations and these borrowings, and accordingly, however segmental a given man's role may seem, he comes to feel himself a 'diffuse' or 'generalized' man of the higher circles, a 'broad-gauge' man. Perhaps such inside experience is one feature of what is meant by 'judgment.'

The key organizations, perhaps, are the major corporations themselves, for on the boards of directors we find a heavy overlapping among the members of these several elites. On the lighter side, again in the summer and winter resorts, we find that, in an intricate series of overlapping circles; in the course of time, each meets each or knows somebody who knows somebody who knows that one.

The higher members of the military, economic, and political orders are able readily to take over one another's point of view, always in a sympathetic way, and often in a knowledgeable way as well. They define one another as among those who count, and who, accordingly, must be taken into account. Each of them as a member of the power elite comes to incorporate into his own integrity, his own honor, his own conscience, the viewpoint, the expectations, the values of the others. If there are no common ideals and standards among them that are based upon an explicitly aristocratic culture, that does not mean that they do not feel responsibility to one another.

All the structural coincidence of their interests as well as the intricate, psychological facts of their origins and their education, their careers and their associations make possible the psychological affinities that prevail among them, affinities that make it possible for them to say of one another: He is, of course, one of us. And all this points to the basic, psychological meaning of class consciousness. Nowhere in America is there as great a 'class consciousness' as among the elite; nowhere is it organized as effectively as among the power elite. For by class consciousness, as a psychological fact, one means that the individual member of a 'class' accepts only those accepted by his circle as among those who are significant to his own image of self.

Within the higher circles of the power elite, factions do exist; there are conflicts of policy; individual ambitions do clash. There are still enough divisions of importance within the Republican party, and even between Republicans and Democrats, to make for different methods of operation. But more powerful than these divisions are the internal discipline and the community of interests that bind the power elite together, even across the boundaries of nations at war.[6]

Notes

1. Cf., for example, David Riesman, in collaboration with Reuel Denney and Nathan Glazer, *The Lonely Crowd* (New Haven: Yale University Press, 1950).

2. See the Hearings of the Pujo Committee, quoted in Richard Hofstadter, *The Age of Reform* (New York: Knopf, 1955), p. 230; and Louis D. Brandeis, *Other People's Money* (New York: Stokes, 1932), pp. 22-3.

3. Richard Hofstadter, op. cit., p. 305.

4. 'Ruling class' is a badly loaded phrase. 'Class' is an economic term; 'rule' a political one. The phrase, 'ruling class,' thus contains the theory that an economic class rules politically. That short-cut theory may or may not at times be true, but we do not want to carry that one rather simple theory about in the terms that we use to define our problems; we wish to state the theories explicitly, using terms of more precise and unilateral meaning. Specifically, the phrase 'ruling class,' in its common political connotations, does not allow enough autonomy to the

political order and its agents, and it says nothing about the military as such. It should be clear to the reader by now that we do not accept as adequate the simple view that high economic men unilaterally make all decisions of national consequence. We hold that such a simple view of 'economic determinism' must be elaborated by 'political determinism' and 'military determinism'; that the higher agents of each of these three domains now often have a noticeable degree of autonomy; and that only in the often intricate ways of coalition do they make up and carry through the most important decisions. Those are the major reasons we prefer 'power elite' to 'ruling class' as a characterizing phrase for the higher circles when we consider them in terms of power.

5. Whittaker Chambers, *Witness* (New York: Random House, 1952), p. 550.

6. For an excellent introduction to the international unity of corporate interests, see James Stewart Martin, *All Honorable Men* (Boston: Little Brown, 1950).

Chapter 12 THE SHORTCOMINGS OF INTEREST-GROUP LIBERALISM

Political scientist THEODORE J. LOWI *of the University of Chicago shares with a growing number of liberals a deep concern over the quality of leadership offered the nation in the years since the New Deal by consensus-conscious administrations that seem to concentrate their efforts, in broker-state manner, on palliating the needs of well-organized elements of the population. The resulting system of "interest-group liberalism," Lowi maintains in the selection that follows, is marred by numerous defects that stultify the effectiveness of its social policies in operation, debase representative democracy and political participation, convert government from a moralistic to a mechanistic institution, and sap the legitimacy of government action and law itself. To what extent do Frederick Lewis Allen's and C. Wright Mills' portraits of American society substantiate Lowi's analysis, even though their conclusions may differ? How would President Truman rate as a "politician" under Lowi's standards of definition?*

In brief sketch, the working model of the interest group liberal is a vulgarized version of the pluralist model of modern political science. It assumes: (1) Organized interests are homogeneous and easy to define, sometimes monolithic. Any "duly elected" spokesman for any interest is taken as speaking in close approximation for each and every member. (2) Organized interests pretty much fill up and adequately represent most of the sectors of our lives, so that one organized group can be found effectively answering and checking some other organized group as it seeks to prosecute its claims against society.[1] And (3) the role of government is one of ensuring access particularly to the most effectively organized, and of ratifying the agreements and adjustments worked out among the competing leaders and their claims. This last assumption is supposed to be a statement of how our democracy works and how it ought to work. Taken together, these assumptions constitute the Adam Smith "hidden hand" model applied to groups.

These assumptions are the basis of the new public philosophy. The policy behavior of old-school liberals and conservatives, of Republicans and Democrats, so inconsistent with liberalism-conservatism criteria, are fully consistent with the criteria drawn from interest-group liberalism: *The most important difference between liberals and conservatives, Republicans and Democrats—however they define themselves—is to be found in the interest groups they identify with. Congressmen are guided in their votes, Presidents in their programs, and administrators in their discretion by whatever organized interests they have taken for themselves as the most legitimate; and that is the measure of the legitimacy of demands.*

It is no coincidence that these assumptions in the interest-group liberal model resemble the working methodology of modern political science. . . . But how did all of this become elevated from a hypothesis about political behavior to an ideology about how a democratic polity ought to work, and then ultimately to that ideology most widely shared among contemporary public men?

Interest-Group Liberalism: An Intellectual History

The opening of the national government to positive action on a large scale was inevitably to have an impact upon political justification just as on political technique. However, the inventors of technique were less than inventive in justifying particular policies at particular times. Hansen, for instance, has observed that Keynes was no dedicated social reformer, nor had he any particular commitments to radically new social ends. Keynes helped discover the modern economic system and how to help it maintain itself, but his ideas and techniques could be used, and indeed have been used, to support many points of view. "Collective bargaining, trade unionism, minimum-wage laws, hours legislation, social security, a progressive tax system, slum clearance and housing, urban redevelopment and planning, education reform," Hansen observed of Keynes, "all these he accepted, but they were not among his preoccupations. In no sense could he be called the father of the welfare state."

Nor was the doctrine of popular government and majority rule, which was so important in the victory of liberalism over conservatism, adequate guidance after the demise of liberalism-conservatism. If one reviews the New Deal period and thereafter, one sees how little propensity Americans have had to use the majority-rule justification. The reasons are fairly apparent. Justification of positive government programs on the basis of popular rule required above all a proclamation of the supremacy of Congress. The abdication of Congress in the 1930s in the passage of the fundamental New Deal legislation could never have been justified in the name of popular government. With all due respect to congressmen, they made little discernible effort to do so. Statutory and investigatory infringements on civil liberties during World War II and during the Cold War, plus the popular support of McCarthyism, produced further reluctance to fall back on Congress and majority rule as the fount of public policy wisdom. Many who wished to use this basis anyway sought support in the plebiscitary character of the Presidency. However, "presidential liberals" have had to blind themselves to many complications in the true basis of presidential authority and to the true—the bureaucratic—expression of presidential will.

The very practices that made convincing use of popular-rule doctrine impossible—delegation of power to administrators, interest representation, outright delegation of power to trade associations, and so on—were what made interest-group liberalism so attractive an alternative. And because the larger interest groups did claim large memberships, they could be taken virtually as popular rule in modern dress. Interest-group liberalism simply corresponded impressively well with the realities of power. Thus, it possessed the approval of science as well as some of the trappings of popular rule. Political scientists, after all, were pioneers in insisting upon recognition of the group, as well as in helping to elevate the pressure-group system from power to virtue. Political scientists had for a long time argued that the group is the necessary variable in political analysis for breaking through the formalisms of government. However, there was inevitably an element of approval in their methodological argument, if only to counteract the kind of recognition of the group that Steffens and other progressives and Muckrakers were more than willing to accord. In 1929, E. Pendleton Herring concluded his inquiry with the argument that:

> [The national associations] represent a healthy democratic development. They rose in answer to certain needs. . . . They are part of our representative system. . . . These groups must be welcomed for what they are, and certain precautionary regulations worked out. The groups must be understood and their proper place in government allotted, if not by actual legislation, then by general public realization of their significance.

Following World War II, one easily notes among political scientists the widespread acceptance of the methodology and, more importantly here, the normative position. Among political scientists the best expression of interest-group liberalism was probably that of Wilfred Binkley and Malcolm Moos. The fact that it was so prominent in their American government basic textbook suggests that it tended to reflect conventional wisdom among political scientists even in 1948. Binkley and Moos argued that the "basic concept for understanding the dynamics of government is the multi-group nature of modern society or the modern state." Political reality can be grasped scientifically as a "parallelogram of forces" among groups, and the public interest is "determined and established" through the free competition of interest groups: "The necessary composing and compromising of their differences is the practical test of what constitutes the public interest."[2]

The fact that a doctrine has some support in the realities of power certainly helps to explain its appeal as a doctrine. But there were also several strongly positive reasons for the emergence of this particular doctrine. The first, and once perhaps the only, reason, is that it has helped flank the constitutional problems of federalism. Manifestations of the corporate state were once limited primarily to the Extension Service of the Department of Agriculture, with self-administration by the land grant colleges and the local farmers and commerce associations. Self-administration by organized groups was an attractive technique precisely because it could be justified as so decentralized and permissive as to be hardly federal at all. Here began the ethical and conceptual mingling of the notion of organized private groups with the notions of "local government" and "self-government." Ultimately, direct interest-group participation in government became synonymous with self-government, first for reasons of strategy, then by belief that the two were indeed synonymous. As a propaganda strategy it eased acceptance in the courts, then among the locals who still believed the farmer was and should be independent. Success as strategy increased usage; usage helped elevate strategy to doctrine. The users began to believe in their own symbols.

A second positive appeal of interest-group liberalism is strongly related to the first. Interest-group liberalism helps solve a problem for the democratic politician in the modern state where the stakes are so high. This is the problem of enhanced conflict and how to avoid it. The politician's contribution to society is his skill in resolving conflict. However, direct confrontations are sought only by the zealous indeologues and "outsiders." The typical American politician displaces and defers and delegates conflict where possible; he squarely faces conflict only when he must. Interest-group liberalism offers a justification for keeping major combatants apart. It provides a theoretical basis for giving to each according to his claim, the price for which is a reduction of concern for what others are claiming. In other words, it transforms logrolling from necessary evil to greater good. This is the basis for the "consensus" so often claimed these days. It is also the basis for President Kennedy's faith that in our day ideology has given over to administration. It is inconceivable that so sophisticated a person as he could have believed, for example, that his setting of guidelines for wage and price increases was a purely administrative act. Here, in fact, is a policy that could never be "administered" in the ordinary sense of the word. The guidelines provide a basis for direct and regular policy-making between the President (or his agent) and the spokesmen for industry and for labor. This is a new phase of government relations with management and labor, and it is another step consistent with the interest-group liberal criterion of direct access.

The third positive appeal of interest-group liberalism is that it is a direct, even if pathological, response to the crisis of public authority. The practice of dealing only with organized claims in formulating policy, and of dealing exclusively through organized claims in implementing programs, helps create the sense that power need not be power at all, nor control control. If sovereignty is parceled out among the groups, then who's out anything? As Max Ways of *Fortune* enthusiastically put it, government power, group power, and individual power may go up simultaneously. *If* the groups to be controlled control the controls, *then* "to administer does not always mean to rule." The inequality of power is always a gnawing problem in a democratic culture. Rousseau's General Will stopped at the boundary of a Swiss canton. The myth of the group and the group will is becoming the answer to Rousseau in the big democracy.

President Eisenhower talked regularly about the desirability of business-government "partnerships," despite the misgivings in his farewell address about the "military-industrial complex," for he and most other Republicans are interest-group liberals. However, explicit and systematic expression of interest-group liberalism is much more the contribution of the Democrats, and the best formulations can be found among the more articulate Democrats, especially the leading Democratic intellectuals, Professors John Kenneth Galbraith and Arthur Schlesinger, Jr.

To Professor Galbraith, "Private economic power is held in check by the countervailing power of those who are subject to it. The first begets the second." Concentrated economic power stimulates other business interests (in contrast to the Smithian consumer), which organize against it. This results in a natural tendency toward equilibrium. But Galbraith is not really writing a theoretical alternative to Adam Smith; he is writing a program of government action. For he admits to the limited existence of effective countervailing power and proposes that where it is absent or too weak, government policy should seek out and support or, where necessary, create the organizations capable of countervailing. Government thereby pursues the public interest and makes itself superfluous at the same time. This is a surefire, nearly scientific guide to interest-group liberalism.

Professor Schlesinger's views are summarized for us in the campaign tract he wrote in 1960. To Schlesinger, the essential difference between the Democratic and Republican parties is that the Democratic party is a truly multi-interest party in the grand tradition extending back to Federalist No. 10. In power, it offers multi-interest administration and therefore ought to be preferred over the Republican party; and:

> What is the essence of a multi-essence administration? It is surely that the leading interests in society are all represented in the interior processes of policy formation—which can be done only if members or advocates of these interests are included in key positions of government. . . .

This theme Schlesinger repeated in his more serious and more recent work, *A Thousand Days*. Following his account of the 1962 confrontation of President

Kennedy with the steel industry and the later decision to cut taxes and cast off for expansionary rather than stabilizing, fiscal policy, Schlesinger concludes:

> The ideological debates of the past began to give way to a new agreement on the practicalities of managing a modern economy. There thus developed in the Kennedy years a national accord on economic policy—a new consensus which gave hope of harnessing government, business, and labor in rational partnership for a steadily expanding American economy.

A significant point in the entire argument is that the Republicans would disagree with Schlesinger on the *facts* but not on the *basis* of his distinction. The Republican rejoinder would be, in effect, "Democratic administrations are *not* more multi-interest than Republican." And, in my opinion, this would be almost the whole truth. . . .

The Costs of Interest-Group Liberalism

For all the political advantages interest-group liberals have in their ideology, there are high costs involved. Unfortunately, these costs are not strongly apparent at the time of the creation of a group-based program. As Wallace Sayre has observed, the gains of a change tend to be immediate, the costs tend to be cumulative. However, it takes no long-run patience or the spinning of fine webs to capture and assess the consequences of group-based policy solutions. Three major consequences are suggested and assessed here: (1) the atrophy of institutions of popular control; (2) the maintenance of old and creation of new structures of privilege; and (3) conservatism, in several senses of the world. . . .

(1) In *The Public Philosophy,* Walter Lippmann was rightfully concerned over the "derangement of power" whereby modern democracies tend first toward unchecked elective leadership and then toward drainage of public authority from elective leaders down into their constituencies. However, Lippmann erred if he thought of constituencies only as voting constituencies. Drainage has tended toward "support group constituencies," and with special consequence. Parceling out policy-making power to the most interested parties destroys political responsibility. A program split off with a special imperium to govern itself is not merely an administrative unit. It is a structure of power with impressive capacities to resist central political control.

Besides making conflict-of-interest a principle of government rather than a criminal act, participatory programs shut out the public. To be more precise, programs of this sort tend to cut out all that part of the mass that is not specifically organized around values strongly salient to the goals of the program. They shut out the public, first, at the most creative phase of policy-making—the phase where the problem is first defined. Once problems are defined, alliances form accordingly and the outcome is both a policy and a reflection of superior power. If the definition is laid out by groups along lines of established group organization, there is always great difficulty for an amorphous public to be organized in any other terms.

The public is shut out, secondly, at the phase of accountability. In programs in which group self-administration is legitimate, the administrators are accountable primarily to the groups, only secondarily to the President or Congress as institutions. In brief, to the extent that organized interests legitimately control a program there is functional rather than substantive accountability. This means questions of equity, balance, and equilibrium to the exclusion of questions of overall social policy and questions of whether or not the program should be maintained or discontinued. It also means accountability to experts first and amateurs last; and an expert is a man trained and skilled in the mysteries and technologies of the program. This is the final victory of functional over substantive considerations. These propositions are best illustrated by at least ten separate, self-governing systems in agriculture alone (representing over ten billion dollars per year in spending and lending). There are many other, although perhaps less dramatic, illustrations. . . .

Finally, there is a conspiracy to shut out the public. One of the assumptions underlying direct group representation is that on the boards and in the staff and among the recognized outside consultants there will be regular countervailing, checks, and balances. In Schattschneider's terms, this would be expected to expand the "scope of conflict." But there is nothing inevitable about that, and the safer assumption might well be the converse. One meaningful illustration, precisely because it is an absurd extreme, is found in the French system of interest representation. Maurice Byé reports that as the Communist-controlled union, the CGT, intensified its participation in post-war government it was able to influence representatives of interests other than employee interests. In a desperate effort to insure the separation and counterpoise of interests on the boards, the government issued the decree that "each member of the board must be *independent of the interests he is not representing.*" Review of the politics of agriculture and of five major efforts of postwar Administrations to bring the ten separate self-governing agriculture systems under a minimum of central control suggests that perhaps Byé's case may not be an absurd extreme. It is only the limiting case of a tendency in all similarly organized programs.

(2) Programs following the principles of interest-group liberalism create privilege, and it is a type of privilege particularly hard to bear or combat because it is touched with the symbolism of the state. The large national interest groups that walk the terrains of national politics are already fairly tight structures of power. We need no more research to support Michels' iron tendency toward oligarchy in these "private governments." Pluralists ease our problem of abiding the existence of organized interests by characterizing oligarchy as simply a negative name for organization: In combat people want and need to be organized and led. Another, somewhat less assuaging, assertion of pluralism is that the member approves the goals of the group or is free to leave it for another, or can turn his attention to one of his "overlapping memberships" in other groups. But however true this may be in pluralistic *politics,* everything changes when some of the groups are co-opted by the state in pluralistic government. The American Farm Bureau Federation is no "voluntary association" insofar as it is a legitimate functionary in Extension work. Such groups as the NAHB, NAREB, NAACP, or NAM are no ordinary lobbies after they become part of the "interior processes of policy formation."

The more clear and legitimized the representation of a group or its leaders in policy formation, the less voluntary is membership in that group and the more necessary is loyalty to its leadership for people who share the interests in question. And, the more clear the official practice of recognizing only organized interests, the more hierarchy is introduced into the society. It is a well-recognized and widely appreciated function of formal groups in modern societies to provide much of the necessary everyday social control. However, when the very thought processes behind public policy are geared toward those groups they are bound to take on much of the involuntary character of *public* control. The classic example outside agriculture is probably the Rivers and Harbors Congress, a private agency whose decisions in the screening of public works projects have almost the effect of law. And, as David Truman observes, arrangements where "one homogeneous group is directly or indirectly charged with the administration of a function . . . [in a] kind of situation that characterizes the occupational licensing boards and similar "independent" agencies . . . have become increasingly familiar in regulatory situations in all levels of government."

Even when the purpose of the program is the uplifting of the underprivileged, the administrative arrangement favored by interest-group liberalism tends toward creation of new privilege instead. Urban redevelopment programs based upon federal support of private plans do not necessarily, but do all too easily, become means by which the building industry regularizes itself. A Federal Housing Administration run essentially by the standards of the National Association of Real Estate Boards (NAREB) became a major escape route for the middle class to leave the city for suburbia rather than a means of providing housing for all. Urban redevelopment, operating for nearly two decades on a principle of local government and local developer specification of federal policy, has been used as an effective instrument for Negro removal. Organizing councils for the poverty program have become first and foremost means of elevating individual spokesmen for the poor and of determining which churches and neighborhood organizations shall be the duly recognized channels of legitimate demand. Encouragement of organization among Negroes and the white and nonwhite poor is important. Early recognition of the few among many emerging leaders and organizations as legitimate administrators or policy-makers seriously risks destroying the process itself. . . .

(3) Government by and through interest groups is in its impact conservative in almost every sense of that term. Part of its conservatism can be seen in another look at the two foregoing objections: Weakening of popular government and support of privilege are, in other words, two aspects of conservatism. It is beside the point to argue that these consequences are not intended. A third dimension of conservatism, stressed here separately, is the simple conservatism of resistance to change. David Truman, who has certainly not been a strong critic of self-government by interest groups, has, all the same, identified a general tendency of established agency-group relationships to be "highly resistant to disturbance.".... *If this is already a tendency in a pluralistic system, then agency-group relationships must be all the more inflexible to the extent that the relationship is official and legitimate.*

The war-on-poverty pattern, even in its early stages, provides a rich testing ground. I observed above that early official co-optation of poverty leaders creates privilege before, and perhaps instead of, alleviating poverty. Another side of this war is the war the established welfare groups are waging against the emergence of the newly organizing social forces. Old and established groups doing good works might naturally look fearfully upon the emergence of competing, perhaps hostile, groups. That is well and good—until their difference is one of "who shall be the government?" Conservatism then becomes necessary as a matter of survival.

The tendency toward the extreme conservatism of sharing legitimate power with private organizations is possibly stronger still in programs more strictly economic. Adams and Gray reviewed figures on assignment of FM radio broadcasting licenses and found that as of 1955, 90 per cent of the FM stations were merely "little auxiliaries" of large AM networks. They also note that the same pattern was beginning to repeat itself in FCC licensing of UHF television channels. The mythology may explain this as a case of "interest-group power," but that begs the question. Whatever power was held by the network was based largely on the commitment the FCC implied in the original grants of licenses. Having granted exclusive privileges to private groups in the public domain (in this case the original assignment of frequencies) without laying down practical conditions for perpetual public retention of the domain itself, the FCC had actually given over sovereignty. The companies acquired property rights and legally vested interests in the grant that interefere enormously with later efforts to affect the grant. Thus, any FCC attempt to expand the communications business through FM would deeply affect the positions and "property" of the established AM companies and networks. Issuing FM licenses to new organizations would have required an open assault on property as well as the established market relations. Leaving aside all other judgments of the practice, it is clearly conservative. Granting of licenses and other privileges unconditionally, and limiting sovereignty by allowing the marketing of properties to be influenced by the possession of the privilege, are practices also to be found in oil, in water power, in the newer sources of power, in transportation, in the "parity" programs of agriculture. ...

There are social and psychological mechanisms as well as economic and vested interests working against change. As programs are split off and allowed to establish self-governing relations with clientele groups, professional norms usually spring up, governing the proper ways of doing things. These rules-of-the-game heavily weight access and power in favor of the established interests. . . . This is all the more true as interests actually become not merely groups but parties represented by name and bloc in a legislature. Even in less formalized situations, legitimizing a group gives it the advantages of exposure and usage as well as direct power, access, and privilege.

The New Representation

Leaders in all democracies probably have at least one common trait: They are ambivalent toward political power. If their lives are dedicated to achieving it, their spirits are tied up with justifying it. American leaders possess this common trait to an uncommon degree. American leaders were, as a consequence, very late to insist upon expansion of the scope of government. That expansion did finally begin to take place, but it only intensified the ambivalence toward power: *With each significant expansion of government in the past century there has been a crisis of public authority.* Social movements, international crises, and varieties of lesser events may trigger off the expansion, but once it occurs in the United States the sense of distress is not ended but simply takes for a while a newer form. For *each such expansion of government and its ensuing crisis of authority has been accompanied by demands for equally significant expansion of representation.* Our ambivalence toward power has thus brought about regular improvements in the mechanisms of representation.

The clearest case in point is the political aftermath of the first big revolution in Federal power, the regulatory revolution that began with the passage of the Interstate Commerce Act of 1887. The political results of the expansion were more immediate and effective than the economic consequences of the statutes themselves. The agrarian movements became the populist movement of the 1890s and the progressive movement of the 1900s. The call went out for congressional reform in nominating processes, ballot reform, decentralization of House leadership. The results were dramatic: "Reed's Rules," Amendment XVII, the direct primary movement, the Australian ballot, the "Speaker Revolt." This was also the period of initial formation of national pressure groups.

In the Wilson period, progressivist expansion of government and revision of the mechanisms of representation were even more intimately interconnected: Female suffrage (Amendment XIX), the short ballot, initiative, referendum and recall, great extension of direct primaries, the commission form of city government, and the first and early demands for formal interest-representation—leading to formal sponsorship of the formation of the Chamber of Commerce and the farm bureau movement, the establishment of the separate Departments of Labor and Commerce, the first experiments with "self-regulation" during World War I industrial mobilization.

The Roosevelt Revolution involved similar relations between government and the demand for representation. The full expression of the pattern was delayed by World War II, but the immediate expression was profound and lasting. It was the theory and practice of the administrative process. It is at this point, as implied earlier, that political scientists and young lawyers trained in the new sociological law becme the high priests. The progressive spirit had been replaced. Demands for representation continued but in these new directions. Administrative law, especially the creation of new agencies, was at first an expression of demands for representation of the new interests which lacked access in Congress and the courts. Interest-group liberalism implied a further formalization and generalization of these particular demands for representation, just as progressivism implied formalization of the earlier types of demands. Obviously the more traditional, progressive demands did not end. Reapportionment, the slow coming of age of the Negro politically and economically—beginning with white primary abolition—the politics leading up to the Administrative Procedure Act, the congressional reforms of 1946 (LaFollette-Monroney Act) are all, in one way or another, traditional progressivist responses to expansion of governmental power. But these reforms were nonetheless over-shadowed by the newer demand inspired and guided by interest-group liberalism. The new halo words alone imply the extent to which the new type of claim now dominates: "interest representation," "cooperation," "partnership," "self-regulation," "delegation of power," "local option," "grass roots," "creative federal-ism," "community action," "maximum feasible participation," and that odd con-tribution from the New Left—which seems unable to escape established thought patterns—"participatory democracy."

In whatever form, the function of representation is the same: to deal with the problem of power—to bring the democratic spirit into some kind of psychological balance with the harsh reality of the coerciveness of government. But there the similarity between progressivism and interest-group liberalism ends. The ultimate consequences of the interest-group liberal solutions are infinitely inferior to the solutions of progressivism. That proposition is precisely what this chapter attempted to articulate. . . .

The interest-group liberal solution to the problem of power provides the system with stability by spreading a sense of representation. But it is the inferior solution because this kind of representation comes at the probable expense of genuine flexibility, of democratic forms, and of legitimacy. The progressivist solutions built greater instabilities into the system by reducing the time lag between social change and the structure and policy of government. But that was supposedly the purpose of representation, and in the process the procedures of the system and the legiti-macy of its policies were clearly more likely to be reinforced. Flexibility and legitimacy are likely to be further reduced by the oligopolistic character of the interest-group liberal's mechanisms of representation, because (1) the number of competitors is deliberately reduced to the most interested and best organized; (2) this tends to eliminate rather than encourage political competition; and (3) this is bound to involve some exchange of legitimacy for the false comfort of stability and the false impression that the problem of power has been solved.

Finally, the interest-group liberal solution to the problem of power is inferior to the progressivist solution because it is basically antagonistic to formalism. All of the foregoing propositions tend to document this in one way or another; put in this general formulation they reveal still further the extent to which some profound requirements of democracy are being weakened. The least evident, yet perhaps the most important, aspect of this is the antagonism of interest-group liberalism to law. Traditional, progressivistic expansions of representation are predicated on the assumption that law is authoritative and that therefore one must seek to expand participation in the making of laws. The "new representation" extends the principle of representation over into administration, since it is predicated on the assumption that lawmaking bodies and conventional procedures cannot and ought not make law. This may be the most debilitative of all the features of interest-group liberalism, for it tends to derange almost all established relations and expectations in the democratic system. It renders formalism impossible. It impairs legitimacy by converting government from a moralistic to a mechanistic institution. It impairs the self-correctiveness of positive law by the very flexibility of its broad policies and by the bargaining, co-optation, and incrementalism of its implementing processes. It impairs the very process of administration itself by delegating to administration alien materials—policies that are not laws. Interest-group liberalism seeks pluralistic government, in which there is no formal specification of means or of ends. In pluralistic government there is therefore no substance. Neither is there procedure. There is only process.

Notes

1. It is assumed that "countervailing power" usually crops up somehow. Where it does not, government ought to help create it. See John Kenneth Galbraith, *American Capitalism* (Boston: Houghton Mifflin, 1952).

2. In order to preserve value-free science, many pluralists ("group theorists") denied public interest altogether, arguing instead that there is a "totally inclusive interest" and that it is best served by letting groups interact without knowing what it is.

Guide for Further Reading

Time, the unfolding of subsequent events, and scholarship have now combined to give us the beginning of a historical perspective on the Truman years, and to enable us to formulate the issues about which future historians of the period are likely to focus their research and debates. President Truman's own recollection of the events of his administration may be found in his two-volume *Memoirs* (Garden City, N. Y., 1955, 1956), subtitled *Years of Decision* and *Years of Trial and Hope*. Among existing biographical studies of the period's star performer are Jonathan Daniels, *The Man of Independence* (Philadelphia, Pa., 1950), Frank McNaughton and Walter Hehmeyer, *Harry Truman: President* (New York, 1958), Cabell Phillips, *The Truman Presidency* (New York, 1966), and Alfred Steinberg, *The Man from Missouri* (New York, 1962). See especially Richard S. Kirkendall's essay on Truman in Morton Borden, ed., *America's Eleven Greatest Presidents* (Chicago, 1971). For the political milieu in which Truman was schooled see Lyle W. Dorsett, *The Pendergast Machine* (New York, 1968). Considerable material on Truman is contained in

Richard E. Neustadt, *Presidential Power: The Politics of Leadership* (New York, 1960), and Walter Johnson, *1600 Pennsylvania Avenue: Presidents and People since 1929* (Boston, 1960).

An invaluable reference work for the Truman administration and the postwar era is Richard S. Kirkendall, ed., *The Truman Period as a Research Field* (Columbia, Mo., 1967), which also suggests fruitful areas for further research. Many of the important documents are collected in Barton J. Bernstein and Allen J. Matusow, eds., *The Truman Administration: A Documentary History* (New York, 1968). See also *Public Papers of the Presidents: Harry S. Truman, 1945-1953*, 8 vols. (Washington, D. C., 1961-1966), General works surveying the postwar years are Herbert Agar, *The Price of Power: America since 1945* (Chicago, 1957), and Eric Goldman's sprightly written *The Crucial Decade and After: America, 1945-1960* (New York, 1960).

The literature on the origins and development of the Cold War is already super-abundant, and grows larger week by week.

For surveys of the worsening of American-Russian relations in the early postwar years see Albert Carr, *Truman, Stalin and Peace* (New York, 1950), Herbert Feis, *From Trust to Terror: The Onset of the Cold War, 1945-1950* (New York, 1971), William H. McNeill, *America, Britain, and Russia: Their Cooperation and Their Conflict, 1941-1946* (New York, 1953), and W. L. Neumann, *After Victory: Churchill, Roosevelt, Stalin and the Making of the Peace* (New York, 1967). More detailed is a series of other books authored by Feis: *Churchill, Roosevelt, Stalin: The War They Waged and the Peace They Sought* (Princeton, N. J., 1953), *Between War and Peace: The Potsdam Conference* (Princeton, N. J., 1960), and *Japan Subdued: The Atomic Bomb and the End of the War in the Pacific* (Princeton, N. J., 1961).

For specific issues the following works may be consulted. On Yalta: Richard Fenno, ed., *The Yalta Conference* (New York, 1955), John Snell, *et.al.*, eds., *The Meaning of Yalta* (New Orleans, 1956), Diane Shaver Clemens, *Yalta* (New York, 1971), and Athan Theoharis, *The Yalta Myths* (Columbia, Mo., 1971). On arms control: Paul R. Baker, ed., *The Atomic Bomb: The Great Decision* (New York, 1968), Bernard Beckhoefer, *Postwar Negotiations for Arms Control* (Washington, D. C., 1961), Joseph Lieberman, *The Scorpion and the Tarantula: The Struggle to Control Atomic Weapons, 1945-1949* (Boston, 1970), H. L. Nieburg, *Nuclear Secrecy and Foreign Policy* (New York, 1964), Robert Gilpin, *American Scientists and Nuclear Weapons Policy* (Princeton, N. J. 1962), and Joseph Nogee, *Soviet Policy toward International Control of Atomic Energy* (South Bend, Ind., 1961). On Berlin and West Germany: Lucius D. Clay, *Decision in Germany* (New York, 1950), W. Phillips Davison, *The Berlin Blockade* (Princeton, N. J., 1958), Laurence Martin, "The American Decision to Rearm Germany," in Harold Stein, ed., *American Civil-Military Relations* (Birmingham, Ala., 1963), Jean Smith, *The Defense of Berlin* (Baltimore, Md., 1963), and Harold Zink, *The United States in*

Germany, 1944-1955 (Princeton, N. J., 1957). On the Truman Doctrine and the Marshall Plan: Joseph Jones, *The Fifteen Weeks* (New York, 1955), and Harry B. Price, *The Marshall Plan and Its Meaning* (Ithaca, N. Y., 1955). See also Robert E. Osgood, *NATO: The Entangling Alliance* (Chicago, 1962).

For American policy in the Far East and the Communist victory in China see Kenneth S. Latourette, *The American Record in the Far East, 1945-1951* (New York, 1953), Harold M. Vinacke, *The United States and the Far East, 1945-1951* (Stanford, Calif., 1952), Edwin O. Reischauer, *The United States and Japan* (Cambridge, Mass., 1957), John K. Fairbank, *The United States and China* (Cambridge, Mass., 1958), Herbert Feis, *The China Tangle* (Princeton, N. J., 1953), Tang Tsou, *America's Failure in China, 1941-1950* (Chicago, 1963), and U. S. Department of State, *United States Relations with China* (Washington, D. C., 1949).

Memoirs and books written by participants in the formulation of America's early Cold War policies include Dean Acheson, *Present at the Creation: My Years in the State Department* (New York, 1969), James Byrnes, *Speaking Frankly* (New York, 1947) and *All in One Lifetime* (New York, 1958), Tom Connally, *My Name is Tom Connally* (New York, 1954), John Foster Dulles, *War or Peace* (New York, 1950), James Forrestal, *The Forrestal Diaries,* ed. Walter Millis (New York, 1955), W. Averell Harriman, *Peace with Russia?* (New York, 1959), George F. Kennan, *Memoirs, 1925-1950* (New York, 1967), *American Diplomacy, 1900-1950* (Chicago, 1951), *Russia, the Atom, and the West* (New York, 1957) and *Russia and the West under Lenin and Stalin* (New York, 1961), Robert Murphy, *Diplomat Among Warriors* (New York, 1964), Walt W. Rostow, *Dynamics of Soviet Society* (New York, 1952), Walter Bedell Smith, *My Three Years in Moscow* (New York, 1950), Edward Stettinius, Jr., *Roosevelt and the Russians: The Yalta Conference,* ed. Walter Johnson (New York, 1951), and Arthur Vandenberg, *The Private Papers of Senator Vandenberg,* ed. Arthur Vandenberg, Jr. (New York, 1952). See also Louis L. Gerson, *John Foster Dulles* (New York, 1967), Arnold Rogow, *James Forrestal* (New York, 1964), and George Curry, "James F. Byrnes," Robert Ferrell, "George C. Marshall," and Richard Walker, "E. R. Stettinius, Jr.," in *The American Secretaries of State and Their Diplomacy,* ed. Robert Ferrell, Vols. XIV, XV (New York, 1965, 1966).

Contemporary dissenters from the Truman administration's foreign policies, motivated by varying considerations, included Walter Lippmann, *The Cold War: A Study in U. S. Foreign Policy* (New York, 1947), Henry Wallace, *Toward World Peace* (New York, 1948), Robert A. Taft, *A Foreign Policy for Americans* (New York, 1951), and Hans Morgenthau, *In Defense of the National Interest* (New York, 1951). See also the very useful compendium of essays edited by Thomas G. Paterson, *Cold War Critics: Alternatives to American Foreign Policy in the Truman Years* (Chicago, 1971).

Nevertheless, for the most part President Truman did an excellent job selling his "get tough" stance not only to Congress and the two major parties, but to the American public as well. (See H. Bradford Westerfield, *Foreign Policy and Party Politics: Pearl Harbor to Korea* [New Haven, Conn., 1955], and Norman Graebner, *The New Isolationism* [New York, 1956]). Consequently, the "orthodox" American view of the Cold War, as originally set forth by the administration, dominated both popular and scholarly writings on the subject until well into the 1960s. (See, for example, John Spanier's influential *American Foreign Policy since World War II* (New York, 1962 and subsequent editions).

The unfolding 1960s, however, brought a "thaw" in American-Russian relations, growing American commitments in the Far East and other distant parts of the world, mounting pressures for social reform at home, and the emergence of the New Left as an articulate element in American society. Along with these developments, "revisionist" interpretations of the Cold War, which shifted blame for the postwar impasse in varying degrees to American ineptitude, wrongheadedness, or malevolent design, gained increasing acceptance. Among the earliest revisionist studies were William Appleman Williams, *American-Russian Relations, 1781-1947* (New York, 1952) and *The Tragedy of American Diplomacy* (Cleveland, O., 1959), Denna F. Fleming, *The Cold War and Its Origins,* 2 vols. (Garden City, N. Y., 1961), and Staughton Lynd, "How the Cold War Began," *Commentary* (November, 1960). By the end of the decade the revisionist bookshelf included also such works as Gar Alperovitz, *Atomic Diplomacy: Hiroshima and Potsdam* (New York, 1965) and *Cold War Essays* (Garden City, N. Y., 1970), David Horowitz, *The Free World Colossus: A Critique of American Foreign Policy in the Cold War* (New York, 1965) and *Empire and Revolution* (New York, 1969), Harry Magdoff, *The Age of Imperialism: The Economics of U. S. Foreign Policy* (New York, 1969), Barton J. Bernstein, "American Foreign Policy and the Origins of the Cold War," and other essays compiled in Barton J. Bernstein, ed., *Politics and Policies of the Truman Administration* (Chicago, 1970), and two books by Gabriel Kolko, *The Politics of War: The World and United States Foreign Policy, 1943-1945* (New York, 1968) and *The Roots of American Foreign Policy,* (Boston, 1969), which perhaps represented the most severe indictment of American Policy yet produced by the New Left. Christopher Lasch provided a useful survey of this literature in "The Cold War, Revisited and Pre-visioned," *New York Times Magazine,* January 14, 1968, while Robert W. Tucker subjected it—as well as the orthodox American interpretation handed down from the Truman administration—to rigorous examination in *Nation or Empire? The Debate over American Foreign Policy* (Baltimore, Md., 1969) and *The Radical Left and American Foreign Policy* (Baltimore, Md., 1971).

From positions outside the New Left ambit other critics of American orthodoxy contributed works such as Hans Morgenthau's *The Impasse of American Foreign Policy* (Chicago, 1962) and *A New Foreign Policy for the United States* (New York, 1969), and J. William Fulbright's *The Arrogance of Power* (New York, 1967). At times the battle waxed hot as defenders of American policy picked up the cudgels on behalf of a "large," or even "imperial," role for the United States in the postwar world: see, for example, Walt W. Rostow, *The United States in the World Arena* (New York, 1960), and George Liska, *Imperial America: The International Politics of Primacy* (Baltimore, Md., 1967).

On the whole, however, the passing of time has fostered a process of cross-fertilization, and mutual give-and-take, among the various schools of Cold War scholarship, as becomes evident in comparing the relatively moderate positions now held by Arthur Schlesinger, Jr., once a vociferous "liberal Cold Warrior," and Lloyd C. Gardner, formerly an ardent exponent of New Left viewpoints. (See Schlesinger, Jr., "The Orgins of the Cold War," *Foreign Affairs* [October, 1967], which is reproduced in this volume, and Gardner, *Architects of Illusion: Men and Ideas in American Foreign Policy, 1941-1949* [Chicago, 1970]). Among recent studies that reflect this more detached and eclectic approach are Stephen E. Ambrose, *The Rise to Globalism: American Foreign Policy since 1938* (Baltimore, Md., 1971), Lloyd C. Gardner, Arthur Schlesinger, Jr., and Hans Morgenthau, *The Origins of the Cold War* (Waltham, Mass., 1970), Norman Graebner, *Cold War Diplomacy* (New York, 1962), Louis Halle, *The Cold War as History* (London, 1967), Martin Herz, *Beginnings of the Cold War* (Bloomington, Ind., 1966), Walter LaFeber, *America, Russia, and the Cold War, 1945-1966* (New York, 1967), and Marshall Shulman, *Stalin's Foreign Policy Reappraised* (Cambridge, Mass., 1963) and *Beyond the Cold War* (New Haven, Conn., 1966).

Probably the most direct and disturbing domestic repercussion of the Cold War during the Truman years consisted in the issues it raised concerning internal Communist subversion, the administration's countermeasures, and the rise of McCarthyism. On the general problems involved see Ralph Brown, *Loyalty and Security* (New Haven, Conn., 1958), Robert Cushman, *Civil Liberties in the United States* (Ithaca, N. Y., 1956), Harold Lasswell, *National Security and Individual Freedom* (New York, 1950), Earl Latham, *The Communist Controversy in Washington* (Cambridge, Mass., 1966), Richard Longaker, *The Presidency and Individual Liberties* (Ithaca, N. Y., 1961), and Samuel Stouffer, *Communism, Conformity, and Civil Liberties* (New York, 1955). On Communist operations in the United States see Whittaker Chambers, *Witness* (New York, 1956), Harold Chase, *Security and Liberty: The Problem of Native Communists, 1947-1955* (Garden City, N. Y., 1955), Louis Coser and Irving Howe, *The American Communist Party* (New York, 1957), Morris Ernst and David Loth, *Report on the American Communist* (New York, 1952), Max Kampelman, *The Communist Party vs. the CIO* (New York, 1957), Wilson Record, *The Negro and the Communist Party* (Chapel Hill, N. C., 1951), David Shannon, *The Decline of American Communism* (New York, 1959), and Nathaniel Weyl, *Battle Against Disloyalty* (New York, 1951). On early congressional inquiries into the field of disloyalty and subversion see Rober Carr, *The House Committee on Un-American Activities, 1945-1950* (Ithaca, N. Y., 1952), and Walter Goodman, *The Committee: The Extraordinary Career of the House Com-*

mittee on Un-American Activities (New York, 1968). On the Alger Hiss case see Fred Cook, *The Unfinished Story of Alger Hiss* (New York, 1958), Alistair Cooke, *A Generation on Trial: U. S. A. vs. Alger Hiss* (New York, 1950), Alger Hiss, *In the Court of Public Opinion* (New York, 1957), Earl Jowitt, *The Strange Case of Alger Hiss* (New York, 1953), and Ralph deToledano and Victor Lasky, *Seeds of Treason: The True Story of the Hiss-Chambers Tragedy* (New York, 1950).

Concerning the nature and propriety of the Truman administration's loyalty and security program, consult Athan Theoharis, *Seeds of Repression: Harry S. Truman and the Origins of McCarthyism* (Chicago, 1971), wherein the author expands upon the article reproduced in this volume. For an assessment more favorable to the administration see Alan D. Harper, *The Politics of Loyalty: The White House and the Communist Issue, 1946-1952* (Westport, Conn., 1970). Other writings on the subject include Alan Barth, *The Loyalty of Free Men* (New York, 1951), Francis Biddle, *The Fear of Freedom* (New York, 1951), Eleanor Bontecou, *The Federal Loyalty and Security Program* (Ithaca, N. Y., 1953), Elmer Davis, *But We Were Born Free* (New York, 1952), Carey McWilliams, *Witch Hunt: The Revival of Heresy* (Boston, 1950), and Clair Wilcox, ed., *Civil Liberties Under Attack* (Philadelphia, Pa., 1951). The Supreme Court's record during these years is reviewed in Oswald Fraenkel, *The Supreme Court and Civil Liberties* (New York, 1952), and C. H. Pritchett, *Civil Liberties and the Vinson Court* (Chicago, 1954).

On McCarthyism—its leader, its nature, and its constituency—see Jack Anderson and R. W. May, *McCarthy* (Boston, 1952), Daniel Bell, ed., *The New American Right* (New York, 1955) later enlarged and reissued as *The Radical Right* (Garden City, N. Y., 1963), William F. Buckley, Jr. and L. Brent Bozell, *McCarthy and His Enemies* (Chicago, 1954) which presents a defense of the Wisconsin senator, Roy Cohn, *McCarthy* (New York, 1968) written by the Senator's chief assistant, Robert Griffith, *The Politics of Fear: Joseph R. McCarthy and the Senate* (Lexington, Ky., 1970), Richard Hofstadter, *The Paranoid Style in American Politics* (New York, 1965) and *Anti-Intellectualism in American Life* (New York, 1963), Earl Latham, ed., *The Meaning of McCarthyism* (Boston, 1968), Allen J. Matusow, ed., *Joseph R. McCarthy* (Englewood Cliffs, N. J., 1970), Joseph R. McCarthy, *McCarthyism, The Fight for America* (New York, 1952), Richard Rovere, *Senator Joe McCarthy* (New York, 1959), and Michael Rogin, *The Intellectuals and McCarthy* (Cambridge, Mass., 1967).

Another source of discord in the postwar years involved the process of reconversion and questions of economic policy. On reconversion and its attendant issues see Jack Peltason, *The Reconversion Controversy* (Washington, D. C., 1950), and a series of articles by Barton J. Bernstein: "The Debate on Industrial Reconversion: The Protection of Oligopoly and Military Control of the War Economy," *American Journal of Economics and Sociology* (April, 1967), "The Removal of War Production Board Controls on Business, 1944-1946," *Business History Review* (Summer, 1965), "The Truman Administration and Its Reconversion Wage Policy," *Labor*

History (Fall, 1965), "Walter Reuther and the UAW-GM Strike of 1945-1946," *Michigan History* (September, 1965), "The Truman Administration and the Steel Strike of 1946," *Journal of American History* (March, 1966), "Clash of Interests: The Postwar Battle between the Office of Price Administration and the Department of Agriculture," *Agricultural History* (January, 1967) and "The Postwar Famine and Price Controls, 1946," *Agricultural History* (October, 1964). Other specialized studies include Lester Chandler, *Inflation in the United States, 1940-1948* (New York, 1951), James Knipe, *The Federal Reserve and the American Dollar: Problems and Policies* (Chapel Hill, N. C., 1965), Henry Murphy, *The Federal Debt in War and Transition* (New York, 1950), A. E. Holmans, *United States Fiscal Policy, 1945-1959* (New York, 1961), and Wilfred Lewis, *Federal Fiscal Policy in the Postwar Recessions* (Washington, D. C., 1962). Useful general studies that help place the economic significance of the Truman years in wider historical perspective are Milton Friedman and Anna Schwartz, *A Monetary History of the United States* (Princeton, N. J., 1963), Bert Hickman, *Growth and Stability in the Postwar Economy* (Washington, D. C., 1961), Robert Lekachman, *The Age of Keynes* (New York, 1965), Herbert Stein, *The Fiscal Revolution in America* (Chicago, 1969), and George A. Steiner, *Government's Role in Economic Life* (New York, 1953). Stephen K. Bailey, *Congress Makes a Law: The Story Behind the Employment Act of 1946* (New York, 1950) relates the legislative history of the measure which "officially"—if vaguely—committed the American government to the principles of Keynesian economics. Edward Flash, *Economic Advice and Presidential Leadership* (New York, 1965) examines the experience, in its earlier years, of the Council of Economic Advisors created by the Employment Act of 1946.

The fate of President Truman's Fair Deal program of economic and social reform may be studied in a growing number of works, in addition to the articles by Neustadt and Bernstein that are reprinted in this volume. The wartime hopes entertained by liberals for a resumption of reform at war's end are portrayed in J. Joseph Huthmacher, *Senator Robert F. Wagner and the Rise of Urban Liberalism* (New York, 1968), and Charles Merriam, "The National Resources Planning Board: A Chapter in American Planning Experience," *American Political Science Review* (December, 1944). On the G. I. Bill of Rights, which constituted one of the most far-reaching welfare measures ever enacted, see David R. B. Ross, *Preparing for Ulysses: Politics and Veterans during World War II* (New York, 1969). On housing measures during the postwar period see Richard O. Davies, *Housing Reform during the Truman Administration* (Columbia, Mo., 1966). On the fight for a federal health program consult James G. Burrow, *AMA: The Voice of American Medicine* (Baltimore, Md., 1963). Labor's role and labor legislation in this period are discussed in Joel Seidman, *American Labor from Defense to Reconversion* (Chicago, 1953), Colston Warne, *et. al.,* eds., *Labor in Postwar America* (New York, 1949), Philip Taft, *The A.F. of L. from the Death of Gompers to the Merger* (New York, 1959), Harry Millis and Emily Brown, *From the Wagner Act to Taft-Hartley*

(Chicago, 1950), C. Wright Mills, *The New Men of Power* (New York, 1948), a study of postwar labor union leadership, C. O. Gregory, *Labor and the Law* (New York, 1958), R. Alton Lee, *Truman and Taft-Hartley: A Question of Mandate* (Lexington, Ky., 1966), Arthur F. McClure, *The Truman Administration and the Problems of Postwar Labor* (Cranbury, N. J., 1969), Gerald Pomper, "Labor and Congress: The Repeal of Taft-Hartley," *Labor History* (Fall, 1961), and Daniel Bell, "Taft-Hartley: Five Years Old," *Fortune* (July, 1952). On farm policy see Allen J. Matusow, *Farm Politics and Policies of the Truman Years* (Cambridge, Mass., 1967), Reo Christenson, *The Brannan Plan: Farm Politics and Policy* (Ann Arbor, Mich., 1959), Charles Hardin, *The Politics of Agriculture* (Glencoe, Ill., 1952), Murray Benedict, *Farm Policies of the United States, 1790-1950* (New York, 1953), Edward Higbee, *Farms and Farmers in an Urban Age* (New York, 1963), and C. C. Taylor, *Rural Life in the United States* (New York, 1949).

The best surveys of the history of the American Negro and the quest for equal rights are John Hope Franklin, *From Slavery to Freedom: A History of American Negroes,* 2d ed., rev. and enl., (New York, 1965), August Meier and Eliot Rudwick, *From Plantation to Ghetto* (New York, 1966), Arnold Rose, *An American Dilemma: The Negro Problem and Modern Democracy* (New York, 1944), Arthur Waskow, *From Race Riot to Sit-In* (Garden City, N. Y., 1966), and C. Vann Woodward, *The Strange Career of Jim Crow* (New York, 1966). The basic reports which sparked the modern battle for civil rights during the Truman administration are President's Committee on Civil Rights, *To Secure These Rights* (Washington, D. C., 1947), and President's Committee on Equality of Treatment and Opportunity in the Armed Services, *Freedom To Serve* (Washington, D. C., 1950). Pertinent studies of the civil rights movement and its various phases during the postwar years include William C. Berman, *The Politics of Civil Rights in the Truman Administration* (Columbus, O., 1971), Barton J. Bernstein, "The Ambiguous Legacy: The Truman Administration and Civil Rights," in Barton J. Bernstein, ed., *Politics and Policies of the Truman Administration* (Chicago, 1970), Arnold Rose, *The Negro in Postwar America* (New York, 1948), Lee Nichols, *Breakthrough on the Color Front* (New York, 1954), Henry Moon, *Balance of Power: The Negro Vote* (New York, 1948), Louis Kesselman, *The Social Politics of FEPC* (Chapel Hill, N. C., 1948), Herbert Garfinkel, *When Negroes March: The March on Washington Movement in the Organizational Politics for FEPC* (Glencoe, Ill., 1959), Louis Ruchames, *Race, Jobs, and Politics* (New York, 1953), and Richard M. Dalfiume, *Desegregation of the United States Armed Forces: Fighting on Two Fronts, 1939-1953* (Columbia, Mo., 1969). Walter White, who headed the National Association for the Advancement of Colored People during the Truman years, has written *A Man Called White* (New York, 1948) and *How Far the Promised Land* (New York, 1955).

On the political stalemate that dominated presidential-congressional and liberal-conservative relations during the late 1930s and into the postwar era the basic book is Samuel Lubell, *The Future of American Politics* (New York, 1952 and subsequent editions), from which a selection is reprinted in this volume. See also Lubell's *The Revolt of the Moderates* (New York, 1956), and James MacGregor Burns, *The Deadlock of Democracy: Four-Power Politics in America* (Englewood Cliffs, N. J., 1963). Two of the key political elements whose differences helped create and sustain that deadlock are examined in Samuel Eldersveld, "The Influence of Metropolitan Party Pluralities in Presidential Elections since 1920: A Study of Twelve Key Cities," *American Political Science Review* (December, 1949), and V. O. Key, Jr., *Southern Politics in State and Nation* (New York, 1949). See also J. Joseph Huthmacher, "Urban Liberalism and the Age of Reform," *Mississippi Valley Historical Review* (September, 1962), and Carl N. Degler, "American Political Parties and the Rise of the City: An Interpretation," *Journal of American History* (June, 1964).

For an authoritative description and analysis of Truman's re-election campaign see Richard S. Kirkendall, "Election of 1948," in Arthur Schlesinger, Jr., ed., *History of American Presidential Elections,* Vol. 4 (New York, 1971). On President Truman's strategy and tactics see, in addition to the extract from Cabell Phillips which is reprinted in this volume, Irwin Ross, *The Loneliest Campaign: The Truman Victory of 1948* (New York, 1968). The superbly titled book by Jules Abels, *Out of the Jaws of Victory* (New York, 1959) recounts Governor Thomas E. Dewey's campaign. On the Dixiecrat movement see Dewey Grantham, Jr., "The South in the Reconstruction of American Politics," *Journal of American History* (September, 1966), Emile B. Ader, *The Dixiecrat Movement: Its Role in Third Party Politics* (Washington, D. C., 1955), S. M. Lemmon, "Ideology of the Dixiecrat Movement," *Social Forces* (December, 1957), and Alberta Lachicotte, *Rebel Senator: Strom Thurmond of South Carolina* (New York, 1966). Charles Wallace Collins, *Whither the Solid South?* (New Orleans, 1947) presents the thinking of one of the chief ideologists of the movement. On Henry A. Wallace and his Progressive Party see Curtis MacDougall, *Gideon's Army,* 3 vols., (New York, 1965-1966), Karl Schmidt, *Henry Wallace: Quixotic Crusade* (Syracuse, N. Y., 1960), Edward and Frederick Schapsmeier, *Prophet in Politics: Henry A. Wallace and the War Years, 1940-1965* (Ames, Iowa, 1970), Allen Yarnell, "The Democratic Party's Response to the Progressive Party in 1948," *Research Studies* (March, 1971), and Alonzo B. Hamby, "Henry A. Wallace, the Liberals, and Soviet-American Relations," *Review of Politics* (1968). See also Hamby's "Sixty Million Jobs and the People's Revolution: The Liberals, the New Deal , and World War II," *Historian* (1966). Also see Angus Campbell, *et. al.*, *The Voter Decides* (Evanston, Ill., 1954).

For background on the New Deal period consult Frank A. Warren III, *Liberals and Communism: The "Red Decade" Revisited* (Bloomington, Ind., 1966), Arthur Schlesinger, Jr., *The Age of Roosevelt: The Coming of the New Deal* (Boston, 1959) and *The Age of Roosevelt: The Politics of Upheaval* (Boston, 1960), and William E. Leuchtenburg, *Franklin D. Roosevelt and the New Deal, 1932-1940* (New York, 1963). On political aspects of the "new liberalism" see Clifton Brock,

Americans for Democratic Action: Its Role in National Politics (Washington, D. C., 1962), Fay Calkins, *The CIO and the Democratic Party* (Chicago, 1952), and Joseph Gaer, *The First Round: The Story of the CIO Political Action Committee* (New York, 1944). For further investigation into this important but neglected subject one should consult the writings of representative liberal ideologists and tacticians during the postwar years. Particularly influential was Arthur Schlesinger, Jr., *The Vital Center* (Cambridge, Mass., 1947). See also, for examples, Max Ascoli, *The Power or Freedom* (New York, 1949), Irwin Ross, *Strategy for Liberals* (New York, 1949), Leland Stowe, *Target: You* (New York, 1949), and Seymour Harris, ed., *Saving American Capitalism* (New York, 1948). Some liberal spokesmen of the period were influenced by the "new realism" expounded by the Protestant theologian Reinhold Niebuhr in such works as *Moral Man and Immoral Society* (New York, 1932), *The Children of Light and the Children of Darkness* (New York, 1944) and *The Irony of American History* (New York, 1952). For the memoirs of a conservative member of Truman's cabinet see Charles Sawyer, *Concerns of a Conservative Democrat* (New York, 1968).

For less elevated aspects of politics under the Truman administration see Blair Bolles, *How to Get Rich in Washington* (New York, 1952), H. H. Wilson, *Congress: Corruption and Compromise* (New York, 1951), Karl Schriftgiesser, *The Lobbyists* (Boston, 1951), and Robert S. Allen and William V. Shannon, *The Truman Merry-Go-Round* (New York, 1950).

The outstanding source on the Korean War and the Truman-MacArthur controversy is United States Senate, 82d Cong., 1st Sess., Committee on Armed Services and Committee on Foreign Relations, *Hearings: Military Situation in the Far East* (Washington, D. C., 1951). The administration viewpoint is argued in President Truman's *Memoirs*, vol. 2 (Garden City, N. Y., 1956), John W. Spanier, *The Truman-MacArthur Controversy and the Korean War* (Cambridge, Mass., 1959), from which an excerpt is reproduced in this volume, Richard Rovere and Arthur Schlesinger, Jr., *The General and the President* (New York, 1951), Trumbull Higgins, *Korea and the Fall of MacArthur* (New York, 1960), and U. S. Department of State, *United States Policy in the Korean Conflict* (Washington, D. C., 1951). It is critically analyzed in the article by Cottrell and Dougherty which is reprinted in this volume. General Douglas MacArthur's case is defended vigorously in his *Reminiscences* (New York, 1964), and in Courtney Whitney, *MacArthur: His Rendezvous with History* (New York, 1956), and Charles A. Willoughby and John Chamberlain, *MacArthur, 1941-1951* (New York, 1954). For the views of generals who served in Korea see Mark W. Clark, *From the Danube to the Yalu* (New York, 1954), and J. Lawton Collins, *War in Peacetime: The History and Lessons of Korea* (Boston, 1968).

General studies of the Korean War include Richard Lowitt, ed., *The Truman-MacArthur Controversy* (Chicago, 1967), Carl Berger, *The Korea Knot* (Philadelphia, Pa., 1964), T. R. Fehrenbach, *In This Kind of War: A Study in Unpreparedness* (New York, 1963), Robert Leckie, *Conflict: The History of the Korean War, 1950-1953* (New York, 1962), and David Rees, *Korea: The Limited War* (New York, 1964). Particular aspects of the episode are considered in R. J. Caridi, *The Korean War and American Politics: The Republican Party as a Case Study* (Philadelphia, Pa., 1968), Leland Goodrich, *Korea: A Study of United States Policy in the United Nations* (New York, 1956), G. D. Paige, *The Korean Decision, June 24-30, 1950* (New York, 1968), and Allen Whiting, *China Crosses the Yalu: The Decision to Enter the Korean War* (New York, 1960).

The concept of "limited war" and the special problems associated with it, and the ability of the American people to sustain such efforts, are discussed in Morton Halperin, *Limited War in the Nuclear Age* (New York, 1963), Henry Kissinger, *Nuclear Weapons and Foreign Policy* (New York, 1957), and Robert E. Osgood, *Limited War: The Challenge to American Strategy* (Chicago, 1957). The relevance to this subject of studies of the American experience in the Indochina crisis of 1954, and subsequently in the Vietnam War is, of course, obvious. See also "On the Protracted War," in *Selected Works of Mao Tse-tung,* vol. II (London, 1954).

A useful compilation of views regarding the state of the American "system" during the Truman years and thereafter is Richard Gillam, ed., *Power in Postwar America* (Boston, 1970). The confidence and pride that pervade Frederick Lewis Allen's *The Big Change: America Transforms Itself, 1900-1950* (New York, 1952), from which a selection is reprinted in this volume, was anticipated and shared by a number of works that appeared during the 1940s and 1950s. Pluralism, countervailing powers, and welfare statism provided the bases for the political science of Wilfred Binkley and Malcolm Moos, *A Grammar of American Politics* (New York, 1950), David B. Truman, *The Governmental Process* (New York, 1951), and V. O. Key, Jr., *Politics, Parties, and Pressure Groups* (New York, 1942); the economics of A. A. Berle, Jr., *The Twentieth-Century Capitalist Revolution* (New York, 1954), and John Kenneth Galbraith, *American Capitalism: The Concept of Countervailing Power* (Boston, 1952); and the optimistic statements of liberal thinkers and publicists such as Daniel Bell, *The End of Ideology* (Glencoe, Ill., 1960), Russell Davenport and the editors of *Fortune, U.S.A., the Permanent Revolution* (New York, 1951), Mario Einaudi, *The Roosevelt Revolution* (New York, 1959), David Lilienthal, *Big Business: A New Era* (New York, 1953), Massimo Salvadori, *The Economics of Freedom: American Capitalism Today* (New York, 1959), and Arthur Schlesinger, Jr.'s very influential *The Vital Center* (Cambridge, Mass., 1947). More recent studies in the same tradition include Robert A. Dahl, *Pluralist Democracy in the United States: Conflict and Consent* (Chicago, 1967), and Arnold Rose, *The Power Structure: Political Process in American Society* (New York, 1967).

The factors that the pluralists relied upon as the chief guarantors of freedom have been subjected to increasing examination and skepticism in more recent years by commentators who share the "Establishment liberals" ends, but who doubt the workability or efficacy of their means. Works that fall into this school of scrutiny, in addition to Theodore J. Lowi's *The End of Liberalism* (New York, 1969), a section of which is reproduced in this volume, include Kenneth Boulding, *The Organizational Revolution* (New York, 1953), Arthur Ekirch, *The Decline of American Liberalism* (New York, 1955), Henry Kariel, *The Decline of American Pluralism* (Stanford, Calif., 1961), Walter Lippmann, *Essays in the Public Philosophy* (Boston, 1955), Grant McConnell, *The Decline of Agrarian Democracy* (Berkeley, Calif., 1953) and *Private Power and Public Democracy* (New York, 1966), and William Foote Whyte's popular book, *The Organization Man* (New York, 1956). For the evolving thought of John Kenneth Galbraith see *The Affluent Society* (Boston, 1958), *The New Industrial State* (Boston, 1967) and *How to Control the Military* (Garden City, N. Y., 1969).

Much more thoroughgoing in their revisionism, of course, are those analysts who predicate their views on an entirely different perception of the actual distribution of power in American society than that depicted by the Establishment liberals. The so-called "military-industrial-political elite" is examined from various perspectives in an anthology edited by Norman L. Crockett, *The "Power Elite" in America* (Boston, 1970). The seminal studies along this line of inquiry include, in addition to C. Wright Mills' *The Power Elite* (New York, 1956), an excerpt from which is reprinted in this volume, Robert A. Brady, *Business As a System of Power* (New York, 1943), Walter Adams and Horace Grey, *Monopoly in America: The Government as Promoter* (New York, 1955), and Paul A. C. Koistinen, "The 'Industrial-Military Complex' in Historical Perspective: World War I," *Business History Review* (Winter, 1967) and "The 'Industrial-Military Complex' in Historical Perspective: The InterWar Years," *Journal of American History* (March, 1970), which trace the phenomenon to periods earlier than those emphasized by Mills. The 1960s evoked an outpouring of sharply critical writings on the power elite and its component parts: see, for example, Richard J. Barnet, *The Economy of Death* (New York, 1970), Omer L. Carey, ed., *The Military-Industrial Complex and U. S. Foreign Policy* (Pullman, Wash., 1969), Fred Cook, *The Warfare State* (New York, 1962), G. William Dumhoff, *Who Rules America?* (Englewood Cliffs, N. J., 1967), David Horowitz, ed., *Corporations and the Cold War* (New York, 1969), Sidney Lens, *The Military-Industrial Complex* (Philadelphia, Pa., 1970), Seymour Melman, *Pentagon Capitalism: The Political Economy of War* (New York, 1970), Morton Mintz and Jerry S. Cohen, *America, Inc.: Who Owns and Operates the United States* (New York, 1971), which quickly became a best-seller, and William Proxmire, *Report from Wasteland: America's Military-Industrial Complex* (New York, 1970), written by a United States Senator.

For varying interpretations of the degree of concentration and control that characterizes American business and its role in modern American life see Raymond Bauer, *et. al., American Business and Public Policy* (New York, 1963), Earl F. Cheit, ed., *The Business Establishment* (New York, 1964), Andrew Hacker, ed., *The Corporation Take-Over* (New York, 1964), Morrell Heald, *The Social Responsibilities of Business: Company and Community, 1900-1960* (Cleveland, O., 1970), and Francis X. Sutton, *et. al., The American Business Creed* (Cambridge, Mass., 1956). For a profile of the military that differs significantly from that of Mills, *et al,* see Samuel P. Huntington, *The Soldier and the State* (Cambridge, Mass., 1957). On the matter of income distribution see Gabriel Kolko, *Wealth and Power in the America: An Analysis of Social Class and Income Distribution* (New York, 1962). As usual, statistics must be handled cautiously: see also Simon Kuznets, *Shares of Upper Income Groups in Income and Savings* (New York, 1953), and Dwight Macdonald, "Our Invisible Poor," *The New Yorker* (1963).

On the state of Marxist analysis of American society see Paul Sweezy, *The Future as History: Essays and Reviews on Capitalism and Socialism* (New York, 1953), Paul Baran and Paul Sweezy, *Monopoly Capitalism: The American Economic and Social Order* (New York, 1966), and William Appleman Williams, *The Great Evasion* (New York, 1964).

For a sampling of views of American conservatives during the war and postwar years see William F. Buckley, Jr., ed., *American Conservative Thought in the Twentieth Century* (Indianapolis and New York, 1970). Outstanding works in this category include Friedrich A. Hayek, *The Road to Serfdom* (Chicago, 1944), Ludwig van Mises, *Human Action* (New Haven, Conn., 1949), and Milton Friedman, *Capitalism and Freedom* (Chicago, 1962). See also Peter Viereck, *Conservatism Revisited* (New York, 1950), William F. Buckley, Jr., *Up From Liberalism* (N. Y., 1959), Henry Hazlitt, *The Great Idea* (New York, 1951), Russell Kirk, *The Conservative Mind* (Chicago, 1953) and *A Program for Conservatives* (Chicago, 1954), Clinton Rossiter, *Conservatism in America: The Thankless Persuasion* (New York, 1955), William S. White, *The Taft Story* (New York, 1954), and Russell Kirk and James McClellan, *The Political Principles of Robert A. Taft* (N. Y., 1967).

Wartime and postwar studies of the American character and of the American system that stand apart and also deserve attention are James Burnham, *The Managerial Revolution* (New York, 1941), David Riesman with Nathan Glazer and Reuel Denney, *The Lonely Crowd: A Study of the Changing American Character* (New Haven, Conn., 1950), and C. Wright Mills, *White Collar: The American Middle Classes* (New York, 1951).

Highlights of the Truman years are portrayed visually in the NBC documentary film, *Not So Long Ago* (1965, 54 mins.). See also the CBS production, *You Are There: V-J Day* (1956, 27 mins.). The devastation wrought by the first atom bombs is awesomely depicted in *Hiroshima-Nagasaki, August, 1945* (Center for Mass Communications of Columbia University Press, n.d., 16 mins.), and *Tale of Two Cities* (U.S. War Department, 1946, 14 mins.). Biographical studies of the president on film include *Harry S. Truman* (David L. Wolper, 1964, 52 mins.).

The development of the Cold War is marked by the contrasting attitudes toward Russia and Communism presented, on the one hand, in the pro-Russian Hollywood fictionalized version of Joseph E. Davies' *Mission to Moscow* (1943, 124 mins., starring Walter Huston, Ann Harding, and Oscar Homolka) and, on the other hand, the various documentaries portraying the Communist "menace" that were pro-duced after the war's end: see, for example, *The Truth about Communism* (n.d., 78 mins., featuring Ronald Reagan) and *The Hoaxsters* (MGM, 1952, 36 mins.). See also *American Foreign Policy, Confrontation, 1945-1953* (NBC, 1966, 32 mins.), *American Foreign Policy: Containment in Asia* (NBC, 1966, 32 mins.), and *George Kennan Discusses Soviet Objectives* (U.S. Department of Defense, 1954, 58 mins.).

On the Korean War see *That War in Korea* (NBC, 1966, 79 mins.), *Korea – 38th Parallel* (David L. Wolper, 1965, 50 mins.), *MacArthur versus Truman* (David L. Wolper, 1964, 25 mins.), *Milestones of the Century: The Korean Conflict, 1948-1953* (Pathé News, 1960, 24 mins.), *Why Korea?* (Teaching Film Custodians, 1957, 30 mins.), *Korea: The Long Road to Peace* (March of Time, 1953, 28 mins.), and *Korea Story* (U.S. Information Agency, 1953, 20 mins.)

On McCarthyism see *Charge and Countercharge: A Film of the Era of Senator Joseph R. McCarthy* (Emile deAntonio, 1968, 43 mins.), *Joseph McCarthy* (David L. Wolper, 1964, 26 mins.), and *McCarthy versus Welch* (David L. Wolper, 1964, 25 mins.).

Some of the major social problems of the Truman years were treated sensitively and effectively in fictionalized Hollywood feature films. On the problems of return-ing veterans see *The Best Years of Our Lives* (Samuel Goldwyn Productions, 1946, 170 mins., starring Frederic March, Myrna Loy, Dana Andrews, Theresa Wright, Harold Russell, and Virginia Mayo). On anti-Semitism see *Gentlemen's Agreement* (20th-Century Fox Productions, 1947, 146 mins., with Gregory Peck, Dorothy McGuire, John Garfield, and Celeste Holm), on prejudice against Japanese-Americans, *Bad Day at Black Rock* (MGM, 81 mins., with Spencer Tracy, Robert Ryan, Walter Brennan, and Lee Marvin), and on black Americans in the service, *Home of the Brave* (produced by Stanley Kramer, 1949, 85 mins., starring Lloyd Bridges, Steve Brodie, Frank Lovejoy, and James Edwards). On the persistence of racism and bigotry in America, see also the excellent documentary, *Strange Victory* (produced by Barnet L. Rossett, Jr., 1948 with an epilogue added in 1966, 77 minutes). On labor racketeering see the David L. Wolper documentary, *Kefauver versus the Syndicates* (1964, 25 mins.), and the classic Hollywood feature film *On the Waterfront* (produced by Sam Spiegel, 1954, 108 mins., starring Marlon Brando, Karl Malden, Lee J. Cobb, Eva Marie Saint, and Rod Steiger).